Contents

VIRGINIA WOOLF

Introduction

by Claire Sprague

I

In Virginia Woolf's first novel, *The Voyage Out*, Terence Hewet confides to Rachel Vinrace: " 'I want to write a novel about Silence . . . the things people don't say.' " [1]

"The things people don't say" were the things Virginia Woolf and her contemporaries, James Joyce and D. H. Lawrence, wanted to say. They shared an interest in making silence speak, in giving a tongue to the complex inner world of feeling and memory and in establishing the validity of that world's claim to the term "reality." That subjective reality came to be identified with the technique rather loosely called "stream of consciousness." [2] The debt some have claimed Mrs. Woolf owes to Marcel Proust, Dorothy Richardson, Henri Bergson or Joyce is less important as demonstrable specific indebtedness than as a symptom of "the dominant metaphysical bias of a whole generation." [3] Literary historians invariably make a trio of Joyce, Woolf and Lawrence, agreeing that they share this "metaphysical bias." We are, however, becoming as much aware of their singularities as of their shared attitudes and techniques. It is doubtful, for example, that Woolf and Lawrence used the famed stream of consciousness technique at all.

In a number of unexpected ways Woolf and Lawrence may be usefully compared. Each tended to attract disciples and antagonists in a way that made reasonably objective criticism during their lifetime almost impossible. Symbol and allegory hunters have come forth with

[1] Virginia Woolf, *The Voyage Out* (New York: Harcourt, Brace & World, n.d.), p. 216.

[2] Critics have tried to sharpen the use of the term. See, for example, Frederick J. Hoffman, *Freudianism and the Literary Mind* (Baton Rouge: Louisiana State University Press, 1945), pp. 124–29; Harry Levin, *James Joyce* (Norfolk: New Directions, 1941), pp. 89 ff.; Robert Humphrey, *Stream of Consciousness in the Modern Novel* (Berkeley: University of California Press, 1965), pp. 1–8; Leon Edel, *The Modern Psychological Novel* (New York: Grove Press, 1955), pp. 53–58; Melvin Friedman, *Stream of Consciousness* (New Haven: Yale University Press, 1955), chaps. 1, 6. Despite their efforts the term is likely to remain imprecise.

[3] William Troy, "Virginia Woolf: The Novel of Sensibility," as reprinted in *Literary Opinion in America*, vol. I, ed. Morton Dauwen Zabel (New York: Harper & Row, 1937), p. 324. See this volume, p. 26.

extravagant interpretations of their work. One critic, for example, goes so far as to find the three strokes of the lighthouse equal to the trinity—its long steady stroke representing the Holy Ghost—and the dinner at which Mrs. Ramsay presides a reenactment of the Last Supper.[4] Both Woolf and Lawrence produced a highly personal vision of life in their works—at least by comparison with Joyce. Furthermore, Joyce was not a preacher; Lawrence was; Virginia Woolf was— as a feminist certainly if less certainly as a novelist. But such comparisons are less meaningful than Woolf's own perception that she and Lawrence had "too much in common—the same pressure to be ourselves." [5] Joyce's more objective, encyclopedic, many-leveled prose never gave her the same shock of recognition.

Though so often mentioned together with Joyce and Lawrence, Woolf is neither so highly valued nor so well known as they are. She may partly be the victim of an obscuring personal legend created by her contemporaries. If so, she again recalls Lawrence; for Lawrence the writer was the victim of a far more obscuring personal legend, one arising out of both adulation and animosity and Lawrence's own strident prophetic stance. Happily, Lawrence has already survived his legend. Woolf has yet to survive hers.

A special complication about her legend is her connection with Bloomsbury. As she put it in her diary: "Bloomsbury is ridiculed; and I am dismissed with it." [6] Bloomsbury, a London neighborhood near the British Museum, is where Virginia and her brother Adrian moved after her father's death in 1904. Virginia's sister, Vanessa, and her husband, the art critic, Clive Bell, were already residents of the area. As misapplied as the term "Bloomsbury" has been, Leonard Woolf does consider the application valid as it refers to the years 1912 to 1914 and includes the three Stephens, Bell, himself, Lytton Strachey, John Maynard Keynes, E. M. Forster, Roger Fry, Desmond MacCarthy and Sydney Saxon-Turner. By 1912 all of the members of "old Bloomsbury" "lived geographically in Bloomsbury within a few minutes walk of one another." [7] The roots of Bloomsbury go back to Cambridge where all the men had known one another and had come under the influence of the philosopher G. E. Moore. Friendship was a critical part of his teachings and of the ideals of his admirers. For our purposes Bloomsbury matters more for the esthetic upper

[4] F. L. Overcarsh, "The Lighthouse, Face to Face," *Accent*, X (Winter 1959), 107–23.

[5] *A Writer's Diary* (New York: Harcourt, Brace & World, 1953), p. 177. Hereafter referred to as *AWD*.

[6] *Ibid.*, p. 224.

[7] Leonard Woolf, *Beginning Again* (New York: Harcourt, Brace & World, 1964), pp. 21–22. "Old Bloomsbury" is Leonard Woolf's term; he defines "new Bloomsbury" as Bloomsbury of the 20s and 30s. Strachey and Fry were dead; the three Bell children and David Garnett were additions to the circle.

class aura critics of the 30s saw in it than for what it may have been. For them it cast the same "peculiar atmosphere of influence, manners, respectability" Leonard Woolf had found in the Stephen home.[8]

Even the other novelist of the group attributed to Virginia defects associated with the group and so shared in the climate of opinion which has kept her work relatively unexplored. Although E. M. Forster concludes that she escapes "the Palace of Art," noting that "she was tough, sensitive but tough," his essay as a whole nevertheless reflects the view that Mrs. Woolf lived in an ivory tower during the politically left-oriented 30s, that she was remote from reality (though at times a shrill feminist), ignorant of the class struggle, and, in William Troy's words, "as acutely refined and aristocratic" as Henry James.[9] This criticism became virulent in the mouth of F. R. Leavis and his *Scrutiny* followers. As the daughter of Sir Leslie Stephen, an eminent member of the complicated interlocking intellectual aristocracy of Victorian England, she was related to the major writers, civil servants, editors, publishers, professors and administrators of her day.[10] As such, she excited antagonism. Her own and her father's agnosticism, her deep concern with the status of women, her marriage to a lifetime left-socialist journalist who, despite his Cambridge background, would as a Jew always be an outsider in England, their management of the Hogarth Press which they started in their basement, the death of her nephew, Julian Bell, in the Spanish Civil War and her anxiety over the rise of Hitler—all these at the time honorific participations were ignored in the hyperesthetic portrait created by hostile contemporaries.

Partly she fits this portrait. Partly she is the victim of the romantic middle class notion that the working class has a monopoly on reality. (Her own origins, it should be underscored, are intellectually aristocratic, not aristocratic by class, like Orlando/Vita Sackville–West's.) Also she was a young contemporary—unlike James, who was removed and revered and, by 1916, dead. Perhaps the explanation is partly that uncomplicated for critics who admire Henry James, finding his "refinement" acceptable and hers unacceptable. Mrs. Woolf was never forgiven her origins, nor was she ever forgiven her lapses into sentimentality or bombast although writers like Lawrence or Faulkner were abundantly forgiven theirs.[11]

Contemporaries were probably also influenced in their judgment of

[8] *Ibid.,* p. 75.

[9] Troy, p. 325.

[10] See especially Noel Annan, *Leslie Stephen* (Cambridge: Harvard University Press, 1952).

[11] Henry James "was uneasy at not finding in them the standard of lady-like life and manners which belonged to Hyde Park Gate." Such, according to Leonard Woolf, was the report Sydney Waterlow gave him of James's impression of the Stephen girls. *Sowing* (New York: Harcourt, Brace & World, 1960), p. 121.

Virginia and her works by their knowledge of her mental illness. It may have reinforced for many the frailness and the remoteness they found in her fiction. The publication of *A Writer's Diary* and of Leonard Woolf's autobiographies since her death permit us a more complete picture of the manic-depressive condition which governed her life, erupting in four major breakdowns and suicide attempts. Her death by suicide is more the culmination of a lifelong condition than it is the inability of a sensitive soul to take the bombing of Britain during World War II as some have suggested. In fact, the depression which brought on her death came, as three previous severe depressions did, with the completion of a novel, *Between the Acts*.[12] The testimony of *A Writer's Diary* shows Mrs. Woolf quite able to function under the strain of bombing and the fear of invasion that so totally filled the years 1940 and 1941.

We may therefore conclude that attitudes toward her personality, her origins and her literary-political circle must have conditioned the onesidedness of the portrait that has come down to us and affected the reading of her fiction as "disengaged." Her novels may, however, justifiably claim to have represented a portion of "reality," even of social reality.

For an artist so obsessed with subjective vision, Virginia Woolf was, like D. H. Lawrence ("Never trust the artist. Trust the tale"), unusually insistent on the separation of the self from the artist.[13] During the gestation of *The Waves*, she asked herself: "Who thinks it? And am I outside the thinker? One wants some device which is not a trick." [14] Another diary entry notes, apropos of a visit from Sydney Webb: "Sydney comes and I'm Virginia: when I write I'm merely a sensibility." [15] The time should have arrived when readers and critics may see her more as writer than as Virginia.

The publication of *A Writer's Diary* in 1953 significantly brought that time closer. It permitted a completer picture of Mrs. Woolf's life as a writer and of the genesis and growth of her major novels. It initiated a less partisan reception of her work. The years have also made additional biographical material about her and her circle available. These include Leonard Woolf's autobiographical volumes, John Maynard Keynes's earlier essay, "My Early Beliefs," the two volume biography of Lytton Strachey, the memoirs of Sir Harold Nicolson (the husband of Vita Sackville–West) and those of John Lehmann, one

---

[12] A fifth severe depression that nearly resulted in breakdown occurred while she was correcting proofs of *The Years* in 1936. According to Leonard Woolf in *Downhill All the Way* (New York: Harcourt, Brace & World, 1967), pp. 55, 153, it was his wife's most severe depression since 1913.

[13] *Studies in Classic American Literature* (New York: Doubleday, 1923), p. 13.

[14] *AWD*, p. 142.

[15] *Ibid.*, p. 55.

of the first employees of the Hogarth Press.[16] Letters and manuscripts have also begun to be available.[17] More will become so, to swell the kind of documentation that can impede as well as enlighten. Distance is at least as helpful as context as Lily Briscoe's truism, "So much depends upon distance," reminds us. It may make a more enduring examination of the relationship between art and autobiography more possible than it has heretofore been.

Before the publication of *A Writer's Diary* some seven book length studies had appeared, of which those by R. W. Chambers and James Hafley are easily the best. Hafley's study, although published in 1954, was written before *A Writer's Diary* appeared and is still one of the most provocative studies of Woolf. He contends, for example, that she does not use the stream of consciousness technique, is not indebted to Joyce (a position Leon Edel rejects) and exhibits a pattern and end in her work from first to last novel. Of the book length studies which have followed, Jean Guiguet's has been the most formidably thorough. Guiguet also insists on the unity and design of her work, claiming that the novelist "spent her life rewriting the same book, of which she has given us nine different versions." [18] Perhaps this apparently self-evident judgment must be understood against the earlier charge that her work is amorphous and without focus.

Among the essays, Erich Auerbach's does what E. M. Forster's may have intended to do. His is the rare tribute. An outsider uninvolved in local fashion placed Virginia Woolf in the larger tradition of Western literature, devoting the concluding chapter of his study of the representation of reality in Western literature from Homer to the present, to Virginia Woolf, deciding that she rather than Joyce exemplifies the modern vision of subjective reality.

Auerbach's essay, although published after Mrs. Woolf's death, preceded by some years the publication of *A Writer's Diary*. The latter

[16] Leonard Woolf, *Sowing: 1880–1914* (New York: Harcourt, Brace & World, 1960); *Growing: 1904–1911* (New York: Harcourt, Brace & World, 1961); *Beginning Again: 1911–1918* (New York: Harcourt, Brace & World, 1964); *Downhill All the Way: 1919–1939* (New York: Harcourt, Brace & World, 1967); *The Journey Not the Arrival Matters: 1939–1969* (New York: Harcourt, Brace & World, 1970); J. M. Keynes, *Two Memoirs* (London: R. Hart–Davis, 1949); [written 1938]; Michael Holroyd, *Lytton Strachey* (London: Heinemann, 1967–68), 2 vols.; Harold Nicolson, *Diaries and Letters,* ed. Nigel Nicolson (London: Collins, 1966–68), 3 vols.; John Lehmann, *In My Own Time* (Boston: Little, Brown, 1969).

[17] The Vita Sackville-West letters in Aileen Pippett's biography *The Moth and the Star* (Boston: Little, Brown, 1955) are valuable; the *Virginia Woolf and Lytton Strachey: Letters,* ed. Leonard Woolf and James Strachey (New York: Harcourt, Brace, 1956) are perfunctory. Manuscript materials are, for example, available in the Berg Collection of the New York Public Library and in the British Museum.

[18] Jean Guiguet, *Virginia Woolf and Her Works* (New York: Harcourt, Brace & World, 1965), p. 196.

publication probably stimulated the appearance in February 1956 of an entire issue devoted to Virginia Woolf by the then very new periodical, *Modern Fiction Studies*. That issue suggests the strong early, and still continuing, critical interest in the poetic elements of Mrs. Woolf's fiction, an interest which contributors to this volume like Reuben Brower, Leon Edel, William Troy and others represent—though they are sharply divided about the success, even the advisability, of her attempt to use metaphor structurally. The essays of the 60s, well represented here by critics like Temple, McConnell, Wilkinson, Batchelor, tend to be more sympathetic to Virginia Woolf and to see her as a tougher and more focused writer than she is usually thought to be. The direction they chart is the direction criticism is likely to continue to take.

II

Virginia Woolf shared the restless experimentalism of her generation. The drive to begin anew may be seen as compulsion; it may also be seen as a kind of courage, an artistic strategy that is anything but soft. Before *The Waves* had its name or design, Mrs. Woolf, noting her lack of "any notion what it is to be like," assumed it would be "a completely new attempt," adding, "So I always think." [19]

But each of her completely new attempts did contain constants. One was her need to explore her double vision of reality. Terence and Rachel of her first novel are partly a double personality whose engagement never becomes a marriage. Terence, her surer novelistic self, must complete the awakening of Rachel, her softer, sheltered, more uncertain and highly naive feminine self. The Terence interested in Silence speaks for his author who knows that a novelist is also interested in talk and in objects. The attraction of these two kinds of reality always pulled at Mrs. Woolf. When she divided novels into novels of fact and vision she was expressing a classification she thought inherent in life and in fiction.[20] Contrary to what she seemed to be saying in her famous attack on Wells-Bennett-Galsworthy in her essay, "Mr. Bennett and Mrs. Brown," fact interested her as much as vision. If death was in the midst of life in all her novels, fact was always in the midst of vision.

The technique of writing about talk, a kind of fact, had been developed and perfected in the novel form. But how write about Silence? " 'The difficulty is immense,' " Terence knew and said.[21] The paradox of talk about silence was one Woolf did not care to solve by authorial

[19] *AWD*, p. 131.
[20] *Ibid.*, p. 179.
[21] *The Voyage Out*, p. 216.

objectivity. She is one of the very few modernists who did not want objective (read dramatic) narration or a single center of consciousness. If she ·did write stream of consciousness, she wrote the simplest, the most lucid, probably the most superficial example of it. Her internal discourse is almost never discontinuous, never close to the pre-speech level and always carefully, almost too obviously guided by connectives which place it precisely. She did learn to internalize omniscient comment more skillfully. *Jacob's Room,* for all its departures from her first two novels, is painfully filled with unnecessary and obtrusive author comment. What she puts into her own mouth in that novel she learned to put into the mouths of others or to discard altogether. Although the musings of the London citizens who see the motor car pageant or the skywriting in *Mrs. Dalloway* may not connect various levels of life and reality for all readers, these musings are more skillfully interwoven into the texture of the novel than are the musings in *Jacob's Room.* Mrs. Woolf never wished to subordinate or to hide her omniscient powers. She wished to learn to use them in a new way.

Probably omniscience interested her because she wanted a method that would permit more than one person to speak in a way that dramatic narration would not permit. *Mrs. Dalloway* gave her one method and each of her subsequent novels gave her another. In no novel does one person speak. What she tried to develop may be called a kind of multipersonal method.[22] It was one way for her to "keep form and speed, and enclose everything, everything." [23] This paradoxical and inevitably frustrating aim was always before her.

How include everything when she was "as usual . . . bored by narrative" or obsessed by the inadequacy of the word novel? She called *To the Lighthouse* an elegy, *The Waves* a play-poem, *The Years* an essay-novel. She could say after *Orlando* was finished: "I feel more and more sure that I will never write a novel again," then, after her most daring departure from the novel form, *The Waves,* feel again attracted by traditional novel material and ask, as she was formulating *The Years*: "How give ordinary waking Arnold Bennett life the form of art?" If we were to decide her intentions as a novelist from her essay, "Mr. Bennett and Mrs. Brown," we should agree that she above all wanted to be faithful to Mrs. Brown. She insisted that the novelist never desert Mrs. Brown yet she deserted her frequently, if not always. In fact, a severe and common charge against her is that she did not create character. She may not even have wanted to. She wryly notes that a London *Times* review of *The Waves* praises "my characters when I meant to have none." [24]

[22] Compare Erich Auerbach's use of this term in "The Brown Stocking," *Mimesis* (New York: Doubleday, 1952), pp. 473–74. See this volume, p. 79.

[23] *AWD,* p. 32.

[24] All references in the paragraph are to *AWD,* pp. 83, 109, 179, 122.

Thus she did in a sense constantly fight her medium, forcing it to do what it could not do and perhaps once or twice succeeding in the impossible—in making a work of fiction without character or narrative.

Her first two novels are apprentice works that put in too much and include too little. No later novels took so long or were rewritten so much as *The Voyage Out* and *Night and Day*.[25] The titles suggest her constantly adventuring spirit and equally constant sense of duality— of terror and ecstasy, flux and the moment, fact and vision. The awakening of Rachel to passion, the true subject of *The Voyage Out,* never again engaged Mrs. Woolf. The novel takes far too long to get to its subject and in its effort to include everything superficially uses too many characters. *Night and Day,* invariably taken for social comedy poorly done, may have as its true subject the relation between the sexes, reflecting, like *The Voyage Out,* a deep dissatisfaction with accepted patterns of courtship and marriage. The novel's primary examination of two couples may represent a Woolfian *Women in Love.* The title suggests several things: the movement from couple to couple, the difference between social or day selves and private or night selves and, in one critic's view, the chapters represent a regular and deliberate alternation "between surface description and interior analysis." [26] The novel opens with Katherine Hilbery pouring tea, inwardly noting at the same time that the activity occupies only one fifth of her consciousness. She reminds the reader of Terence's projected novel about Silence and of her author's effort to get more fifths to the surface.

Jacob's Room, like the two earlier novels, is drenched in literary talk and literary allusions. Nothing stands out like Clarissa Dalloway's "Fear no more the heat of the sun" or Mr. Ramsay's "We perished, each alone," though the novel, much shorter than the first two, uses time far more selectively and is more consistent in tone and method than the earlier two. It also displays for the first time the author's characteristic repetition and use of imagery for structural purposes— so much so that the reader forgets he is following a young man chronologically from cradle to grave. But he isn't really following Jacob; Jacob as object is always elusive and indirect. The reader is really following the portrait other people have of Jacob; in that sense his room is another indirect means of looking at him. This new technique makes *Jacob's Room* a first novel.

The room as setting, like England's town, country, and literature, is filled with emotionally charged meaning as settings were always

---

[25] According to Leonard Woolf in *Beginning Again,* Mrs. Woolf rewrote *The Voyage Out* five times and finished it in 1913. Publication was delayed two years due to her breakdown (pp. 81, 87). *Night and Day* took six years to write (pp. 92–93).

[26] Guiguet, pp. 210–11.

again to be except in *The Waves* where setting is only symbol (the Hampton Court reunion, Percival's death in India) and never place as well. Some characters appear only once as they do in *Mrs. Dalloway.* Mrs. Norman and Mrs. Lidgett in *Jacob's Room,* like Mrs. Johnson and others in *Mrs. Dalloway* who join the main plot for a moment when they see the airplane or the motorcade, are examples of the omniscient author's hand held out in the open, manipulating rather than internalizing. The novel recalls later novels in other ways. Its elegiac tone recurs most strongly in *To the Lighthouse.* Its more specific attention to the sudden death of a young man recalls the deaths of Septimus (*Mrs. Dalloway*), Andrew (*To the Lighthouse*), and Percival (*The Waves*)—and of the author's brother, Thoby Stephen.

Thus, interesting as Virginia Woolf's first two novels are, *Jacob's Room* represents her true beginning. From now on her novels came quickly and regularly, usually written in a year, sometimes two, and usually alternating with critical writing.

With her best work still ahead of her, her readers can note John Middleton Murry's warning that *Jacob's Room* was a dead end and be pleased that Mrs. Woolf did not believe him. Her next four works are probably her best. They show her skill in exploring and manipulating time, personality and memory. In *Mrs. Dalloway, To the Lighthouse, Orlando* and *The Waves* intention and achievement are remarkably close.

Mrs. Dalloway and *To the Lighthouse* discard the narrative forms of *The Voyage Out* and *Night and Day* and the traditional cradle to grave chronology of *Jacob's Room.* Both novels integrate past and present. The "tunnelling process" of *Mrs. Dalloway* moves between the present time of one day and the personal past of Clarissa, Peter and Septimus.[27] It also looks forward to the culminating event of the day, Clarissa's party. *To the Lighthouse* deals with a past created in the novel rather than with one that existed prior to the novel as in *Mrs. Dalloway.* Once again, time and memory are handled with wit and risk, although the greater risk in *Mrs. Dalloway* is not the manipulation of memory but the splitting up of personality into a man and a woman who never meet. The greater risk in *To the Lighthouse* is the decision to have the dead heroine preside silently in the memory of the five figures of Part Three and in effect to mastermind the action of that section. The wit of the design lies as much, of course, in the decision to have two long days frame a very brief ten years. Thus, both novels may be said to use the chronology of a day as basic strategy; but Mrs. Woolf has clearly learned how to use and how to escape chronology at the same time.

---

[27] *AWD*, p. 66: "It took me a year's groping to discover what I call my tunnelling process, by which I tell the past by installments, as I have need of it. This is my prime discovery so far."

In *Orlando* and *The Waves* Mrs. Woolf moves further and further away from the kind of modern novel she helped to define. Even in the Woolf canon *Orlando* is a sport, an "essay novel" on English literature, character and manners from Elizabethan times to the present, a fantasy with a main character who changes sex in 1683 and is over 300 years old when the novel closes in 1928. Though begun as a lark, *Orlando* may have served the more serious function of freeing its creator from dependence on the usual novelistic controls. It may have freed her for the creation of *The Waves*, if that novel is, as many critics believe, her best. *The Waves* can be called an anti-novel. The exciting artistic risk of that novel is the splitting up of personality into six voices only tenuously connected to external reality. Bernard, the talkiest of the six, wonders: "Am I all of them?" This novel, of voices without bodies or setting, may be an intellectualized tour-de-force that the common reader Mrs. Woolf prized would never return to, a kind of sport, like *Orlando*.

Her last two novels are re-combinations of familiar fictional strategies, as though the writer were enjoying a conventional holiday—one quite unlike the writer's holiday she said she was taking when she wrote *Orlando*. The principle of selection her mature works so suitably reflect deserts her in *The Years*, but reasserts itself in *Between the Acts* which more effectively evokes England than its predecessor. The counterpoint of a village pageant play which covers the English past against a few hours of present time moves lyrically and unostentatiously within what are essentially traditional novelistic techniques of dialogue and description. *Orlando* may also look ahead to these last two novels which are less interested in personal memory or personality than in nationality, tradition and myth—the dimension Mrs. Woolf was likely to continue to explore had she written more novels.

Although serpent and toad intrude in *Between the Acts*, neither it nor the other later novels contain Holmeses, Bradshaws or Kilmans. Old Giles appears to be speaking for the author when he divides people into "unifiers" and "separatists," but the poles of *Between the Acts* are in fact less sharp. The author's view of human nature seems more accepting despite the brutal and frustrating image of the snake "choked with a toad in its mouth. The snake . . . unable to swallow; the toad . . . unable to die." [28] Lucy Swithin's doubt that people were ever "Victorian" probably reflects her creator's view, one rather different from her hypothesis that "on or about December 1910 human character changed" or her projection that happily did not materialize of Mr. Ramsay as merely patriarchal Victorian.[29] Mrs. Woolf even

---

[28] *Between the Acts* (New York: Harcourt, Brace & World, 1941), pp. 118, 99.
[29] See Virginia Woolf's essay, "Leslie Stephen" (1932) written for the hundredth anniversary of her father's birth: reprinted in *The Captain's Death-Bed and Other*

makes of Lucy the kind of befuddled grab bag religious type she could not earlier have handled sympathetically and has her reading, of all things, H. G. Wells's *Outline of History*. The aggressive and rigid religiosity of a Doris Kilman would be very much out of place in *Between the Acts*. Like the skull under the shawl in *To the Lighthouse*, or the sheep's skull in *Jacob's Room*, snake and toad exist, but the conception of motivation and character is more benign and more complicated in her final novel.

Mrs. Woolf's life as a reader and a critic fed her life as a novelist. Her first publications were reviews for the *Times Literary Supplement*. Her reading was avid and deep, especially in English literature; and she was more the common reader in her taste than the selective or exclusionary reader friends like T. S. Eliot were. Though she chafed under the need to write reviews, she chose not to give them up when she was financially able to do so.[30] They were refreshment and exploration. Novels like *Orlando* and *Between the Acts* are only more obviously connected with her deep involvement in English tradition than are her other novels. Although she has usually been considered more impressionist than formalist as a critic, a recent commentator, Mark Goldman, makes a case for her criticism as formalist in foundation. At least two of her essays have become required reading for anyone interested in modernist fiction theory. In the very frequently anthologized "Modern Fiction" (1919) and "Mr. Bennett and Mrs. Brown" (1924) Mrs. Woolf appears to have articulated the dissatisfactions and the yearnings of a whole artistic generation.

Like Mr. Ramsay, she was acutely sensitive to the criticism of others; unlike him she was pretty good at self-criticism. She lights on the character of Clarissa Dalloway as the point of doubt about *Mrs. Dalloway*: "It may be too stiff, too glittering and tinselly." She finds *Orlando* "too freakish and unequal, very brilliant now and then, . . . a joke" continued too "seriously." She anticipates her own worst critics in her question: "Have I the power of conveying the true reality? Or do I write essays about myself?"[31] Such criticism is a part of the toughness Frank McConnell and other contributors to this volume see in Mrs. Woolf.

Her feminism may be another facet of her toughness, perhaps best seen against her constant sense of opposing states. She describes *Orlando*, and probably herself, as "censuring both sexes equally, as

---

Essays (New York: Harcourt, Brace & World, 1950), pp. 69–75. Gertrude Himmelfarb misreads Mr. Ramsay's character as unchanging and exactly like Mr. Stephen's; in "Mr. Stephen and Mr. Ramsay: The Victorian Intellectual," *Twentieth Century*, CLII (December 1952), 513–25.

[30] According to Leonard Woolf the Woolfs were financially well off only after 1928. See *Downhill All the Way*, p. 145.

[31] *AWD*, pp. 66, 126, 63.

if she belonged to neither." [32] The engagement of her first fictional couple, Terence and Rachel, may postulate a united androgynous self. But the union never takes place; Rachel dies. Only in fantasy, only in *Orlando* can ideal androgyny exist. A witty view, yes; also a shrewd one. Mrs. Woolf's later couples are more separate than Lawrence's; sometimes they seem more separate than united. Clarissa seems closer to Septimus or to Sally Seton than to Richard Dalloway or to Peter Walsh; Mrs. Ramsay closer finally to Lily Briscoe than to Mr. Ramsay. Her women are usually better with feelings and people than her men. Although she can do well by the single woman as artist (Lily Briscoe, Miss LaTrobe), she can be merciless with the single woman as proselytizer (Doris Kilman). She does accept Mary Datchet's devotion to women's rights, but Mary had a man to lose; Doris never did. Her best female figures are wives and mothers—an interesting paradox in a woman violently attacked for her feminism. [33] The artistic relevance of her feminism is likely to receive less partisan examination today as J. B. Batchelor and other critics have shown. [34]

We may come to see Virginia Woolf as less frail in her life and in her art than we have heretofore. Her productivity was, for example, striking. She did not match the torrential outpourings of her father, Sir Leslie Stephen, and other Victorians, but she did write 17 books in 21 years (too much perhaps by current standards). Her illness cannot make us ignore this fact. She appears to have been in life an example of the contrary states she explored in her novels: solid and shifting, male and female, a creature made up of fact and vision, subject to terror and ecstasy. The oppositions she lived and wrote about may, in the words of one critic, be identical, "insofar as one logically 'implies' the other," or contains the other—whether we speak of isolation and connection, uniqueness and anonymity or of any of the other pairings we have used. [35] What Virginia Woolf called the "amphibious" periods of her life ("I'm amphibious still, in bed and out of it.") seem to have been a necessary part of her creative life. She is capable of a detached, even implicitly arrogant, appraisal of her amphibious self: "this state, my depressed state, is the state in which most people usually are." [36]

Two years before her death she thought how interesting it would

[32] *Orlando* (New York: Signet, n.d.), p. 103.

[33] See, for example, Q. D. Leavis' review of *Three Guineas*: "Caterpillars of the Commonwealth Unite," *Scrutiny*, VII (September 1938), 203–14.

[34] See, for example, Herbert Marder, *Feminism and Art* (Chicago: University of Chicago Press, 1968) and Ralph Samuelson, "Virginia Woolf: *Orlando* and the Feminist Spirit," *Western Humanities Review*, XV (Winter 1961), 51–58.

[35] "A Principle of Unity in *Between the Acts*," *Criticism*, VIII (1966), p. 62. See this volume, p. 145.

[36] *AWD*, pp. 85, 195. She also refers to her "odd amphibious life of headache," p. 84.

be to treat the "tremendous experience" of aging, one "not as un-conscious . . . as birth is." This may or may not have been the sub-ject she had in mind at the time of her death. But she was already thinking about her next novel while she was revising *Between the Acts*. "It will be a supported-on-fact book" she had decided.[37] That unwritten work was likely to have been another voyage out.

[37] *AWD*, pp. 292, 331.

Virginia Woolf

by E. M. Forster

When I was appointed to this lectureship the work of Virginia Woolf was much in my mind, and I asked to be allowed to speak on it. To speak on it, rather than to sum it up. There are two obstacles to a summing up. The first is the work's richness and complexity. As soon as we dismiss the legend of the Invalid Lady of Bloomsbury, so guilelessly accepted by Arnold Bennett, we find ourselves in a bewildering world where there are few headlines. We think of *The Waves* and say "Yes—that is Virginia Woolf"; then we think of *The Common Reader*, where she is different, of *A Room of One's Own* or of the preface to *Life as we have known it:* different again. She is like a plant which is supposed to grow in a well-prepared garden bed— the bed of esoteric literature—and then pushes up suckers all over the place, through the gravel of the front drive, and even through the flagstones of the kitchen yard. She was full of interests, and their number increased as she grew older, she was curious about life, and she was tough, sensitive but tough. How can her achievement be summed up in an hour? A headline sometimes serves a lecturer as a life-line on these occasions, and brings him safely into the haven where he would be. Shall I find one today?

The second obstacle is that 1941 is not a good year in which to sum up anything. Our judgments, to put it mildly, are not at their prime. We are all of us upon the Leaning Tower, as she called it, even those of us who date from the nineteenth century, when the earth was still horizontal and the buildings perpendicular. We cannot judge the landscape properly as we look down, for everything is tilted. Isolated objects are not so puzzling; a tree, a wave, a hat, a jewel, an old gentleman's bald head look much as they always did. But the relation between objects—that we cannot estimate, and that is why the verdict must be left to another generation. I have not the least faith that anything which we now value will survive historically (something

"Virginia Woolf" by E. M. Forster. From *Two Cheers for Democracy* (New York: Harcourt, Brace & World, Inc., 1942), pp. 242–58. Originally the Rede Lecture, delivered in the Senate House, Cambridge, 1941. Copyright 1942 by Harcourt, Brace & World, Inc. Reprinted by permission of Harcourt Brace Jovanovich, Inc. and Edward Arnold Publishers Ltd.

which we should have valued may evolve, but that is a different proposition); and maybe another generation will dismiss Virginia Woolf as worthless and tiresome. However, this is not my opinion, nor I think yours; we still have the word, and I wonder whether I cannot transmit some honour to her from the university she so admired, and from the central building of that university. She would receive the homage a little mockingly, for she was somewhat astringent over the academic position of women. "What? I in the Senate House?" she might say. "Are you sure that is quite proper? And why, if you want to discuss my books, need you first disguise yourselves in caps and gowns?" But I think she would be pleased. She loved Cambridge. Indeed, I cherish a private fancy that she once took her degree here. She, who could disguise herself as a member of the suite of the Sultan of Zanzibar, or black her face to go aboard a Dreadnought as an Ethiopian[1]—she could surely have hoaxed our innocent praelectors, and, kneeling in this very spot, have presented to the Vice-Chancellor the exquisite but dubious head of Orlando.

There is, after all, one little life-line to catch hold of: she liked writing. . . .

She liked writing with an intensity which few writers have attained, or even desired. Most of them write with half an eye on their royalties, half an eye on their critics, and a third half eye on improving the world, which leaves them with only half an eye for the task on which she concentrated her entire vision. She would not look elsewhere, and her circumstances combined with her temperament to focus her. Money she had not to consider, because she possessed a private income, and though financial independence is not always a safeguard against commercialism, it was in her case. Critics she never considered while she was writing, although she could be attentive to them and even humble afterwards. Improving the world she would not consider, on the ground that the world is man-made, and that she, a woman, had no responsibility for the mess. This last opinion is a curious one, and I shall be returning to it; still, she held it, it completed the circle of her defences, and neither the desire for money nor the desire for reputation nor philanthropy could influence her. She had a singleness of purpose which will not recur in this country for many years, and writers who have liked writing as she liked it have not indeed been common in any age.

Now the pitfall for such an author is obvious. It is the Palace of Art, it is that bottomless chasm of dullness which pretends to be a palace, all glorious with corridors and domes, but which is really a dreadful hole into which the unwary esthete may tumble, to be seen

---

[1] See Adrian Stephen, *The Dreadnought Hoax*. See, still more, an unpublished paper which she herself once wrote for a Women's Institute, leaving it helpless with laughter.

no more. She has all the esthete's characteristics: selects and manipulates her impressions; is not a great creator of character; enforces patterns on her books; has no great cause at heart. So how did she avoid her appropriate pitfall and remain up in the fresh air, where we can hear the sound of the stable boy's boots, or boats bumping, or Big Ben; where we can taste really new bread, and touch real dahlias? . . . She might have become a glorified diseuse, who frittered away her broader effects by mischievousness, and she did give that impression to some who met her in the flesh; there were moments when she could scarcely see the busts for the moustaches she pencilled on them, and when the bust was a modern one, whether of a gentleman in a top hat or of a youth on a pylon, it had no chance of remaining sublime. But in her writing, even in her light writing, central control entered. She was master of her complicated equipment, and though most of us like to write sometimes seriously and sometimes in fun, few of us can so manage the two impulses that they speed each other up, as hers did.

The above remarks are more or less introductory. It seems convenient now to recall what she did write, and to say a little about her development. She began back in 1915 with *The Voyage Out*—a strange, tragic, inspired novel about English tourists in an impossible South American hotel; her passion for truth is here already, mainly in the form of atheism, and her passion for wisdom is here in the form of music. The book made a deep impression upon the few people who read it. Its successor, *Night and Day*, disappointed them. This is an exercise in classical realism, and contains all that has characterised English fiction, for good and evil, during the last two hundred years: faith in personal relations, recourse to humorous side-shows, geographical exactitude, insistence on petty social differences: indeed most of the devices she so gaily derides in *Mr. Bennett and Mrs. Brown*. The style has been normalised and dulled. But at the same time she published two short stories, *Kew Gardens,* and *The Mark on the Wall.* These are neither dull nor normal; lovely little things; her style trails after her as she walks and talks, catching up dust and grass in its folds, and instead of the precision of the earlier writing we have something more elusive than had yet been achieved in English. Lovely little things, but they seemed to lead nowhere, they were all tiny dots and coloured blobs, they were an inspired breathlessness, they were a beautiful droning or gasping which trusted to luck. They were perfect as far as they went, but that was not far, and none of us guessed that out of the pollen of those flowers would come the trees of the future. Consequently when *Jacob's Room* appeared in 1922 we were tremendously surprised. The style and sensitiveness of *Kew Gardens* remained, but they were applied to human relationships, and to the structure of society. The blobs of colour continue to drift past, but in their midst, interrupting their course like a closely sealed jar, stands the solid figure of a young man. The improbable has occurred; a method essentially poetic and apparently trifling has been applied to fiction. She was still uncertain of the possibilities of the new technique, and *Jacob's Room* is an uneven little book, but it represents her great departure, and her abandonment of the false start of *Night and Day*. It leads on to her genius in its fullness; to *Mrs. Dalloway* (1925), *To the Lighthouse* (1927), and *The Waves* (1931). These successful works are all suffused with poetry and enclosed in it. *Mrs. Dalloway* has the framework of a London summer's day, down which go spiralling two fates: the fate of the sensitive worldly hostess, and the fate of the sensitive obscure maniac; though they never touch they are closely connected, and at the same moment we lose sight of them both. It is a civilised book, and it was written from personal experience. In her work, as in her private problems, she was always civilised and sane on the subject of madness. She pared the edges off this particular malady, she tied it down to being a malady, and robbed it of the evil magic it has acquired through timid or careless thinking; here is one of the gifts we have to thank her for. *To the Lighthouse* is, however, a much greater achievement, partly because the chief characters in it, Mr. and Mrs. Ramsay, are so interesting. They hold us, we think of them away from their surroundings, and yet they are in accord with those surroundings, with the poetic scheme. *To the Lighthouse* is in three movements. It has been called a novel in sonata form, and certainly the slow central section, conveying the passing of time, does demand a musical analogy. We have, when reading it, the rare pleasure of inhabiting two worlds at once, a pleasure only art can give: the world where a little boy wants to go to a lighthouse but never manages it until, with changed emotions, he goes there as a young man; and the world where there is pattern, and this world is emphasised by passing much of the observation through the mind of Lily Briscoe, who is a painter. Then comes *The Waves*. Pattern here is supreme—indeed it is italicised. And between the motions of the sun and the waters, which preface each section, stretch, without interruption, conversation, words in inverted commas. It is a strange conversation, for the six characters, Bernard, Neville, Louis, Susan, Jinny, Rhoda, seldom address one another, and it is even possible to regard them (like Mrs. Dalloway and Septimus) as different facets of one single person. Yet they do not conduct internal monologues, they are in touch amongst themselves, and they all touch the character who never speaks, Percival. At the end, most perfectly balancing their scheme, Bernard, the would-be novelist, sums up, and the pattern fades out. *The Waves* is an extraordinary achievement, an immense extension of the possibilities of *Kew Gardens* and *Jacob's Room*. It is trembling on the edge. A little less—and it would lose its poetry. A little more

—and it would be over into the abyss, and be dull and arty. It is her greatest book, though *To the Lighthouse* is my favourite.

It was followed by *The Years*. This is another experiment in the realistic tradition. It chronicles the fortunes of a family through a documented period. As in *Night and Day*, she deserts poetry, and again she fails. But in her posthumous novel *Between the Acts* she returns to the method she understood. Its theme is a village pageant, which presents the entire history of England, and into which, at the close, the audience is itself drawn, to continue that history; "The curtain rose" is its concluding phrase. The conception is poetic, and the text of the pageant is mostly written in verse. She loved her country—the country that is the countryside, and emerges from the unfathomable past. She takes us back in this exquisite final tribute, and she points us on, and she shows us through her poetic vagueness something more solid than patriotic history, and something better worth dying for.

Amongst all this fiction, nourishing it and nourished by it, grow other works. Two volumes of *The Common Reader* show the breadth of her knowledge and the depth of her literary sympathy; let anyone who thinks her an exquisite recluse read what she says on Jack Mytton the foxhunter. As a critic she could enter into anything—anything lodged in the past, that is to say; with her contemporaries she sometimes had difficulties. Then there are the biographies, fanciful and actual. *Orlando* is, I need hardly say, an original book, and the first part of it is splendidly written: the description of the Great Frost is already received as a "passage" in English literature, whatever a passage may be. After the transformation of sex things do not go so well; the authoress seems unconvinced by her own magic and somewhat fatigued by it, and the biography finishes competently rather than brilliantly; it has been a fancy on too large a scale, and we can see her getting bored. But *Flush* is a complete success, and exactly what it sets out to be; the material, the method, the length, accord perfectly, it is doggie without being silly, and it does give us, from the altitude of the carpet or the sofa-foot, a peep at high poetic personages, and a new angle on their ways. The biography of Roger Fry—one should not proceed direct from a spaniel to a Slade Professor, but Fry would not have minded and spaniels mind nothing—reveals a new aspect of her powers, the power to suppress herself. She indulges in a pattern, but she never intrudes her personality or overhandles her English; respect for her subject dominates her, and only occasionally —as in her description of the divinely ordered chaos of Fry's studio with its still-life of apples and eggs labelled "please do not touch"— does she allow her fancy to play. Biographies are too often described as "labours of love," but the *Roger Fry* really is in this class; one artist is writing with affection of another, so that he may be remembered and may be justified.

Finally, there are the feminist books—*A Room of One's Own* and *Three Guineas*—and several short essays, etc., some of them significant. It is as a novelist that she will be judged. But the rest of her work must be remembered, partly on its merits, partly because (as William Plomer has pointed out) she is sometimes more of a novelist in it than in her novels.

After this survey, we can state her problem. Like most novelists worth reading, she strays from the fictional norm. She dreams, designs, jokes, invokes, observes details, but she does not tell a story or weave a plot, and—can she create character? That is her problem's centre. That is the point where she felt herself open to criticism—to the criticisms, for instance, of her friend Hugh Walpole. Plot and story could be set aside in favour of some other unity, but if one is writing about human beings, one does want them to seem alive. Did she get her people to live?

Now there seem to be two sorts of life in fiction, life on the page, and life eternal. Life on the page she could give; her characters never seem unreal, however slight or fantastic their lineaments, and they can be trusted to behave appropriately. Life eternal she could seldom give; she could seldom so portray a character that it was remembered afterwards on its own account, as Emma is remembered, for instance, or Dorothea Casaubon, or Sophia and Constance in *The Old Wives' Tale*. What wraiths, apart from their context, are the wind-sextet from *The Waves,* or Jacob away from *Jacob's Room!* They speak no more to us or to one another as soon as the page is turned. And this is her great difficulty. Holding on with one hand to poetry, she stretches and stretches to grasp things which are best gained by letting go of poetry. She would not let go, and I think she was quite right, though critics who like a novel to be a novel will disagree. She was quite right to cling to her specific gift, even if this entailed sacrificing something else vital to her art. And she did not always have to sacrifice; Mr. and Mrs. Ramsay do remain with the reader afterwards, and so perhaps do Rachel from *The Voyage Out,* and Clarissa Dalloway. For the rest— it is impossible to maintain that here is an immortal portrait gallery. Socially she is limited to the upper-middle professional classes, and she does not even employ many types. There is the bleakly honest intellectual (St. John Hirst, Charles Tansley, Louis, William Dodge), the monumental majestic hero (Jacob, Percival), the pompous amorous pillar of society (Richard Dalloway as he appears in *The Voyage Out,* Hugh Whitbread), the scholar who cares only for young men (Bonamy, Neville), the pernickety independent (Mr. Pepper, Mr. Banks); even the Ramsays are tried out first as the Ambroses. As soon as we understand the nature of her equipment, we shall see that as regards human beings she did as well as she could. Belonging to the world of poetry, but fascinated by another world, she is always stretching out from her enchanted tree and snatching bits from the flux of daily life as they float past, and out of these bits she builds novels. She would not plunge. And she should not have plunged. She might have stayed folded up in her tree singing little songs like *Blue-Green* in the *Monday or Tuesday* volume, but fortunately for English literature she did not do this either.

So that is her problem. She is a poet, who wants to write something as near to a novel as possible.

I must pass on to say a little—it ought to be much—about her interests. I have emphasised her fondness for writing both seriously and in fun, and have tried to indicate how she wrote: how she gathered up her material and digested it without damaging its freshness, how she rearranged it to form unities, how she was a poet who wanted to write novels, how these novels bear upon them the marks of their strange gestation—some might say the scars. What concerns me now is the material itself, her interests, her opinions. And not to be too vague I will begin with food.

It is always helpful, when reading her, to look out for the passages which describe eating. They are invariably good. They are a sharp reminder that here is a woman who is alert sensuously. She had an enlightened greediness which gentlemen themselves might envy, and which few masculine writers have expressed. There is a little too much lamp oil in George Meredith's wine, a little too much paper crackling on Charles Lamb's pork, and no savour whatever in any dish of Henry James', but when Virginia Woolf mentions nice things they get right into our mouths, so far as the edibility of print permits. We taste their deliciousness. And when they are not nice, we taste them equally, our mouths awry now with laughter. I will not torture this great university of Oxbridge by reminding it of the exquisite lunch which she ate in a don's room here in the year 1929; such memories are now too painful. Nor will I insult the noble college of women in this same university—Fernham is its name—by reminding it of the deplorable dinner which she ate that same evening in its Hall—a dinner so lowering that she had to go to a cupboard afterwards and drink something out of a bottle; such memories may still be all too true to fact. But I may without offence refer to the great dish of Bœuf en Daube which forms the centre of the dinner of union in *To the Lighthouse,* the dinner round which all that section of the book coheres, the dinner which exhales affection and poetry and loveliness, so that all the characters see the best in one another at last and for a moment, and one of them, Lily Briscoe, carries away a recollection of reality. Such a dinner cannot be built on a statement beneath a dish-cover which the novelist is too indifferent or incompetent to remove. Real food is necessary, and this, in fiction as in her home, she knew how to provide. The Bœuf en Daube, which had taken the cook three days to make and had worried Mrs. Ramsay as she did her hair, stands before us "with its confusion of savoury brown and yellow meats and its bay leaves and its wine"; we peer down the shiny walls of the great casserole and get one of the best bits, and like William Bankes, generally so hard to please, we are satisfied. Food with her was not a literary device put in to make the book seem real. She put it in because she tasted it, because she saw pictures, because she smelt flowers, because she heard Bach, because her senses were both exquisite and catholic, and were always bringing her first-hand news of the outside world. Our debt to her is in part this: she reminds us of the importance of sensation in an age which practises brutality and recommends ideals. I could have illustrated sensation more reputably by quoting the charming passage about the florists' shop in *Mrs. Dalloway,* or the passage where Rachel plays upon the cabin piano. Flowers and music are conventional literary adjuncts. A good feed isn't, and that is why I preferred it and chose it to represent her reactions. Let me add that she smokes, and now let the Bœuf en Daube be carried away. It will never come back in our lifetime. It is not for us. But the power to appreciate it remains, and the power to appreciate all distinction.

After the senses, the intellect. She respected knowledge, she believed in wisdom. Though she could not be called an optimist, she had, very profoundly, the conviction that mind is in action against matter, and is winning new footholds in the void. That anything would be accomplished by her or in her generation, she did not suppose, but the noble blood from which she sprang encouraged her to hope. Mr. Ramsay, standing by the geraniums and trying to think, is not a figure of fun. Nor is this university, despite its customs and costumes: she speaks of "the light shining there—the light of Cambridge."

No light shines now from Cambridge visibly, and this prompts the comment that her books were conditioned by her period. She could not assimilate this latest threat to our civilisation. The submarine perhaps. But not the flying fortress or the land mine. The idea that all stone is like grass, and like all flesh may vanish in a twinkling, did not enter into her consciousness, and indeed it will be some time before it can be assimilated by literature. She belonged to an age which distinguished sharply between the impermanency of man and the durability of his monuments, and for whom the dome of the British Museum Reading Room was almost eternal. Decay she admitted: the delicate grey churches in the Strand would not stand for ever; but she supposed, as we all did, that decay would be gradual. The younger generation—the Auden-Isherwood generation as it is convenient to call it—saw more clearly here than could she, and she did not quite

do justice to its vision, any more than she did justice to its experiments
in technique—she who had been in her time such an experimenter.
Still, to belong to one's period is a common failing, and she made the
most of hers. She respected and acquired knowledge, she believed in
wisdom. Intellectually, no one can do more; and since she was a poet,
not a philosopher or a historian or a prophetess, she had not to consider whether wisdom will prevail and whether the square upon the
oblong, which Rhoda built out of the music of Mozart, will ever stand
firm upon this distracted earth. The square upon the oblong. Order.
Justice. Truth. She cared for these abstractions, and tried to express
them through symbols, as an artist must, though she realised the inadequacy of symbols.

> They come with their violins, said Rhoda; they wait; count; nod;
> down come their bows. And there is ripples and laughter like the dance
> of olive trees. . . .
> "Like" and "like" and "like"—but what is the thing that lies beneath
> the semblance of the thing? Now that lightning has gashed the tree and
> the flowering branch has fallen . . . let me see the thing. There is a
> square. There is an oblong. The players take the square and place it
> upon the oblong. They place it very accurately; they make a perfect
> dwelling-place. Very little is left outside. The structure is now visible;
> what is inchoate is here stated; we are not so various or so mean; we
> have made oblongs and stood them upon squares. This is our triumph;
> this is our consolation.

The consolation, that is to say, of catching sight of abstractions.
They have to be symbolised, and "the square upon the oblong" is as
much a symbol as the dancing olive trees, but because of its starkness
it comes nearer to conveying what she seeks. Seeking it, "we are not
so various or so mean"; we have added to the human heritage and
reaffirmed wisdom.

The next of her interests which has to be considered is society. She
was not confined to sensations and intellectualism. She was a social
creature, with an outlook both warm and shrewd. But it was a peculiar
outlook, and we can best get at it by looking at a very peculiar side
of her: her feminism.

Feminism inspired one of the most brilliant of her books—the charming and persuasive *A Room of One's Own;* it contains the Oxbridge
lunch and the Fernham dinner, also the immortal encounter with the
beadle when she tried to walk on the college grass, and the touching
reconstruction of Shakespeare's sister—Shakespeare's equal in genius,
but she perished because she had no position or money, and that has
been the fate of women through the ages. But feminism is also responsible for the worst of her books—the cantankerous *Three Guineas*
—and for the less successful streaks in *Orlando.* There are spots of it
all over her work, and it was constantly in her mind. She was con-

vinced that society is man-made, that the chief occupations of men are the shedding of blood, the making of money, the giving of orders, and the wearing of uniforms, and that none of these occupations is admirable. Women dress up for fun or prettiness, men for pomposity, and she had no mercy on the judge in his wig, the general in his bits and bobs of ribbon, the bishop in his robes, or even on the harmless don in his gown. She felt that all these mummers were putting something across over which women had never been consulted, and which she at any rate disliked. She declined to co-operate, in theory, and sometimes in fact. She refused to sit on committees or to sign appeals, on the ground that women must not condone this tragic male-made mess, or accept the crumbs of power which men throw them occasionally from their hideous feast. Like Lysistrata, she withdrew.

In my judgment there is something old-fashioned about this extreme feminism; it dates back to her suffragette youth of the 1910's, when men kissed girls to distract them from wanting the vote, and very properly provoked her wrath. By the 1930's she had much less to complain of, and seems to keep on grumbling from habit. She complained, and rightly, that though women today have won admission into the professions and trades they usually encounter a male conspiracy when they try to get to the top. But she did not appreciate that the conspiracy is weakening yearly, and that before long women will be quite as powerful for good or evil as men. She was sensible about the past; about the present she was sometimes unreasonable. However, I speak as a man here, and as an elderly one. The best judges of her feminism are neither elderly men nor even elderly women, but young women. If they, if the students of Fernham, think that it expresses an existent grievance, they are right.

She felt herself to be not only a woman but a lady, and this gives a further twist to her social outlook. She made no bones about it. She was a lady, by birth and upbringing, and it was no use being cowardly about it, and pretending that her mother had turned a mangle, or that her father Sir Leslie had been a plasterer's mate. Working-class writers often mentioned their origins, and were respected for doing so. Very well; she would mention hers. And her snobbery—for she was a snob—has more courage in it than arrogance. It is connected with her insatiable honesty, and is not, like the snobbery of Clarissa Dalloway, bland and frilled and unconsciously sinking into the best arm-chair. It is more like the snobbery of Kitty when she goes to tea with the Robsons; it stands up like a target for anyone to aim at who wants to. In her introduction to *Life as we have known it* (a collection of biographies of working-class women edited by Margaret Llewellyn Davies) she faces the fire. "One could not be Mrs. Giles of Durham, because one's body had never stood at the wash-tub; one's hands had never wrung and scrubbed and chopped up whatever the meat is that makes a

miner's supper." This is not disarming, and it is not intended to dis-
arm. And if one said to her that she could after all find out what
meat a miner does have for his supper if she took a little trouble, she
would retort that this wouldn't help her to chop it up, and that it is
not by knowing things but by doing things that one enters into the
lives of people who do things. And she was not going to chop up meat.
She would chop it badly, and waste her time. . . .

There is an admirable hardness here, so far as hardness can be
admirable. There is not much sympathy, and I do not think she was
sympathetic. She could be charming to individuals, working-class and
otherwise, but it was her curiosity and her honesty that motivated her.
And we must remember that sympathy, for her, entailed a tremendous
and exhausting process, not lightly to be entered on. It was not a half-
crown or a kind word or a good deed or a philanthropic sermon or a
godlike gesture; it was adding the sorrows of another to one's own.
Half fancifully, but wholly seriously, she writes:

> But sympathy we cannot have. Wisest Fate says no. If her children,
> weighted as they already are with sorrow, were to take on them that
> burden too, adding in imagination other pains to their own, buildings
> would cease to rise; roads would peter out into grassy tracks; there would
> be an end of music and of painting; one great sigh alone would rise to
> Heaven, and the only attitudes for men and women would be those of
> horror and despair.

Here perhaps is the reason why she cannot be warmer and more
human about Mrs. Giles of Durham.

This detachment from the working-classes and Labour reinforces the
detachment caused by her feminism, and her attitude to society was in
consequence aloof and angular. She was fascinated, she was unafraid,
but she detested mateyness, and she would make no concessions to
popular journalism, and the "let's all be friendly together" stunt. To
the crowd—so far as such an entity exists—she was very jolly, but she
handed out no bouquets to the middlemen who have arrogated to
themselves the right of interpreting the crowd, and get paid for doing
so in the daily press and on the wireless. These middlemen form after
all a very small clique—larger than the Bloomsbury they so tirelessly
denounce, but a mere drop in the ocean of humanity. And since it was
a drop whose distinction was proportionate to its size, she saw no reason
to conciliate it.

"And now to sum up," says Bernard in the last section of *The Waves*.
That I cannot do, for reasons already given; the material is so rich
and contradictory, and ours is not a good vintage year for judgments.
I have gone from point to point as best I could, from her method of
writing to her books, from her problems as a poet-novelist to her
problems as a woman and as a lady. And I have tried to speak of her
with the directness which she would wish, and which could alone

honour her. But how are all the points to be combined? What is the pattern resultant? The best I can do is to quote Bernard again. "The illusion is upon me," he says, "that something adheres for a moment, has roundness, weight, depth, is completed." This, for the moment, seems to be her life. Bernard puts it well. But, as Rhoda indicated in that earlier quotation, these words are only similes, comparisons with physical substances, and what one wants is the thing that lies beneath the semblance of the thing; that alone satisfies, that alone makes the full statement.

Whatever the final pattern, I am sure it will not be a depressing one. Like all her friends, I miss her greatly—I knew her ever since she started writing. But this is a personal matter, and I am sure that there is no case for lamentation here, or for the obituary note. Virginia Woolf got through an immense amount of work, she gave acute pleasure in new ways, she pushed the light of the English language a little further against darkness. Those are facts. The epitaph of such an artist cannot be written by the vulgar-minded or by the lugubrious. They will try, indeed they have already tried, but their words make no sense. It is wiser, it is safer, to regard her career as a triumphant one. She triumphed over what are primly called "difficulties," and she also triumphed in the positive sense: she brought in the spoils. And sometimes it is as a row of little silver cups that I see her work gleaming. "These trophies," the inscription runs, "were won by the mind from matter, its enemy and its friend."

Virginia Woolf: The Novel of Sensibility

by William Troy

> Life is not a series of gig-lamps symmetrically arranged; but
> *a luminous halo, a semi-transparent envelope* surrounding us
> from the beginning of consciousness to the end.

Not only in rhythm and tone but also in the imponderable vagueness of its diction this statement has a familiar ring to the modern ear.
The phrases in italics alone are sufficient to suggest its proper order
and place in contemporary thought. For if this is not the exact voice
of Henri Bergson, it is at least a very successful imitation. Dropped
so casually by Mrs. Woolf in the course of a dissertation on the art of
fiction, such a statement really implies an acceptance of a whole theory
of metaphysics. Behind it lies all that resistance to the naturalistic
formula, all that enthusiastic surrender to the world of flux and individual intuition, which has constituted the influence of Bergson on
the art and literature of the past thirty years. Whether Mrs. Woolf was
affected by this influence directly, or through the medium of Proust
or some other secondary source, is not very important. The evidence
is clear enough in her work that the fundamental view of reality on
which it is based derives from what was the most popular ideology of
her generation. What is so often regarded as unique in her fiction is
actually less the result of an individual attitude than of the dominant
metaphysical bias of a whole generation.

For members of that generation concerned with fiction the philosophy of flux and intuition offered a relief from the cumbersome technique and mechanical pattern of naturalism. (Against even such mild
adherents to the doctrine as Wells and Bennett Mrs. Woolf raised the
attack in *Mr. Bennett and Mrs. Brown*.) Moreover, the new philosophy
opened up sources of interest for the novel which allowed it to dispense
with whatever values such writers as George Eliot and Henry James
had depended on in a still remoter period. Like naturalism, it brought
with it its own version of an esthetic; it supplied a medium which

"Virginia Woolf: The Novel of Sensibility" by William Troy. From *Literary
Opinion in America*, ed. Morton Dauwen Zabel (New York: Harper & Row, Publishers, 1937), pp. 324–37.

involved no values other than the primary one of self-expression. Of course one cannot wholly ignore the helpful co-operation of psycho-analysis. But to distinguish between the metaphysical and the psychological origins of the new techniques is not a profitable task. It is not difficult to understand how the subjective novel could have derived its assumptions from the one field, its method from the other. And the fusion between them had been completed by the time Mrs. Woolf published her little pamphlet. Everybody, in Rebecca West's phrase, was "doing" a novel in the period immediately following the World War. Everybody, that is to say, was writing a quasi-poetic rendition of his sensibility in a form which it was agreed should be called the novel.

Possessing a mind schooled in abstract theory, especially alert to the intellectual novelties of her own time, Mrs. Woolf was naturally attracted by a method which in addition to being contemporary offered so much to the speculative mind. But the deeper causes of the attraction, it is now evident, were embedded in Mrs. Woolf's own temperament of sensibility. The subjective mode is the only mode especially designed for temperaments immersed in their own sensibility, obsessed with its movements and vacillations, fascinated by its instability. It was the only mode possible for someone like Proust; it was alone capable of projecting the sensibility which because it has remained so uniform throughout her work we may be permitted to call Mrs. Woolf's own. Here it happens to be Bernard, in *The Waves,* speaking:

> A space was cleared in my mind. I saw through the thick leaves of habit. Leaning over the gate I regretted so much litter, so much un-accomplishment and separation, for one cannot cross London to see a friend, life being so full of engagements; nor take ship to India and see a naked man spearing fish in blue water. I said life had been imperfect, an unfinished phrase. It had been impossible for me, taking snuff as I do from any bagman met in a train, to keep coherency—that sense of the generations, of women carrying red pitchers to the Nile, of the nightingale who sings among conquests and migrations. . . .

But this might be almost any one of Mrs. Woolf's characters; and from such a passage we can appreciate how perfectly the subjective or "confessional" method is adapted to the particular sensibility reflected throughout her work.

And if we require in turn some explanation for this hieratic cultivation of the sensibility, we need only examine for a moment the nature and quality of the experience represented by most of her characters. From *The Voyage Out* to *The Waves* Mrs. Woolf has written almost exclusively about one class of people, almost one might say one type of individual, and that a class or type whose experience is largely vicarious, whose contacts with actuality have been for one or another reason incomplete, unsatisfactory, or inhibited. Made up of poets, metaphysicians, botanists, water-colorists, the world of Mrs. Woolf is a kind of superior Bohemia, as acutely refined and aristocratic in its way as the world of Henry James, except that its inhabitants concentrate on their sensations and impressions rather than on their problems of conduct. (Such problems, of course, do not even exist for them since they rarely allow themselves even the possibility of action.) Life for these people, therefore, is painful less for what it has done to them than for what their excessive sensitivity causes them to make of it. Almost every one of them is the victim of some vast and inarticulate fixation: Mrs. Dalloway on Peter Walsh, Lily Briscoe in *To the Lighthouse* on Mrs. Ramsay, everyone in *The Waves* on Percival. All of them, like Neville in the last-named book, are listening for "that wild hunting-song, Percival's music." For all of them what Percival represents is something lost or denied, something which must remain forever outside the intense circle of their own renunciation. No consolation is left them but solitude, a timeless solitude in which to descend to a kind of self-induced Nirvana. "Heaven be praised for solitude!" cries Bernard toward the close of *The Waves*. "Heaven be praised for solitude that has removed the pressure of the eye, the solicitation of the body, and all need of lies and phrases." Through solitude these people are able to relieve themselves with finality from the responsibilities of living, they are able to complete their divorce from reality even to the extent of escaping the burden of personality. Nothing in Mrs. Woolf's work serves as a better revelation of her characters as a whole than these ruminations of Mrs. Ramsay in *To the Lighthouse:*

> To be silent; to be alone. All the being and the doing, expansive, glittering, vocal, evaporated; and one shrunk, with a sense of solemnity, to being oneself, a wedge-shaped core of darkness. . . . When life sank down for a moment, *the range of experience seemed limitless.* . . . Losing personality, one lost the fret, the hurry, the stir; and there rose to her lips always some exclamation of triumph over life when things came together in this peace, this rest, this eternity. . . .

What Mrs. Ramsay really means to say is that when life sinks down in this manner the range of *implicit* experience is limitless. Once one has abandoned the effort to act upon reality, either with the will or the intellect, the mind is permitted to wander in freedom through the stored treasures of its memories and impressions, following no course but that of fancy or simple association, murmuring Pillicock sat on Pillicock's Hill or Come away, come away, Death, "mingling poetry and nonsense, floating in the stream." But experience in this sense is something quite different from experience in the sense in which it is ordinarily understood in referring to people in life or in books. It does not involve that active impact of character upon reality which provides the objective materials of experience in both literature and life. And if it leads to its own peculiar triumphs, it does so only through a dread of being and doing, an abdication of personality and a shrinking into the solitary darkness.

Because of this self-imposed limitation of their experience, therefore, the characters of Mrs. Woolf are unable to *function* anywhere but on the single plane of the sensibility. On this plane alone is enacted whatever movement, drama, or tragedy occurs in her works. The movement of course is centrifugal, the drama unrealized, the tragedy hushed. The only truly dramatic moments in these novels are significantly enough precisely those in which the characters seem now and again to catch a single brief glimpse of that imposing world of fact which they have forsworn. The scenes we remember best are those like the one in *Mrs. Dalloway* in which the heroine, bright, excited and happy among the guests at her party, is brought suddenly face to face with the fact of death. Or like the extremely moving one at the end of *To the Lighthouse* in which Lily Briscoe at last breaks into tears and cries aloud the hallowed name of Mrs. Ramsay. In such scenes Mrs. Woolf is excellent; no living novelist can translate these nuances of perception in quite the same way; and their effect in her work is of an occasional transitory rift in that diaphanous "envelope" with which she surrounds her characters from beginning to end.

II

For the novelist of sensibility the most embarrassing of all problems, of course, has been the problem of form. From Richardson to Mrs. Woolf it has been the problem of how to reconcile something that is immeasurable, which is what experience as *feeling* very soon becomes, with something that is measured and defined, which has remained perhaps our most elementary conception of art. In the eighteenth century the impulse toward reconciliation was undoubtedly less acute than it has become today: Richardson and Sterne were working in a medium which did not yet make serious pretensions to being opposed to poetry and drama as a distinct art form. There was not yet a Flaubert or a Tolstoy, a Turgenev or a Henry James. Feeling was enough; and feeling was allowed to expand in volumes whose uncontrollable bulk was an eloquent demonstration of its immeasurability. But when at the turn of the present century, under distinguished philosophical auspices, feeling was restored to the novel, when the sensibility finally triumphed over the floundering nineteenth-century Reason, no such artistic insouciance was possible for anyone at all conscious of the literary tradition. In Proust we see the attempt to achieve form on a large scale through the substitution of a purely metaphysical system for the various collapsing frameworks of values—religious, ethical, and scientific—on which the fiction of the nineteenth century had depended.

In Joyce it is through a substitution of quite a different kind, that of a
particular myth from the remote literary past, that the effort is made
to endow the treasures of the sensibility with something like the *inte-
gritas* of the classical estheticians. And in the case of Mrs. Woolf, who
is in this respect representative of most of the followers of these two
great contemporary exemplars, the pursuit of an adequate form has
been a strenuous one from first to last.

In her earliest two books, to be sure, this strain is not too clearly apparent. But *The Voyage Out,* although an interesting novel in many
respects, is notably deficient in what we usually designate as narrative
appeal. In retrospect the excellence of the dialogue, the skill with
social comedy, the objective portraiture of character—all traditional
elements which Mrs. Woolf has since chosen to discard—seem remarkable. But already one can observe a failure or reluctance to project
character through a progressive representation of motives, which provides the structure in such a novelist as Jane Austen, for example,
whom Mrs. Woolf happens to resemble most in this novel. For an
ordered pattern of action unfolding in time Mrs. Woolf substitutes a
kind of spatial unity (the setting is a yacht at sea and later a Portuguese
hotel), a *cadre,* so to speak, within which everything—characters, scenes
and ideas—tends to remain fixed and self-contained. This would be
an altogether true description if it were not for the promise of some
larger development in the love affair that emerges at the end. But even
here, in Mrs. Woolf's first novel, no fulfillment is allowed; death is in-
voked; death supplies a termination which might not otherwise be
reached since none is inherent in the plan. *Night and Day* is an effort
to write a novel on a thoroughly conventional model, and the result is
so uncertain that we can understand the rather sudden turning to a
newer method. It is as if Mrs. Woolf had persuaded herself by these
experiments (how consciously we may judge from her essay *Mr. Bennett
and Mrs. Brown*) that her view of personality did not at all coincide
with the formal requirements of the conventional novel. Of course she
was not alone in this discovery for there already existed the rudiments
of a new tradition, whose main tendency was to dispense with form for
the sake of an intensive exploitation of method.

Despite the number of artists in every field who assume that an innovation in method entails a corresponding achievement in form, method
cannot be regarded as quite the same thing as form. For the novelist all
that we can mean by method is embraced in the familiar phrase "the
point of view." As his object is character his only method can be
that by which he endeavors to attain to a complete grasp and understanding of that object. "Method" in fiction narrows down to nothing
more or less than the selection of a point of view from which character
may be studied and presented. The drastic shift in the point of view
for which Henry James prepared English fiction has undeniably re-

sulted in many noticeable effects in its form or structure. But it is not yet possible to declare that it has resulted in any *new* form. Dorothy Richardson, in the opening volume of *Pilgrimage,* was among the first to apply this new method but in none of the volumes which followed has she allied it to anything like a consistent form. What Mrs. Woolf absorbed from Miss Richardson, from May Sinclair and from James Joyce, all of whom had advanced its use before 1918, was therefore only method, and not form. In the collection of sketches called *Monday or Tuesday* Mrs. Woolf definitely announced her affiliation with the new tradition. But such pieces as "Kew Gardens" and "The Mark on the Wall" were so slight in scope that they could make their appeal (like the essays of Lamb, for example) without the aid of any formal order or plan. Not until *Jacob's Room* does Mrs. Woolf attempt to use the method at any length, and in this book, with which her larger reputation began, we can first perceive the nature of the problem suggested by her work.

In one sense, the structure of *Jacob's Room* is that of the simplest form known to story-telling—the chronicle. From its intense pages one is able to detach a bare continuity of events: Jacob goes to the seashore, to Cambridge, to Greece, to the War. But what his creator is manifestly concerned with is not the relation of these events to his character, but their relation to his sensibility. The latter is projected through a poetic rendering of the dreams, desires, fantasies and enthusiasms which pass through his brain. The rendering is poetic because it is managed entirely by images, certain of which are recurrent throughout—the sheep's jaw with yellow teeth, "the moors and Byron," Greece. The theme also would seem to be a kind of poetic contrast between the outward passage of events and the permanence of a certain set of images in the mind. It happens that there is enough progression of outward events to give the book about as much movement as any other biographical (or autobiographical) chronicle. But one cannot point to any similar movement, any principle of progressive unity in the revelation of all that implicit life of the hero which makes up the substance of the book. As a sensibility Jacob remains the same throughout; he reacts in an identical fashion to the successive phenomena of his experience. Since he reacts only through his sensibility, since he does not act directly upon experience, he fails to "develop," in the sense in which characters in fiction usually develop. Instead of acting, he responds, and when death puts an end to his response, the book also comes to an end. "What am I to do with these?" his mother asks at the close, holding up an old pair of shoes, and this bit of romantic pathos is all the significance which his rich accumulation of dreams and suffering is made to assume in our minds.

In *Mrs. Dalloway* there is a much more deliberate use of recurrent images to identify the consciousness of each of the characters. The ef-

fort is not toward an integration of these images, for that would amount
to something which is opposed to Mrs. Woolf's whole view of personality. It is toward no more than the emphᵃsis of a certain rhythm in
consciousness, which is obviously intended to supply a corresponding
rhythm to the book as a whole. Moreover, in this work use is made for
the first time of an enlarged image, a symbol that is fixed, constant and
wholly outside the time-world of the characters. The symbol of Big
Ben, since it sets the contrast between physical time and the measureless
duration of the characters' inner life, serves as a sort of standard or
center of reference. But neither of these devices, it should be realized,
has anything directly to do with the organization of character: rhythm,
the rhythm of images in the consciousness, is not the same thing as
an order of the personality; the symbol of Big Ben is no real center
because it exists outside the characters, is set up in contrast with them.
By means of these devices carried over from lyric poetry, a kind of
unity is achieved which is merely superficial or decorative, corresponding to no fundamental organization of the experience.

In her next book, however, Mrs. Woolf goes much further toward
a fusion of character and design. *To the Lighthouse,* which is probably
her finest performance in every respect, owes its success not least to the
completeness with which the symbol chosen is identified with the will of
every one of the characters. The lighthouse is the common point toward
which all their desires are oriented; it is an object of attainment or
fulfillment which gives direction to the movements of their thought and
sensibility; and since it is thus associated with them it gives a valid
unity to the whole work. Moreover, alone among Mrs. Woolf's works,
To the Lighthouse has for its subject an action, a single definite action,
"*going* to the lighthouse," which places it clearly in the realm of narrative. In fact, as narrative, it may be even more precisely classified as an
incident. The sole objection that might be raised on esthetic grounds
is whether Mrs. Woolf's method has not perhaps caused her to extend
her development beyond the inherent potentialities of this form. The
question is whether such a narrow structure can support the weight of
the material and the stress of its treatment. More relevant to the present
question, however, is the consideration that so much of the success of
the book rests on the unusally happy choice of symbol, one that is very
specially adapted to the theme, and not likely to be used soon again.
Not many more such symbols occur to the imagination.

Certainly Mrs. Woolf does not make use of the same kind of symbol
in her next novel; for in *The Waves* she returns to the devices of
rhythm and symbolical contrast on which she depended in her earlier
books. (*Orlando* is not a novel, but a "biography," and has only to
follow a simple chronological order. Whatever hilarious variations its
author plays on the traditional concept of time do not affect her ad-

herence to this simple order.) In *The Waves* Mrs. Woolf again presents her characters through the rhythm of images in the brain, again bases her structure on a contrast between these and a permanent symbol of the objective world. There is, first of all, the image or set of images which serves as a *motif* for each of the characters: for Louis, a chained beast stamping on the shore, for Bernard, the willow tree by the river; for Neville, "that wild hunting-song, Percival's music." And also there is the cumulative image of each of their lives taken as a whole set in a parallel relationship to the movements of the sea.

Such a parallel, of course, is not an unfamiliar one. "Dwellers by the sea cannot fail to be impressed by the sight of its ceaseless ebb and flow," remarks Frazer in *The Golden Bough*, "and are apt . . . to trace a subtle relation, a secret harmony, between its tides and the life of man." What is unique is Mrs. Woolf's effort to expand what is usually no more than an intuition, a single association, a lyrical utterance to the dimensions of a novel. In one sense this is accomplished by a kind of multiplication: we are given six lyric poets instead of the usual one. For what Mrs. Woolf offers is a rendering of the subjective response to reality of six different people at successive stages in their lives. We are presented to them in childhood, adolescence, youth, early and late middle-age. *"The waves broke on the shore"* is the last line in the book, and from this we are probably to assume that at the close they are all dead. Such a scheme has the order of a chronicle, of a group of parallel biographies, but Mrs. Woolf is much more ambitious. Each period in her characters' lives corresponds to a particular movement of the sea; the current of their lives at the end is likened to its "incessant rise and fall and rise and fall again." In addition, the different periods correspond to the changing position of the sun in the sky on a single day, suggesting a vision of human lives *sub specie aeternitatis*. (The ancillary images of birds, flowers and wind intensify the same effect.) The theme is best summed up by one of the characters in a long monologue at the end: "Let us again pretend that life is a solid substance, shaped like a globe, which we turn about in our fingers. Let us pretend that we can make out a plain and logical story, so that when one matter is despatched—love for instance—we go on, in an orderly manner to the next. I was saying there was a willow tree. Its shower of falling branches, its creased and crooked bark had the effect of what remains outside our illusions yet cannot stay them, is changed by them for the moment, yet shows through stable, still, with a sternness that our lives lack. Hence the comment it makes; the standard it supplies, the reason why, as we flow and change, it seems to measure." In conception and form, in method and style, this book is the most poetic which Mrs. Woolf has yet written. It represents the extreme culmination of the method to which she has applied herself exclusively since

Monday or Tuesday. It is significant because it forces the question whether the form in which for her that method has resulted is not essentially opposed to the conditions of narrative art.

For this form is unmistakably that of the extended or elaborated lyric; and criticism of these novels gets down ultimately to the question with what impunity one can confuse the traditional means of one literary form with the traditional means of another. This is no place to undertake another discussion of the difference between poetry and prose —or, more particularly, the difference between the lyrical and the narrative. It is a difference which we immediately recognize, and which criticism has always rightly recognized, even when it has not been altogether certain of its explanation. . . .

The objection to the lyrical method in narrative is that it renders impossible the peculiar kind of interest which the latter is designed to supply. By the lyrical method is meant the substitution of a group of symbols for the orderly working-out of a motive or a set of motives which has constituted the immemorial pattern of narrative art. Perhaps the simplest definition of symbols is that they are things used to stand for other things; and undoubtedly the most part of such a definition is the word "stand." Whatever operations of the imagination have gone on to produce them, symbols themselves become fixed, constant, and static. They may be considered as the end-results of the effort of the imagination to fix itself somewhere in space. The symbol may be considered as something *spatial*. Symbols are thus ordinarily used in lyric poetry, where the effort is to fix ideas, sentiments, or emotions. By themselves, of course, symbols in poetry are no more than so many detached, isolated and unrelated points in space. When projected separately, as in the poetry of the Imagist school, or in too great confusion, as in much contemporary poetry, they do not possess any necessary meaning or value to the intelligence: the worlds that they indicate are either too small or too large to live in. Moreover, whether separate or integrated into a total vision symbols are capable of being grasped, like any other objects of space, by a single and instantaneous effort of perception. . . .

When narrative based itself on a simple chronological record of action, it was assured of a certain degree of interest. When, later, it based itself on an arrangement of action which corresponded to an orderly view of life or reality, it attained to the very high interest of a work of art. As long as it based itself firmly on action according to one pattern or another, it was certain of some degree of interest. To understand the nature of the satisfaction which we seem to take in the representation of reality in a temporal order we should have to know more about certain primitive elements of our psychology than science has yet been able to discover. It is enough to recognize that whatever the reasons this satisfaction is rooted in our sense of *time*. It is enough to realize that this is the basis of the appeal which narrative has made through the whole history of fiction, from the earliest fables of the race to the most complex "constructions" of Henry James. For this reason, for example, description has always occupied a most uncertain place in fiction. Description, which deals with things rather than events, interposes a space-world in the march of that time-world which is the subject of fiction. For this reason the use of poetic symbols in fiction, as in all Mrs. Woolf's work since *Monday or Tuesday,* seems to be in direct contradiction to the foundations of our response to that form.

III

Because it is in an almost continuous state of moral and intellectual relaxation that Mrs. Woolf's characters draw out their existence, they can be projected only through a more or less direct transcription of their consciousness. Such a qualification is necessary, however, for the method here is rarely if ever as direct as that of Joyce or his followers. Between the consciousness and the rendition of it there is nearly always interposed a highly artificial literary style. This style remains practically uniform for all the characters; it is at once individual and traditional. The effect of its elegant diction and elaborately turned periods is to make one feel at times as if these sad and lonely people were partly compensated for the vacuity of their lives by the gift of casting even their most random thoughts in the best literary tradition. For some of them, like Bernard in *The Waves* (or is it the author herself speaking?), language is more than a compensation; it has an absolute value in itself: "A good phrase, however, seems to me to have an independent existence." Others may go to religion, to art, to friendship, but Mrs. Woolf's people more often than not go "to seek among phrases and fragments something unbroken." It is as if they seek to net the world of time and change with a phrase, to retrieve the chaos with words. For this reason the presentation of character by Mrs. Woolf gets down finally to a problem of style, to the most beautiful arrangement of beautiful words and phrases.

Here also Mrs. Woolf is pre-eminently the poet; for as an unwillingness to use motives and actions led to her substitution of poetic symbols in their stead so is she also compelled to use a metaphorical rather than a narrative style. In this practice of course she is not without precedent; other novelists have relied on metaphor to secure their finest effects of communication. But while such effects are ordinarily used to heighten the narrative, they are never extended to the point where they assume an independent interest. In Mrs. Woolf's books metaphorical writing is not occasional but predominate; from the beginning it has subordinated every other kind; and it was inevitable that it should one day be segmented into the purely descriptive prose-poems of *The Waves.*

No sooner is the essentially poetic character of this writing admitted than one is confronted with the whole host of problems associated with the general problem of imagery in poetry. It happens, however, that the peculiar use of imagery in Mrs. Woolf's prose suggests among other things a particular distinction, and one which has not been often enough made, although it was recognized by both Coleridge and Baudelaire, a distinction between two kinds of sensibility.

Of the two kinds of sensibility that we can identify in examining works of poetry the first would seem to be incapable of receiving impressions except through the prism of an already acquired set of language symbols. It is as if poets with this type of sensibility are uncontrollably *determined* in the kind of response they can make to reality. And because they are so determined in their initial response they are determined also in their manner of expression. The original language-symbols, acquired through culture, training, or unconscious immersion in some tradition, are infinitely perpetuated in their writing. At its worst such writing is anemic and invertebrate, like the minor verse of any period or like the earlier work of many excellent poets. In such verse the language gives the effect of having occasioned the feeling more often than the feeling the language. At its most sophisticated, however, this verse is capable of achieving a certain superficial quality of distinction all its own. . . . It may consist in the pure musicalization of language through the draining of all specific content from the imagery that we find in Mallarmé or (on a lower plane) in Swinburne. . . .

The other type of sensibility, of course, is in the habit of receiving direct impressions, of forming images which possess the freshness, uniqueness, and body of the original object. It has the faculty of creating new language-symbols to convey what it has perceived or, as sometimes happens, of re-creating traditional symbols with enough force to make them serve again. . . . It is the difference between writing which secures a certain effectiveness through being recognizable in a particular tradition and writing which is an exact verbal equivalent for a precise emotion or set of emotions. It is the difference, among the writers of our time, between Conrad Aiken and T. S. Eliot, or between Thornton Wilder and Ernest Hemingway. And in the most characteristic lines of the best writers of any time it is this latter kind of sensibility that we can see at work. We see it in Antony's rebuke to Cleopatra:

> I found you as a morsel, cold upon
> Dead Caesar's trencher

or in Baudelaire's

> J'ai cherché dans l'amour un sommeil oublieux;
> Mais l'amour n'est pour moi qu'un matelas d'aiguilles

or in Yeats'

> I pace upon the battlements and stare
> On the foundations of a house, or where
> Tree, like a sooty finger, starts from the earth.

In prose fiction, when the language approaches the precision and density of poetry, it is a result of the same necessity on the part of author or character, under stress of exceptional feeling, to seize upon his experience for the particular image or images necessary to express his state. The only difference is that the images of fiction are likely to be less remote, less "difficult" perhaps, than those of poetry. And the reason of course is that the images are likely to arise out of the immediate background of the novel. No better example of this can be offered than in the speech in *Wuthering Heights* in which Catherine, in her delirium, shakes the feathers out of her pillow:

> That's turkey's . . . and this is a wild duck's; and this is a pigeon's. Ah, they put pigeons' feathers in the pillows—no wonder I couldn't die! . . . And here is a moor-cock's; and this—I should know it among a thousand—it's a lapwing's. Bonny bird; wheeling over our heads in the middle of the moor. It wanted to get to its nest, for the clouds had touched the swells, and it felt rain coming.

In Mrs. Woolf's novels, as replete with imagery as they are, the effect is never quite the same as in this passage from Emily Brontë. The images that pass through in her characters' minds are rarely seized from any *particular* background of concrete experience. There are few of them which we have not encountered somewhere before. They belong not so much to the particular character as to the general tradition of literature. The effect is of an insidious infiltration of tradition into the sensibility. And this effect is the same whether it is a straight description by the author, as in *To the Lighthouse:*

> The autumn trees, ravaged as they are, take on the flash of tattered flags kindling in the gloom of cool cathedral caves where gold letters on marble pages describe death in battle and how bones bleach and burn far away on Indian sands. The autumn trees gleam in the yellow moonlight, in the light of harvest moons, the light which mellows the energy of labour, and smooths the stubble, and brings the wave lapping blue to the shore.

or a presentation of mood, as in *Mrs. Dalloway:*

> Fear no more, says the heart. Fear no more, says the heart, committing its burden to some sea, which sighs collectively for all sorrows, and renews, begins, collects, lets fall. And the body alone listens to the pass-

ing bee; the wave breaking; the dog barking, far away barking and
barking.

or a translation of ecstasy, as in *The Waves:*

> Now tonight, my body rises tier upon tier like some cool temple
> whose floor is strewn with carpets and murmurs rise and the altars stand
> smoking; but up above, here in my serene head, come only fine gusts of
> melody, waves of incense, while the lost dove wails, and the banners
> tremble above tombs, and the dark airs of midnight shake trees outside
> the open windows.

From such examples it should be apparent to what extent the sensibility here is haunted by the word-symbols of the past. The consciousness of each of these characters is a Sargasso Sea of words, phrases,
broken relics of poetry and song. The phrases which rise to the surface
are like bright shells resonant with the accumulated echoes of their
past histories. Some of them have the familiar charm of cherished
heirlooms; only a few retain completely whatever power to stir the
imagination they may once have had. Almost all of them depend for
their effect on their associations to the cultivated mind rather than
on their ability to evoke the fullness and immediacy of concrete experience. And the reason of course is that there is insufficient experience
of this sort anywhere reflected in the course of Mrs. Woolf's work.

It is also clear in such passages how Mrs. Woolf has come more and
more to cultivate language for its own sake, to seek in phrases some
"independent existence" which will give them an absolute beauty in
themselves. But detached from experience as they are they attain to no
more substantial beauty than that of a charming virtuosity of style. It
is not the beauty but the cleverness of Mrs. Woolf's writing which is
responsible for the final effect on the reader. "No woman before Virginia Woolf has used our language with such easy authority," wrote
the late Sara Teasdale. Indeed few writers of either sex have written
English with the same mastery of traditional resources, the same calculated effectiveness, the same facility. And when this facile tradition-
alism is allied with an appropriate subject, as in a frank burlesque like
Orlando, the result is truly brilliant. It is only when it is used as the
vehicle for significant serious thoughts and emotions, as in the larger
portion of Mrs. Woolf's work, that its charm seems false, its authority
invalid, and its beauty sterile.

It is only fair to point out what would seem to be a sincere self-
questioning in the long monologue at the end of *The Waves.* Bernard,
the inveterate phrasemonger, recalling the scene in which he and his
friends first heard of Percival's death, remembers that they had compared him to a lily. "So the sincerity of the moment passed," Bernard
cries, "so it had become symbolical; and that I could not stand. Let us
commit any blasphemy of laughter and criticism rather than exude

this lily-sweet glue; and cover him over with phrases." Perhaps it is too much to read into this lapse into sincerity on the part of a single character a confession of dissatisfaction by the author with the kind of language that she has been using all along in her work. But while such an interpretation may be too eager there is at least the implication that she is aware that reality when it is encountered is something far too important to be covered over with beautiful phrases. The vague hope is thrown out that in her later work she may finally be tempted to give us Percival himself, that she may spare him from death and allow him a more solid existence than he ever enjoyed in the minds and memories of his friends.

But no sooner is this idea expressed than one is reminded of the profound changes that would have to happen in Mrs. Woolf's whole metaphysical outlook before any such hope could be realized. For every element of her work that we have considered—her form, her method of characterization, her style even—is affected by the same fundamental view of personality at its root. These elements of form and of style can hardly be expected to change as long as the view which determines them remains unchanged. And nothing in Mrs. Woolf's recent work, it must be admitted, justifies the belief that this view is likely to be changed in the near future.

Characters and Human Relations

by Jean Guiguet

It can be said without exaggeration that critics have unanimously reproached Virginia Woolf with a certain inability to create characters.[1] None of her heroes or heroines, not even Clarissa Dalloway or Mrs. Ramsay, impress the reader's imagination with that precision, richness and vitality which ensure an independent and convincing existence for characters in fiction. It is moreover significant that the heroes of her first two novels, and the secondary figures in her more original works, are those that stand out most sharply. Helen Ambrose, St. John Hirst, the four protagonists of *Night and Day* particularly, Mrs. Flanders, Bonamy, Sandra Wentworth Williams, Sir William Bradshaw, Sally Seton, Charles Tansley, Carmichael, Mrs. Swithin, Mrs. Manresa and a score of other silhouettes, sketched in with a few gestures, attitudes and phrases, thanks to their manageable simplicity, leave a lively and living impression on the reader. But except for the heroes of the two early novels, these figures are obviously caricatures rather than portraits. Their slightness, and the restricted place they occupy in the books, makes it difficult if not impossible to base on them a study of Virginia Woolf's characterization. None the less, the contrast they present with figures like Clarissa Dalloway or Mrs. Ramsay, and even more with the protagonists of *The Waves,* provides an opportunity for preliminary comments which are surely essential to any discussion of this side of Virginia Woolf's art.

The primary quality of all these characters, the one which ensures for them a convincing presence in the novels and the power of surviving in our memories, is their very limitedness. They are fixed, static, in every respect. They have a history, a profession, a passion or a mania, a gesture, an attitude or a turn of phrase that defines them; and their fidelity to themselves is unfailing; thus they are, and thus they remain.

[1] Apart from various authors of reviews, F. Delattre is the first to have stressed this aspect of Virginia Woolf's art. Among more recent criticisms, that of D. S. Savage is particularly harsh (cf. *The Withered Branch,* p. 95).

Around them the author has, like St. John Hirst, traced the chalk circle which gives them being but which also confines them. They correspond exactly to the traditional notion of personality, made of a bundle of more or less complex tendencies and manifested by constant reactions. All the characters named above are of the same nature. Between a Katherine Hilbery and a Sally Seton, a Ralph Denham and a Bonamy or a Charles Tansley, there is only a difference of degree or, if you like, of richness and complexity. The diversity of the situations, the detail of the analyses that give the heroes of *Night and Day* a different stature (which does not mean a different density) from the figures in the later novels, should not deceive us. The accumulation of circumstances, the multiplicity and complication of events involving multiple and complicated reactions, arouse our curiosity, foster our interest in the characters and may even lead us to believe that this description is the essential part of the novel. We have seen that this is not so. This traditional painting of characters of traditional type is here merely the survival of a technique which was inadequate to the author's intention and which she used for lack of a better, still undiscovered one. The following books, just as much as the essays on the art of fiction, amply prove that Virginia Woolf had other ambitions. The fact that she retained this mode of characterization for her secondary figures, for Dr. Crane in *The Waves* or Mrs. Manresa in *Between the Acts,* far from being a concession to the method, or a residue from it, is on the contrary an implied criticism of it, and brings out the more sharply the essential features of the method by which she intended to replace it. In fact, these figures have no reality, no existence of their own; they make a momentary appearance in the field of vision of the chief protagonists, and it is the two-dimensional image which they leave as they pass, in the latters' accumulated experience, that the novelist reproduces. They may have colour and movement enough to give the illusion of life, but it is merely an illusion. They lack two essential traits to attain human reality as Virginia Woolf perceived it from the very first and as she tried to express it later: imprecision of outline and an infinite potentiality for renewal and creation. There is no indeterminate zone around their desires, their will, their feelings or ideas which might leave room for hesitation, doubt, and in the final analysis anguish. None of these walkers-on could say, like Louis in *The Waves,* "I am conscious of flux, of disorder; of annihilation and despair." Enclosed within their security, their certitude, they are immune to questioning from without or within. They are clockwork figures, wound up once and for all, functioning in season and out of season with equal blindness and self-confidence. They are never taken by surprise and can never surprise anyone else. They have the solidity and permanence of material objects. It is owing to this, no doubt, that they leave a vivid and enduring impression in the reader's mind. But quite obviously Viriginia

Woolf never believed in the effectiveness or value of so crude a method of representation. From *The Voyage Out* to *The Years,* through the medium of Hewett and North to, quote only these two, she never ceased to say so: "These little snapshot pictures of people left much to be desired, these little surface pictures that one made, like a fly crawling over a face, and feeling here's the nose, here's the brow." [2] If these characters exist, it is only for the superficial, hasty observer, used to this convenient formulation of his fellows, which has the backing of a whole literary and psychological tradition. Though they seem substantial, and acquire importance from the foreground position they occupy, the four heroes of *Night and Day* have no more than this elementary reality. . . . If we consider that Terence Hewet and above all Rachel Vinrace in *The Voyage Out* are far less sharply outlined, blurred by their mutual contacts, which make them part of one another, and at the same time by the multiple points of view from which they are presented, we are tempted to see in *Night and Day* a deliberate application of the traditional technique and psychology, being tried out by Virginia Woolf in order to test their possibilities and ascertain her own resources and limitations. It is basically the least characteristic of her novels, but a necessary experiment in order to exorcise any temptation to follow the beaten path. . . .

"Vague and universal" was E. M. Forster's verdict on *The Voyage Out*; "vague and inconclusive" Virginia Woolf had written a few months earlier to sum up her impression of one of Chekhov's stories, which seemed to her characteristic of those elements in Russian literature that exerted a revivifying influence on the contemporary English novel.[3] This is the aspect, at first sight a negative one, which may be considered the essential weakness of Virginia Woolf's characters, not only in her first novel where she unconsciously followed her own bent, but in those of her maturity where she tried out all the resources of writing in turn in order to convey that haziness without which any representation of that essential object of the artist's quest, "whether we call it life or spirit, truth or reality," [4] is merely a vain and disappointing counterfeit.

The specific question of characters and their function in the novel, of the way of portraying them and conveying their personality, is not tackled directly in the article of 1919. We have to wait until 1924 for "Character in Fiction," better known under the title "Mr. Bennett and Mrs. Brown," to find, if not the solution, at any rate a precise analysis of the data of the problem:

---

[2] *The Y[ears]* p. 341 (317).
[3] Cf. "Modern Novels," *TLS,* April 10, 1919 (E. M. Forster's comment is mentioned in the Diary on Nov. 6, 1919); under the title "Modern Fiction in Common Reader 1." See p. 193 (157); also *ibid.,* p. 223 (180), in "The Russian Point of View."
[4] Cf. [*The*] C[*ommon*] R[*eader*] I p. 188 (153): "Whether we call it life or spirit, truth or reality, this, the essential thing, has moved off, or on. . . ."

I believe that all novels begin with an old lady in the corner opposite. I believe that all novels, that is to say, deal with character, and that it is to express character—not to preach doctrines, sing songs, or celebrate the glories of the British Empire, that the form of the novel, so clumsy, verbose, and undramatic, so rich, elastic, and alive, has been evolved.[5]

Winifred Holtby, who usually offers interesting interpretations of the novels, seems not to have taken into account the context when she quotes this phrase to assert that "Mrs. Woolf holds that in novel writing, character creation is the all-important quality." [6] She thus ignores that essential reservation that follows this apparent concession to the traditional laws of the genre.[7]

To express character, I have said; but you will at once reflect that the very widest interpretation can be put upon these words. . . . You see one thing in character, and I another. You say it means this, and I that. And when it comes to writing each makes a further selection on principles of his own. Thus Mrs. Brown can be treated in an infinite variety of ways, according to the age, country, and temperament of the writer.[8]

Moreover, despite the effort at elucidation to which Virginia Woolf was driven, first by her difficulties in the composition of *Jacob's Room*, then by her researches for *Mrs. Dalloway* and her controversy with Arnold Bennett, it is clear that at this period she had not yet completely broken free from that central convention of the novel which forms an essential part of any definition of the genre. She had only cast off its formal restrictions, the method of creation, those tools so skilfully handled by the Edwardians and yet, to her mind, so inadequate.[9] If the failure of Wells, Bennett and Galsworthy to satisfy her, if her sense that the stuff with which such figures as Dr. Watson and Hilda Lessways are padded out is irrelevant and external incited her to discover something else, at the same time the example of the great novels— *War and Peace, Vanity Fair, Tristram Shandy, Madame Bovary* . . . —maintained, alive and active, the fascination of that element which seems to distil and transmit the essence of these masterpieces: their characters. The result of this conflict between what she rejects and what she accepts is particularly noticeable in *Jacob's Room* and *Mrs. Dalloway*, and, to a lesser degree, in *To the Lighthouse*. Without seeking to minimize the wish to make something new, nor the originality of the

---

[5] [*The*] C[*aptain's*] D[*eath*] B[*ed*], pp. 96–7 (102).

[6] Winifred Holtby, *Virginia Woolf*, p. 151.

[7] Other critics have made the same mistake, whether or not they realized that this assertion of the novelist's did not correspond to the basic meaning of her work. Cf. for instance John Graham, in the opening paragraph of his article "Time in the Novels of Virginia Woolf" *Univ. of Toronto Quarterly*, XVIII (Jan. 1949), pp. 186–201.

[8] CDB p. 97 (102–3).

[9] Cf. *Ibid.*, pp. 104 (110) and 106 (112).

means employed to attain her ends, the fact remains that the presentation of one or several beings, the creation of characters, is one of the
determining factors in the composition of these three novels. The very
titles of the first two are significant in this respect. As regards the third,
remember how, at its inception, Virginia Woolf envisaged this book:
"This is going to be fairly short; to have father's character done complete in it; and mother's . . ." [10] Considering these works at a little
distance, we can now see how, from one to the next, the lure of character diminishes. *Jacob's Room* is dominated by the desire to present
character as she conceives it, in opposition to the conceptions and
methods of her contemporaries. She takes her hero almost from the
cradle and follows him to his death. She eliminates any sort of plot,
to devote herself solely to portraiture. Even if this elimination is, in
itself, rich with other implications as to the theory of the novel, it none
the less contributes to concentrating our interest on the portrayal of
her hero. Jacob may have become discontinuous, but he remains chronological. But after all, if discontinuity is an essential part of reality,
which is blurred to the point of being destroyed in the traditional type
of narrative, it may on the other hand be only an inevitable condition
of the literary art: an exhaustive chronicle is an impossibility; and by
one of its distinctive features, *Jacob's Room* conforms to type.

If the figure of Clarissa Dalloway dominates Virginia Woolf's fourth
novel and, on the whole, leaves a clearer impression than Jacob, it is
because she seems to be concentrated in a single day and place; a
concentration which has a synthetic power akin to that of the plot in
the traditional novel. This result, which is repeated with Mrs. Ramsay
in *To the Lighthouse,* is to the credit of Virginia Woolf's art. But
what matters to us here is the profound nature of these characters, who,
while remaining autonomous individuals, reveal a dependence and a
diffusion which *Jacob's Room* had described from the outside without
succeeding in integrating it. Around Jacob there were other figures,
which like mirrors or the walls of his room showed us his reflection or
his shadows; it was through these reflections and shadows that he
existed, and to a large extent he *was* them—whence his difficulty in
being Jacob. On the contrary, with the figures that surround Clarissa
and Mrs. Ramsay, even the flimsiest, or to use E. M. Forster's term
the flattest of them, such as Richard Dalloway or Mr. Bankes, the
function of reflector is only a secondary one. In fact, they are essentially
a part of the central figure. They converge towards her to mingle and
blend with her substance, in the case of Clarissa. Inversely, in the case
of Mrs. Ramsay, she turns towards them and is diffused into them. In
either case, this blurring of outlines and this fusion of beings reveals
an order of reality entirely different from that which the terms character, personality, hero normally imply. What we have here is no

---

[10] A W[riter's] D[iary] p. 76 (75).

longer somebody or something; . . . what we have is a nexus of relations, a manifold participation in all that lies around, absorbing it all into his own substance, which is constantly altered by this contact. It no longer *is*; it *becomes*. This profound alteration of the nature of a character, which Virginia Woolf achieved in three stages, was already implicit in what she wrote of the heroes of the great novels:

> . . . . if you think of these books, you do at once think of some character who has seemed to you so real (I do not by that mean so lifelike) that it has the power to make you think not merely of it itself, but of all sorts of things through its eyes—of religion, of love, of war, of peace, of family life, of balls in country towns, of sunsets, moonrises, the immortality of the soul. . . .[11]

However, although these lines show that Virginia Woolf does not consider characters as the end of the novel but only as a means, if we compare this text with the one from which it was derived, published six months earlier, we see that she did not reach this position all at once. Referring to the same heroes, she had then written:

> They love, they joke, they hunt, they marry, they lead us from hall to cottage, from field to slum. The whole country, the whole society is revealed to us through the astonishing vividness and reality of the characters.[12]

"The astonishing vividness and reality of the characters" which brought about this revelation and which consequently were deemed essential features are relegated to the background in the later text; moreover, Virginia Woolf is careful to distinguish what seems real from what is merely lifelike. Besides, in the paragraph where she contrasts the Russian novel with the Victorian novel, although she only defines a negative aspect of these characters that fascinate her, she uses an image which, echoing that in which a few months previously she had described the method used in *Mrs. Dalloway*, suggests an unexplored wealth of visions and presentiments: "These are characters without any features at all. We go down into them as we descend into some enormous cavern." [13] True, what I have called the lure of the character, exerted by figures like Natasha, Becky Sharp or Emma Bovary, remains. But, following the evolution we have just examined, which occurred

---

[11] "Mr. Bennett and Mrs. Brown," CDB, originally "Character in Fiction," *Criterion,* July 1924.
[12] "Mr. Bennett and Mrs. Brown," *New York Evening Post,* Literary Review, Nov. 17, 1923, reprinted in *Nation and Athenaeum,* Dec. 1, 1923.
[13] "Mr. Bennett and Mrs. Brown," *Nation & Athenaeum,* Dec. 1, 1923, p. 342. Since V. W. speaks in her diary on June 19th of her answer to Bennett [AWD p. 57 (56)] we may assume that the article was written during that summer. The similarity of expression noted here inclines one to think that it might be more profitable to seek for the artistic sources of *Mrs. Dalloway* in the Russian novel than in James Joyce.

during the last months of 1923, this lure loses its restrictive power. . . .

I shall not dwell upon that essential reality, with its manifold names, which constitutes the true subject of Virginia Woolf's books; I shall only stress the progressive adaptation of her characters to the aim that the novelist assigns to them. . . . To . . . deprive [human beings] of the opacity and rigidity which makes masks and puppets of them instead of the filters, the living beings that they are, such is the goal towards which Virginia Woolf slowly gropes her way, from *Jacob's Room* to *To the Lighthouse,* finally reaching in *The Waves* the elimination of all that is alien and heterogeneous to this pure sensibility. I should point out here that by the term sensibility, used somewhat loosely, I mean all the activity of the psyche that extends from sensation to thought, but in which the predominance of receptivity, of the whole phase of contact and absorption, is such that the word seems preferable to any other. The progress in the three novels that may be described as preparatory or experimental can be defined by an increased inwardness of impressions and of expression. The surface contacts which mould Jacob are combined, in *Mrs. Dalloway,* with inner resonances, the exploration of deep caverns. In this region what had been mere contiguity, juxtaposition, becomes fusion and connectedness. And it is to the constant shift from one to the other, the balance between the outer and the inner, between the periphery and the centre, the object and the subject, that Clarissa owes the firmness and clarity of outline which the heroes of the later novels lack. Mrs. Ramsay retains something of it, but to a lesser degree. The first pages of *To the Lighthouse* are characteristic in this respect. Recollections of her walk with Charles Tansley, and Charles Tansley himself, are inextricably fused in Mrs. Ramsay's mind: the landmarks of time and space which mark out people and events are practically obliterated. Yet, slender as they have become, the book still retains a scaffolding of events and circumstances which, even when they are only in parentheses, guarantee a certain integrity to individuals, keep them separate from one another and from the outside world. It is only in *The Waves* that Virginia Woolf achieves absolute homogeneity. Instead of preserving on the one hand a centre of apprehension, *Mrs. Dalloway's* "unseen part of us, which spreads wide," [14] even if reduced to the abstract form of a kind of figurative symbol like Mrs. Ramsay's "wedge-shaped core of darkness," [15] and on the other hand all that comes to it from the universe and from existence, there remains only pure apprehension: the subject-object duality which had proved a stumbling block to Mr. Ramsay and Lily Briscoe in their different ways is finally reabsorbed in a monism which is also a phenomenologism. These terms, which suggest rationally constructed systems, con-

[14] Cf. *Mrs. D[alloway]*, p. 232 (232).
[15] Cf. *To the L[ighthouse]*, p. 99 (95).

trary as they may be to the spirit of our author and thereby risky to use, are none the less useful if we wish to penetrate fully the meaning of her work. In spite of the hesitations and uncertainties of vocabulary, it is this metaphysical attitude that underlies Virginia Woolf's vision as revealed in her finest work.

The elimination of plot and of spatio-temporal determinations is complementary to the disintegration of the character. They are all ways of denying matter, whether the material nature of objects which petrifies their qualities, or that of our bodies which limits the infinite potentialities of human beings for expansion and participation. In the centre of the universe—we may say, too, at the beginning and at the end, so as not to lay more stress on the spatial than on the temporal, both moreover being symbolic and conventional—at its heart and always, there is what we call "I," without being able to state its nature more precisely. It is the sole and ultimate sum of everything, and it is, itself, the whole world reflected in itself. But these two terms, the I on the one hand and the Universe on the other, are beyond our grasp; no definition can circumscribe them, no description can account for them. This is what Virginia Woolf gradually discovered, between *Jacob's Room* and *To the Lighthouse.* The only reality accessible between these two phantoms is the relationship between them, that function of the "soul," the inner life, or just *life,* which is sensation, emotion, feeling, desire, will, ideas, to use words which are not quite accurate, since they have acquired, by their use through the ages and in various philosophies, a variety of meanings. All the moments and all the aspects of this activity have an essential common character; they are appearances, phenomena, phantasms; they arise, they alter, they remain, they disappear, they arise once more, and we can neither control nor account for these metamorphoses: this is reality, this is truth—the only ones to which we have access, all the rest being only a mode of representation, a convention, an algebra, convenient perhaps but illusory.

This power of absorption and transmutation is what we find in its purest state in *The Waves.* Whatever critics may have said for or against it, whatever they may have looked for or found in it, Virginia Woolf sought neither to create nor to present characters.[16] Many expressions, noted during an attempt to summarise the intentions of this novel, point to the same refusal. And at the same time Virginia Woolf was realising her ambition to express life, love, nature, death, conveyed through this consciousness which is one and yet many, faceless and nameless. It seems futile to criticise *The Waves* by suggesting, as Daiches and other critics have done, that the novelist has merely substituted one convention for another. Such an attitude implies that this convention is arbitrary, a mere artifice. . . . If we look closely at

[16] Cf. AWD p. 175 (170).

the meaning of the work, we immediately realise that this convention is the actual answer to the question which haunts and dominates all Virginia Woolf's writing: *What* are we? *Who* are we? From Rachel to Bernard, none of her characters has hitherto brought a satisfactory solution to this riddle. But beyond all the hypothetical and approximate formulae they may offer, either directly through being as their creator made them, or indirectly through what they say, the form of *The Waves* asserts that man is essentially a consciousness, that is to say a potential of relations, whose centre is everywhere and whose circumference is nowhere, and which creates itself at the same time as it creates the universe. . . .

I have intentionally dwelt on *The Waves* in this attempt to formulate Virginia Woolf's theory, and if I have not referred to *Orlando,* it is because, while perfectly consistent with the conceptions that underlie *The Waves,* it only gives their reverse side, so to speak. We see all the framework, all the seams. The element of fantasy, of discursiveness and caricature in *Orlando* is indeed not without its explanatory value, but thereby deprives the book of the atmosphere and the resonances essential to a reality which is better conveyed by half tones, blurred contours and suggestion than by sharp outlines and colours, or by formulae.

On the other hand it seems to me that Virginia Woolf's two last novels can be considered as attempts to exploit, in a generalized fashion, the principles put into practice in a state of purity, so to speak, in *The Waves.* In *The Years* we have not so much a return to realism, as some critics have thought, realism of the external world and realism of character, as a concern with expressing the same manifold relations, the same obscure intermingling of consciousnesses with one another and with the universe. None of the Pargiters, and none of their satellites, despite appearances, can claim more individuality, autonomy or precision than Rhoda or Louis. Like these, each is a focus of irradiation of that nebula, their inextricably intermingled consciousness. Eleanor, Milly, Delia, Rose, Martin, Morris, Edward alternate like the voices in *The Waves,* separate, meet, scatter and come together again through chronological vicissitudes that permeate them and cling to them in the same fashion. They go through childhood, schooldays, professional and family life and love, just like the characters in the previous novel. Delia gathers them all together, moved by the same impulse as Bernard. She takes the same rose to consider its ephemeral brilliance. The speech which is to sum things up, the final assessment, is never uttered; but is it needed? The summing-up is there: confusion and fusion, separation and unity, despair and resolution— and the riddle which had baffled all Bernard's dialectic is expressed only in the sibylline song of the two children who appear at the party in the first light of dawn.

The difference of treatment between Bernard's monologue and the party in "Present Day" reflects the difference between *The Waves* and *The Years*. Whereas in the first we had the concentration of a laboratory experiment, in the second Virginia Woolf has tried direct observation. Instead of the deliberately arranged voices of her faceless protagonists, she has sought to preserve "the human voice at its natural speaking level" [17] and, by gradual steps, around these voices, the whole complex of space and time in which they sound, and in which words take on their immediate and superficial meaning. This attempt in no way contradicts her vision of beings nor her vision of reality. If, from the point of view of aesthetic success, it is ill-fated, it nevertheless confirms her theories by its very failure. To express the one on the level of the many, to express a relation on the level of the extremes which this relation is intended to bring together, means restoring materialism and dualism. All the skill, all the artifice intended to reabsorb these heterogeneous elements are used in vain; the recurrence of analogous situations, the duplication of characters by one another, the dislocation of an event in the various consciousnesses that apprehend it, the contrast between words and thoughts in simple juxtaposition, the whole system of echoes, leitmotivs, subtle intertwinings, do not penetrate the real substance of the novel. These characters, being too ponderous, betray their vocation and their essence, while their vocation and their essence dissolve away the garment of flesh they have tried to put on.

The bareness of *Between the Acts* brings us back to a more homogeneous vision. If the intermittent emergence of a few clearly drawn secondary figures, such as Mrs. Manresa and Mr. Streatfield the clergyman, or even the sharpness of outline in which the apparently central figures of Isa and Giles are sometimes held stationary, may suggest that Virginia Woolf was trying out a compromise analogous to that of *The Years*, this hypothesis will not stand up to examination. The rudiments of physical presence and personal history attached to their names are not intended to define them, to set them up against one another, but solely to outline those superficial contacts from which their deeper relations spring and spread in an obscure tangle, all that open system of attractions, repulsions and participations which Virginia Woolf sought to substitute for the closed system of contiguity and the reactions of personality. The first scene, which brings together the Haineses, Bartholomew and Isa, is characteristic in this respect. A few touches seem to promise portraits: Mrs. Haines's protruberant eyes, Isa's curls, the haggard face of the gentleman farmer. But in fact this shorthand is only superficially, or rather parenthetically, characterological. It is focussed entirely on the feelings, in the broadest

[17] The Y p. 445 (411).

sense of the term, that these people experience for one another: the repulsion and contempt inspired by Mrs. Haines; the suggestions of youth, carelessness, intimacy and sensuality that emanate from Isa; Haines's rough, inarticulate masculinity. These physical details are not meant to distinguish the characters, any more than the details of their status ("Mr. Oliver of the Indian Service, retired," "her husband, the stockbroker") but to provide implicit causes and reasons for the atmosphere of jealousy, contempt, tenderness and desire that pervades these four pages.

The extreme simplification of the general plan, the elimination of the circumstantial, lead here to a result analogous to that obtained in *The Waves* by different means. The pageant provides under a symbolic form the wealth of events, of facts, that broadens the setting and gives substance to those one-day relations without arousing the uncertainty and ambiguity which the direct angle of approach had introduced into *The Years*.

If I have made some reservations as to the success of this novel taken as a whole,[18] I believe none the less that from this restricted point of view it constitutes the end of Virginia Woolf's quest, integrating all her successive discoveries, realising that novel of silence dreamed of by Hewett in *The Voyage Out*—the novel of all that which, not yet having reached the level of speech, has been preserved from the treachery and sclerosis of words. It is only when the reality of behind the scenes, the flow of life between the acts, in a word all that true reality of which we are granted a glimpse through and beyond the world of people and things, has been expressed that the curtain rises to let the characters appear and speak; it is time then for the novelist to stop, for neither these words nor these appearances are her reality.

The walls of Jacob's room had flung back to us a single name, that echoed through the years to the seaside childhood of the ghostly hero. Percival, invisible and mute, had remained a myth in the inner lives, inextricably interconnected, of the voices in *The Waves*. "What need have we of words to remind us? Must I be Thomas? You Jane?" is the question asked in *Between the Acts*. The answer lies in the totality of the novel, which denies the validity of a sign whose meaning the earlier novels had sought in vain. There are no personalities; there are no characters; there is only the inner life, a centre of fusion and assimilation whose individuality and autonomy are only apparent and usurped.

[18] [In Chapter V of M. Guiguet's book; not here represented.]

Something Central Which Permeated:
Virginia Woolf and 'Mrs. Dalloway'

by Reuben Brower

> *It was something central which permeated . . .*
> *Mrs. Dalloway*

The best preparation for understanding *Mrs. Dalloway* is to read *The Tempest,* or *Cymbeline,* or, better still, *A Winter's Tale.* One might go further and say that in her singleness of vision and in her handling of words, Virginia Woolf has a Shakespearean imagination. If that sounds like nonsense—and it may—perhaps by the end of this chapter the reader will agree that it sounds "so like sense, that it will do as well."

Mrs. Dalloway has a story and some characters—by conventional standards, a fragmentary dramatic design—but the fragments of which the novel is composed would not seem related or particularly significant without another sort of connection. [The dramatic sequences are connected through a single metaphorical nucleus, and the key metaphors are projected and sustained by a continuous web of subtly related minor metaphors and harmonizing imagery.]

Once we have seen this design and the vision of experience it implies, we shall understand why *Mrs. Dalloway* takes the form it does, why as a story it has properly no beginning or ending. It opens one morning with Clarissa Dalloway in the midst of preparing for a party; it closes in the early hours of the next morning with Clarissa very much involved in giving the party. The major event of her day is the return of Peter Walsh, the man she had almost married instead of Richard Dalloway, a successful M.P. Clarissa and Richard have a daughter, Elizabeth, who is temporarily attached to a religious fanatic, a woman with the Dickensian name of Miss Kilman. There is also in the novel another set of characters who at first seem to have no connection with Clarissa and her world: Septimus Smith, a veteran of

"Something Central Which Permeated: Virginia Woolf and 'Mrs. Dalloway'" by Reuben Brower. From *The Fields of Light* (New York: Oxford University Press, 1951), pp. 123–157. Reprinted by permission of the author and Oxford University Press.

the First World War, and his Italian wife, Rezia, a hatmaker by trade. Septimus, who is suffering from shell shock, is being treated—somewhat brutally—by a hearty M.D., Dr. Holmes. During the day of Clarissa's preparations, Septimus visits Sir William Bradshaw, an eminent psychiatrist, who recommends rather too firmly that Septimus should be taken to a sanatorium. In the late afternoon, as Dr. Holmes comes to take him away, Septimus jumps from the balcony of his room and kills himself. That evening, Sir William Bradshaw reports the story of his death at Clarissa's party.

Readers of the novel will recognize this outline as more or less accurate, but they will want to add that the impression it gives is very remote from their remembered experience of *Mrs. Dalloway*. For the peculiar texture of Virginia Woolf's fiction has been lost. The ebb and flow of her phrasing and the frequent repetition of the same or similar expressions, through which her characteristic rhythmic and metaphorical designs are built up, have completely disappeared.

No one needs to be shown that the novel is full of odd echoes. The Shakespearean tag, "Fear no more," occurs some six or seven times; certain words turn up with surprising frequency in the various interior monologues: "life," "feel," "suffer," "solemn," "moment," and "enjoy." Less obvious, and more peculiar to Virginia Woolf is the recurrence in the individual monologues of expressions for similar visual or aural images. Some of these images—the aeroplane and the stopped motorcar are examples—connect separate dramatic sequences in a rather artificial way; but others, such as Big Ben's striking and the marine images, often connect similar qualities of experience and so function as symbolic metaphors. There are many repeated words, phrases, and sentences in the novel, besides those already quoted, which gradually become metaphorical: "party," "Holmes and Bradshaw," "there she was," "plunge," "wave" and "sea," "sewing," "building" and "making it up," "Bourton," et cetera. Almost innumerable continuities, major and minor, may be traced through the various recurrent expressions; but as compared with Shakespeare's practice in *The Tempest,* the continuities are less often built up through the use of explicit metaphors. The repeated word does not occur in a conventional metaphorical expression, and its metaphorical value is felt only after it has been met in a number of contexts. Virginia Woolf's most characteristic metaphors are purely symbolic.

I can indicate from the adjective "solemn" how a recurrent expression acquires its special weight of meaning. By seeing how metaphor links with metaphor, the reader will also get a notion of the interconnectedness of the entire novel. The word appears on the first page of *Mrs. Dalloway*:

> How fresh, how calm, stiller than this of course, the air was in the early morning; like the flap of a wave; the kiss of a wave; chill and sharp and

yet (for a girl of eighteen as she then was) solemn, feeling as she did, standing there at the open window, that something awful was about to happen . . .

It is echoed at once, on the next page, in the first account of Big Ben's striking (an important passage in relation to the whole novel):

> For having lived in Westminster—how many years now? over twenty, —one feels even in the midst of the traffic, or waking at night, Clarissa was positive, a particular hush, or solemnity; an indescribable pause; a suspense (but that might be her heart, affected, they said, by influenza) before Big Ben strikes. There! Out it boomed. First a warning, musical; then the hour, irrevocable. The leaden circles dissolved in the air.

"Solemn," which on our first reading of the opening page had only a vague local meaning of "something awful about to happen," is now connected with a more particularized terror, the fear of a suspense, of a pause in experience. Each time that "solemn" is repeated in subsequent descriptions of Big Ben, it carries this additional meaning. The word recurs three times in the afternoon scene in which Clarissa looks across at an old woman in the next house:

> How extraordinary it was, strange, yes, touching, to see the old lady (they had been neighbours ever so many years) move away from the window, as if she were attached to that sound, that string. Gigantic as it was, it had something to do with her. Down, down, into the midst of ordinary things the finger fell making the moment solemn.

And a little further on:

> . . . Big Ben . . . laying down the law, so solemn, so just . . . on the wake of that solemn stroke which lay flat like a bar of gold on the sea.

In the early morning scene near the end of the book, Clarissa goes to the window, again sees the old lady, and thinks, "It will be a solemn sky . . . it will be a dusky sky, turning away its cheek in beauty." In all but the last passage there is some suggestion in the imagery of Big Ben's stroke coming down and marking an interruption in the process of life. By the end of the book we see the significance in the use of "solemn" on the first page in a passage conveying a sharp sense of freshness and youth. The terror symbolized by Big Ben's "pause" has a connection with early life, ". . . one's parents giving it into one's hands, this life, to be lived to the end." The "something awful . . . about to happen" was associated with "the flap of a wave, the kiss of a wave"; the "solemnity" of life is a kind of "sea-terror" (so Shakespeare might express it in *The Tempest*). Wave and water images recur in other "solemn" passages: "the wave," "the wake," "the leaden circles dissolved in the air." So, through various associations, "solemn" acquires symbolic values for the reader: some terror of entering the sea of experience and of living life and an inexplicable fear of a "suspense" or interruption.

While following a single symbolic adjective in *Mrs. Dalloway,* we have seen that it was impossible to interpret one continuity apart from several others. Various expressions—"solemn," "wave," "Big Ben," "fear," and "pause"—kept leading us toward the key metaphor of the book. The metaphor that links the continuities and gives unity to the dramatic design of *Mrs. Dalloway* is not a single, easily describable analogy, but two complementary and extremely complex analogies which are gradually expressed through recurrent words and phrases and through the dramatic pattern of the various sequences. Though they are salient in the sequences of nearly all the main characters, they are best interpreted from Clarissa's, since her experience forms the center of attention for the reader.

One of the two metaphorical poles of the novel emerges in a passage that comes just after the first account of Big Ben's striking:

> Such fools we are, she thought, crossing Victoria Street. For Heaven only knows why one loves it so how one sees it so, making it up, building it round one, tumbling it, creating it every moment afresh; but the veriest frumps, the most dejected of miseries sitting on doorsteps (drink their downfall) do the same; can't be dealt with, she felt positive, by Acts of Parliament for that very reason: they love life. In people's eyes, in the swing, tramp, and trudge; in the bellow and the uproar; the carriages, motor cars, omnibuses, vans, sandwich men shuffling and swinging; brass bands; barrel organs; in the triumph and the jingle and the strange high singing of some aeroplane overhead was what she loved; life; London; this moment of June.

The key phrase here is "they love life," and what is meant by "life" and "loving it" is indicated by the surrounding metaphors—"building it," "creating it every moment," "the swing, tramp, and trudge"—and also by the various images of sights, sounds, and actions.

"Life" as expressed in Mrs. Dalloway's morning walk (and in the walks of Peter and of her daughter Elizabeth) consists first in the doings of people and things and in the active perception of them. To meet Clarissa's approval, people "must do something," as she did in "making a world" in her drawing room, in "assembling" and "knowing" all sorts of individuals, in running her house, and in giving "her parties," which were for her "life." But the perception, the savoring of these doings of oneself and of others is itself a creation. For Mrs. Dalloway, "enjoying" and "loving" is "creating" and "building up," not passive enjoyment. Life is experienced in successively created "moments"; the sense of succession, of process, is inseparable from Clarissa's feeling about life; it is implicit in her movement along the streets, "this astonishing and rather solemn progress with the rest of them, up Bond Street." She thinks of "all this" as *going on* without her." ("This" and "all this" also become metaphors for life.) Later, in Elizabeth's experience of going up Fleet Street, all these metaphors are explicitly combined: "this van; this life; this procession." To live, then, is to enter into the process of action and active perception, to be absorbed in the successive moments: ". . . yet to her it was absolutely absorbing; all this."

But the sense of being absorbed in the process is inseparable from a fear of being excluded, from the dread that the process may be interrupted. The progress is a "solemn" one, the adjective suggesting (as elsewhere) the terror of "plunging" into experience. The sense of being *in* experience is inseparable from the sense of being *outside* of it:

> She sliced like a knife through everything; at the same time was outside, looking on. She had a perpetual sense, as she watched the taxi cabs, of being out, out, far out to sea and alone; she always had the feeling that it was very, very dangerous to live even one day.

Though the terror lies in having to go through with life, paradoxically the escape from terror lies in building up delight and sharing in the process:

> Even now, quite often if Richard had not been there reading the *Times,* so that she could crouch like a bird and gradually revive, send roaring up that immeasurable delight, rubbing stick to stick, one thing with another, she must have perished.

The central metaphor of Clarissa's narrative (and of the novel) is thus twofold: the exhilarated sense of being a part of the forward moving process and the recurrent fear of some break in this absorbing activity, which was symbolized by the "suspense" before Big Ben strikes. We are to feel all sorts of experiences qualified as at once "an absorbing progression" and "a progression about to be interrupted." Such in crudely schematic terms are the two analogies which make up the metaphorical nucleus of the novel. As my analysis has indicated, this complex metaphor is expressed through countless variant minor metaphors and images.

Both of the major aspects of the metaphor are intricately linked in the wonderful sewing scene in which Clarissa's old lover, Peter Walsh, returns to announce his plans for a second marriage:

> Quiet descended on her, calm, content, as her needle, drawing the silk smoothly to its gentle pause, collected the green folds together and attached them, very lightly, to the belt. So on a summer's day waves collect, overbalance, and fall; collect and fall; and the whole world seems to be saying "That is all" more and more ponderously, until even the heart in the body which lies in the sun on the beach says too, That is all. Fear no more, says the heart. Fear no more, says the heart, committing its burden to some sea, which sighs collectively for all sorrows, and

renews, begins, collects, lets fall. And the body alone listens to the passing bee; the wave breaking; the dog barking, far away barking and
barking.

Through the wave simile the opening statement expands in a metaphorical bloom which expresses in little the essence of the novel. The
quiet, calm, and content (Clarissa's absorption in what she is doing)
and the rhythmic movement of the needle are the points in the immediate situation from which the two main meanings of the key
metaphor grow. The comparison between sewing and wave movements draws in these further levels of meaning, thanks to the nice
preparation of earlier scenes and the delicate adjustment of those
that follow. There are the wave and sea images which have been
appearing when Clarissa recalls the terror of early life or when she
hears Big Ben's solemn stroke. Much later in the novel, there is
Clarissa at her party in her "silver-green mermaid's dress . . . lol-
loping on the waves." Here, in the scene with Peter, as in the final
party scene, the waves mainly symbolize Clarissa's complete absorption in her life: "That is all"—the phrase she had used twice while
shopping and which had come back in her musings on "the solemn
progress up Bond Street." There is for the heart at this moment
nothing but the process, and the individual becomes a mere percipient
body, intensely aware of the immediate sensation. But the moment
has a dual value, as has been suggested by the oblique allusions to
solemnity and terror ("waves," "ponderously," "That is all"). So the
reader is perfectly prepared for the return of "Fear no more," which
it is now clear suggests both freedom from fear and the fear of interruption, meanings which are dramatized in the scene that immediately follows.

Clarissa's quiet is rudely shaken by the sound of the front-door bell:

> "Who can—what can," asked Mrs. Dalloway (thinking it was out-
> rageous to be interrupted at eleven o'clock on the morning of the day
> she was giving a party), hearing a step on the stairs. She heard a hand
> upon the door. She made to hide her dress, like a virgin protecting
> chastity, respecting privacy.

The nature of the interruption, the return of her former lover, Peter
Walsh, and her gesture, "like a virgin protecting chastity, respecting
privacy," point to another analogy in *Mrs. Dalloway*, which is simply
a special aspect of the "life" metaphor. We might call it the "destroyer" theme. Peter's coming in temporarily destroys Clarissa's do-
mesticity, even her marriage. As a lover Peter had allowed her no
independence, and as a husband he would have been intolerable,
leaving her no life of her own. Clarissa reasserts herself and her life
by calling after him as he leaves, "Remember my party to-night!"
Peter is one of those who would cut her off from her way of living by

making her into another person: he is one of the "destroyers of the privacy of the soul." Compulsion of this sort is a special form of the "suspense" in life's exhilarating process. The "suspense" may be fear itself, or the sense of time's passing, or death, or a failure in personal relationships, or, finally, the loss of independence which results from love or hatred or officiousness.

We shall now see to what a remarkable extent the central metaphor penetrates and organizes the novel. The dramatic sequences of the principal characters are all linked with Clarissa's through a shuttling pattern of verbal reminiscences. (Curious readers may amuse themselves by finding dozens more than can be cited here.) Although "life" is peculiarly the key figure in Clarissa's experience, it is important in that of other characters, including Septimus and Miss Kilman, who are unable to "live" as Clarissa does.

We may begin with Peter Walsh, who as a lover has the role of one of the "interrupters" and "destroyers." But in the two accounts of his walks through London, he shows much of Clarissa's eager experience of life. He sets off on his morning walk, speaking rhythmically her parting words, "Remember my party, remember my party." He then "marches up Whitehall" as she has gone "up Bond Street," and he too "makes up" life (his mild "escapade with the girl"). During his evening walk, he expresses Clarissa's sense of enjoyment:

> Really it took one's breath away, these moments . . . absorbing, mysterious, of infinite richness, this life.

Elizabeth also shares her mother's perceptiveness, and in her bus ride has an experience closely paralleling Clarissa's morning walk. As all three characters pass through the "procession" of experience, they savor life as a series of exquisite moments, a sensation summed up by the motif of the scene in which Richard brings Clarissa the roses: "Happiness is this."

The crude parallel between the roles of Mrs. Dalloway and Septimus is obvious; the finer relations and how they are expressed may be best seen by tracing the links made through the "life" metaphor. While Clarissa usually feels her inclusion *in* everything and only occasionally feels *outside,* Septimus is almost always "alone" and unable to connect with the world about him. He had "felt very little in the war," and "now that it was all over, truce signed, and the dead buried, he had, especially in the evening, these thunder-claps of fear. He could not feel." Rezia, his wife, is his refuge from fear, though like Mrs. Dalloway she too has moments of panic when she cries, "I am alone; I am alone!" But she is shown as having some of Mrs. Dalloway's gift for active enjoyment, and through her Septimus is for once able to recover his power of feeling and to enter into the real life around him. The moment comes near the end of his narrative, in the late afternoon, as he lies on a sofa while Rezia is making a hat. The writing in this scene shows wonderfully the way in which Virginia Woolf moves from one narrative plane to another via image and metaphor. (The parallel with Shakespeare is obvious.)

Immediately preceding the scene comes the episode of Elizabeth's bus ride, with "this van; this life; this procession." These metaphors are then echoed in a long description of cloud movements which cast changing lights on the moving buses; the transition to Septimus takes place as he watches the "goings and comings" of the clouds. The movements and colors referred to and the verbal rhythm ("watching watery gold glow and fade") prepare us easily for the return of the wave and sea imagery of Clarissa's and Peter's monologues:

> Outside the trees dragged their leaves like nets through the depths of the air; the sound of water was in the room and through the waves came the voices of birds singing. Every power poured its treasures on his head, and his hand lay there on the back of the sofa, as he had seen his hand lie when he was bathing, floating, on the top of the waves, while far away on shore he heard dogs barking and barking far away. Fear no more, says the heart in the body; fear no more.

The last words anticipate the next phase of the scene. Septimus, watching Rezia sew a hat, temporarily loses himself in his interest in her activity: "She built it up, first one thing, then another, she built it up, sewing." (The "building" is an echo of the "life" metaphor, and the sewing is now symbolic.) Septimus begins to note actual objects around him, as Rezia gives him assurance that real things are real: "There she was, perfectly natural, sewing." The words, "There she was" (also the concluding sentence of the novel) are an exact repetition of one of Peter's earlier remarks about Clarissa, where they signified her "extraordinary gift, that woman's gift, of making a world wherever she happened to be." Septimus' participation in life is interrupted, as was Clarissa's, by one of the compellers, Dr. Holmes. His suicide is a protest against having his life forcibly remade by others.

In the figure of Sir William Bradshaw we get an almost allegorical representation of a "destroyer." His talk of keeping a "sense of proportion" and his tactful questions are a screen for his firm intention of getting patients to do what he thinks best. There is a close relation, we are told, between preaching proportion and being a converter, for Proportion has a sister, Conversion, who "feasts on the wills of the weakly." Clarissa also is pursued by a compeller of this less lovely type, the horrendous if pious spinster, Miss Kilman. She ruins Clarissa's enjoyment of life and is shown as having herself no capacity for delight (if we overlook her perverse fondness for chocolate éclairs!). In the mock-heroic tea-table scene she fails in her attempt to exert a negative influence over Elizabeth, who leaves to go to her mother's party. As Miss Kilman questions Elizabeth, the reader recalls that Mrs. Dalloway's parting words to Miss Kilman and her daughter had been those she had used to Peter: "Remember my party!" Her words are symbolic of defiance. ✳

Just after this episode the mysterious old lady makes the first of her two appearances, the value of which can now be seen. The old lady, Clarissa says, was "merely being herself." "There was something solemn in it—but love and religion would destroy that, whatever it was, the privacy of the soul." "Solemn" connects this "privacy" theme, symbolized by the old lady, with the attitudes expressed through the key metaphor of the novel, especially with the precarious and terrifying sense of enjoyment. To experience life, terror and all, we must be left alone.

All of the related analogies that make up the key metaphor are combined near the end of the novel, at the point when Bradshaw tells Clarissa of Septimus' death and when Clarissa, reflecting on its meaning, looks out of the window at the old lady going to bed. Bradshaw, a man "capable of some indescribable crime—forcing your soul, that was it—," momentarily ruins her party ("in the middle of my party, here's death, she thought . . ."). But Clarissa immediately recognizes that Septimus' death has a further meaning in relation to his life and hers. By killing himself Septimus had defied the men who make life intolerable, and though he had "thrown it away," he had not lost his independence of soul. This (in so far as we can define it) is "the thing" he had preserved. By contrast Clarissa had sacrificed some of this purity. She had made compromises for the sake of social success, "She had schemed; she had pilfered." But she had not given in to Peter, and by marrying Richard she had been able to make a life of her own. The delight, though impure, remained. The old lady, in her second appearance as in her first, symbolizes the quiet maintenance of one's own life, which is the only counterbalance to the fear of "interruption" whether by death or compulsion.

This scene shows in the highest degree the concentration of various dramatic relationships through a central metaphor. What we would emphasize here is Virginia Woolf's literary feat in achieving this result—literary in the primitive sense of Frost's pun, "feat of words." The unity of her design depends on the building up of symbolic metaphors through an exquisite management of verbal devices: through exact repetitions, reminiscent variations, the use of related eye and ear imagery, and the recurrence of similar phrase and sentence rhythms. The novel has as a result a unique closeness of structure which is only slightly dependent on story, though also supported by the time patterns which David Daiches has chosen to emphasize. What is most remarkable is the way in which so many different experiences have been perceived through a single metaphorical vision: the lives of Clarissa, Peter, Richard, Septimus, and Rezia as glimpsed at various periods, and of Elizabeth at the moment of growing up. Most of the characters are seen, too, in some relation to the persons who "make life intolerable": Miss Kilman, Holmes, Bradshaw, and Peter in his role as lover. Experience, rich and various in its range, has struck the mind of the novelist at a single angle and been refracted with perfect consistency. This singleness in reception and expression, as evidenced in the metaphorical design, is what we mean by integrity of imagination in Virginia Woolf.

But there are certainly points in the novel at which this singleness of vision shows signs of strain. Philistine readers have observed that the men of the novel are not full-blooded or are barely "men" at all —a type of criticism that could be applied with disastrous results to *Tom Jones,* or *Emma,* or *The Portrait of a Lady.* But the strain that is truly a sign of weakness appears in the relating of dramatic elements through the central metaphorical nucleus. That Peter is no man—whether we mean not lifelike or not masculine—is a relevant comment only because of the symbolic role in which he is sometimes cast. As a lover he stands in Clarissa's thoughts for one of the dark "forcers of the soul"; but in much of his behavior he is described as a womanish sort of person who has little power to manage himself or to move others. In one rather embarrassing episode, Peter's half-imaginary pursuit of a young girl, Virginia Woolf is apparently attempting to present his passionate side. The lack of lively sensuous detail in this narrative contrasts very badly with the glowing particularity of Mrs. Dalloway's walk through Bond Street or with the vividness of Peter's impressions of a London evening, while by way of a poor compensation there is a good deal of generalized emotional language: "vast philanthropy," "exquisite delight," "mournful tenderness," "laughing and delightful," et cetera. Peter calls this "making up" an "exquisite amusement," which is in this instance a painfully accurate label. The metaphor ceases to be an instrument through which experience is connected for us in a new relation and remains a simple declaration of a connection never made.

On occasion Virginia Woolf becomes so fascinated with this instrument that she elaborates the metaphor out of all proportion to its expressive value. (*The Waves* is a kind of metaphorical monster of this sort.) The purest and most interesting example of such elaboration in *Mrs. Dalloway* comes just after Peter's imaginary flirtation, the interlude of "the solitary traveller." The passage—which is not a dream, though it covers the time while Peter is sleeping—is an enlarged symbolic version of Peter's experience with the girl and in part an expression of his desire for a more satisfactory relationship with Clarissa. As various echoes show, it is, like the experience on the street, a grand example of "making up," a vision of the consolatory woman who gives the kind of understanding which Peter had attributed to the girl and which he had not found in Clarissa. It is in a picturesque sense a beautiful passage, but merely beautiful, a piece which could be detached with little loss. The detailed picture of the woman, the evening, the street, and the adorable landlady does not increase or enrich our knowledge of Peter or of anyone else in the book.

Perhaps the most obvious examples of metaphorical elaboration for its own sake are the super-literary, pseudo-Homeric similes which adorn various pages of *Mrs. Dalloway*. Whether they are in origin Proustian or eighteenth-century Bloomsbury, we could wish that they might be dropped. Here is a relatively short example from the scene following the sewing passage:

> "Well, and what's happened to you?" she said. So before a battle begins, the horses paw the ground; toss their heads; the light shines on their flanks; their necks curve. So Peter Walsh and Clarissa, sitting side by side on the blue sofa, challenged each other. His powers chafed and tossed in him. He assembled from different quarters all sorts of things; praise; his career at Oxford; his marriage, which she knew nothing whatever about; how he had loved; and altogether done his job.

The contrast between such a literary pastiche and the wave-sewing simile shows us in part what is wrong. The particular sense images, "paw," "toss," "light shines," are not grounded on the dramatic and narrative level, since there is no preparation for this Homeric horseplay in the account of Clarissa's and Peter's talk and gestures. (By contrast the wave motion was anticipated through describing Clarissa's movements as she sewed.) So the reader is unprepared to take the further jump to the psychological levels of the metaphor. The efforts to show any similarity in Peter's internal "chafings" and "tossings" come too late. The metaphor is crudely explained; but it doesn't work. Such simulations—like Peter's escapade and the solitary traveller's vision—are verbally inert matter, sending no radiations through the reader's experience of the novel.

But what is vital in the writing of *Mrs. Dalloway* is both more nearly omnipresent and more unobtrusive. To say, as I did at the beginning of this, that Virginia Woolf creates a Shakespearean pattern of metaphor tells us something, of course; but to see how she connects diverse moments of experience by playing on a single analogy, or on a single word, tells us much more. As Clarissa is thinking of the death of Septimus Smith, she says to herself: "But this young man who had killed himself—had he plunged holding his treasure?" She has just recalled that he had "plunged" by "throwing himself from a window," which in turn echoes his earlier agonies ("falling through the sea, down, down") and his actual death ("flung himself vigorously, violently down"). But Septimus' "plunge" recalls experiences of a very different sort in Clarissa's social life:

> . . . as she stood hesitating one moment on the threshold of her drawing-room, an exquisite suspense, such as might stay a diver before plunging while the sea darkens and brightens beneath him. . .

"Darkens" suggests that "plunge" has also a more fearful significance, as we saw on the first page of the novel:

> What a lark! What a plunge! For so it had always seemed to her, when, with a little squeak of the hinges, which she could hear now, she had burst open the French windows and plunged at Bourton into the open air. How fresh, how calm, stiller than this of course, the air was in the early morning; like the flap of a wave; the kiss of a wave; chill and sharp and yet (for a girl of eighteen as she then was) solemn, feeling as she did, standing there at the open window, that something awful was about to happen . . .

Septimus' plunge from the window is linked with those earlier windows and "the triumphs of youth" and thereby with the exhilarating and "solemn" sense of delight in life's process (the "treasure"). This twofold sense of life is constantly being expressed through the central metaphor of *Mrs. Dalloway*. The recurrence of a single word is a quiet indication of the subtlety and closeness of the structure which Virginia Woolf was "building up" as she wrote this novel.

The Novel as Poem

by Leon Edel

Virginia Woolf was not one of the architects of the stream-of-consciousness novel. She read Joyce, Proust, and Dorothy Richardson and absorbed their lesson. Her peculiar contribution to the novel of subjectivity lay in her awareness almost from the first that she could obtain given effects of experience by a constant search for the condition of poetry. The influence of James Joyce upon her is much more profound than is generally believed. Indeed, she herself was prompt to seize upon *Ulysses* as a transcendent work long before it was published and only a few chapters had been serialized. She wrote at the time:

> Anyone who had read the *Portrait of the Artist as a Young Man* or, what promises to be a far more interesting work, *Ulysses,* now appearing in the *Little Review,* will have hazarded some theory ... as to Mr. Joyce's intention. On our part, with such a fragment before us, it is hazarded rather than affirmed; but whatever the intention of the whole, there can be no question but that it is of the utmost sincerity and that the result, difficult or unpleasant as we may judge it, is undeniably important. ... Mr. Joyce ... is concerned at all costs to reveal the flickerings of that innermost flame which flashes its messages through the brain, and in order to preserve it he disregards with complete courage whatever seems to him adventitious, whether it be probability, or coherence, or any other of those signposts which for generations have served to support the imagination of a reader when called upon to imagine what he can neither touch nor see. ... If we want life itself, here surely we have it.

She was to have reservations about Joyce, but these were to be, in effect, afterthoughts. The impression he made on her was powerful. Her first two novels, *The Voyage Out* and *Night and Day,* published in 1915 and 1919, were conventional enough. The narrative proceeded in a traditional progression and there was no attempt to go very far into the minds of the characters. There are, however, interesting por-

"The Novel as Poem" by Leon Edel. From *The Modern Psychological Novel* (New York: Grosset and Dunlap, Inc., 1964), pp. 123–36. Copyright © 1964 by Leon Edel. Reprinted by permission of the author and the William Morris Agency, Inc.

tents of what was to come (as there are in the short stories in which she was experimenting). In *The Voyage Out* one of the characters observes: "What I want to do in writing novels is very much what you want to do when you play the piano, I expect. We want to find out what's behind things, don't we?—Look at the lights down there scattered about anyhow. Things I feel come to me like lights. . . . I want to combine them. . . . Have you ever seen fireworks that make figures? . . . I want to make figures."

In this novel a woman looks at a circular, iridescent patch in the river, watching it with fascination and weaving thoughts around it. The patch is like the distant series of lights; it is the pin-point of experience, the grains of sand, the mark on the wall around which Virginia Woolf will have the mind accumulate its associations. Her method seems to be a focusing of the mind in this fashion, in the way in which animals and people—and notably in certain types of mental ailments—will look at some pinpoint with a fascination all-absorbing, unable to tear themselves away from it. Such a focusing occurs in the works of Mrs. Woolf, and around this she gives us the cluster of emotion and memory. By this process she achieves a remarkable, shimmering effect of experience. Light, tone, colour play through her cadenced works in a constant search for mood and with no attempt to impart an individual character to the style of thought. There is no attempt at portrait painting; rather does she try to evoke a state of feeling by a kind of mental poesy. The same vein of poetry runs through all the minds she creates for us. It is as if she had created a single device or convention, to be applied universally, in the knowledge that the delicacy of her perception, the waves of feeling, will wash over her readers as she washes them over her characters.

This is alike her achievement and its fatal flaw. The bright flame-like vividness of her books creates beautiful illuminated surfaces. There is no tragic depth in them, only the pathos of things lost and outlived, the past irretrievable or retrieved as an ache in the present. And in this she has fused the example of Proust as of Joyce. I think of *Mrs. Dalloway* as a Joycean novel, diluted, and washed and done in beautiful water-colour; and *To the Lighthouse* is Proustian in its time-sense, but again the medium is a kind of water-colour of the emotions.

Like Proust and Joyce, Virginia Woolf clearly expressed her aesthetic of fiction. Once she had grasped the lesson of her two great predecessors, she seems to have known exactly how she would apply it. But her definition of fiction is more impressionistic than the carefully evolved analysis Proust made of his *métier,* or the Aquinian aesthetic of Joyce. She adds little to what has been said, and once we divest her ideas of the eloquence in which they are clothed, we find them rather thin and unoriginal. Precisely because it has become one of her most quoted passages, I want to repeat here Virginia Woolf's account of what she believed should be the material of the novel of subjectivity:

> Examine for a moment an ordinary mind on an ordinary day. The mind receives a myriad impressions—trivial, fantastic, evanescent, or engraved with the sharpness of steel. From all sides they come, an incessant shower of innumerable atoms; and as they fall, as they shape themselves into the life of Monday or Tuesday, the accent falls differently from of old; the moment of importance came not here but there; so that if a writer were a free man and not a slave, if he could write what he chose, not what he must, if he could base his work upon his own feeling and not upon convention, there would be no plot, no comedy, no tragedy, no love interest or catastrophe in the accepted style, and perhaps not a single button sewn on as the Bond Street tailors would have it. Life is not a series of gig lamps symmetrically arranged but a luminous halo, a semi-transparent envelope surrounding us from the beginning of consciousness to the end. Is it not the task of the novelist to convey this varying, this unknown and uncircumscribed spirit, whatever aberration or complexity it may display, with as little mixture of the alien and external as possible? We are not pleading merely for courage and sincerity; we are suggesting that the proper stuff of fiction is a little other than custom would have us believe it.

This is very beautifully stated, but I am tempted to suggest that Benjamin Constant expressed it much more succinctly long before. I translate freely:

> Man's feelings are mixed and confused; they are composed of a multitude of varied impressions which escape observation; and words, always clumsy and too general, may well serve to designate but never to define them.

Virginia Woolf tried to catch the shower of innumerable atoms, the vision of life, the iridescence, the luminous halo. It was her way of circumventing the clumsiness of words. She went on to specify:

> Let us record the atoms as they fall upon the mind in the order in which they fall, let us trace the pattern, however disconnected and incoherent in appearance, which each sight or incident scores upon that consciousness. . . . Any method is right, every method is right, that expresses what we wish to express, if we are writers; that brings us closer to the novelist's intention, if we are readers . . . everything is the proper stuff of fiction, every feeling, every thought, every quality of brain and spirit is drawn upon; no perception comes amiss.

This, however, comes much more closely to describing the writing of Dorothy Richardson than the art of Virginia Woolf. However much Mrs. Woolf might assert the need to record the shower of atoms "in the order in which they fall," she neither accepted that order, nor believed in describing their frequent incoherence. Her method was that of the lyric poet. She was interested in the sharpened image, the moment, the condensed experience. She saw the world around her as if it were a sharp knife cutting its way into her being.

From James Joyce, Virginia Woolf seems to have obtained a certain sense of *oneness* and the isolation that resides within it: from him she learned how to give meaning to the simultaneity of experience. London is to Mrs. Dalloway what Dublin is to Leopold Bloom. But her London is a large canvas background with light cleverly playing over it and, unlike Joyce, her people are distillations of mind and flesh. Clarissa Dalloway's day in London, also a day in June, as in *Ulysses,* begins at nine in the morning and finishes early the next morning. (Indeed, in most of Mrs. Woolf's fiction, time is reduced to a few hours, so that even in *To the Lighthouse,* where a number of years are bridged in the middle passage, "Time Passes," it is but to link two single days at each end of that period.) Clarissa Dalloway walks through London, and the people around her form an encircling wave as she goes to Bond Street or strolls along the Green Park, while in the midst of the day the big bronze accents of Big Ben remind us of the ticking of mechanical time while we move in and out of Mrs. Dalloway's mind and the minds of the other characters in the story.

The book's structure seems largely to be modelled on the multiple-scened chapter in *Ulysses* which is tied together by the progress of the vice-regal cavalcade through Dublin's streets. We are in many minds in the streets of London. But Mrs. Dalloway's mind, and that of Septimus Warren Smith, hold the centre of the book as did those of Bloom and Dedalus in *Ulysses.* The entire inwardness of the book, its limited time-scheme, the use of multiple views, so that we feel we have seen London through many eyes—and so are aware of it through many awarenesses—the glimpsing of certain characters and then the glimpse of them anew through the perceptions of the principal characters—all this becomes a subtle conversion to simpler ends of the Joycean complexities. But if Bloom and Dedalus are a father and son who meet for a brief moment at the end of a long day symbolically, as Odysseus met Telemachus after a lifetime of wanderings, Clarissa Dalloway and Septimus Smith seem to be two facets of the same personality—indeed, the projection by Virginia Woolf of two sides of herself. Mrs. Woolf's diary shows that she conceived this novel as an attempt to show "the world seen by the sane and the insane side by side." And we know from her own preface to it that she first intended Septimus to have no existence: it was Clarissa who was to die or to kill herself at the end of her London day and her brilliant party. Finally, she envisaged Septimus as a "double" of Clarissa.

But how is he the double—Septimus the insane, Clarissa the sane? What connections, we might ask, unify them? They never actually meet, as Bloom and Dedalus did, although their paths converge during the day; and it is the doctor of Septimus, the clumsy inept Harley Street psychiatrist, who brings to Clarissa's party the little bit of news that Septimus has committed suicide. The imparting of this bit of information, a mere incident in a big city, remote from Clarissa, plunges her nevertheless into a deep fantasy and identification with the unknown man who is now dead.

> What business had the Bradshaws to talk of death at her party? A young man had killed himself. And they talked of it at her party—the Bradshaws talked of death.

So far it is the intrusion of unpleasant reality, and Clarissa is hard at work trying to submerge her feelings. Then comes identification:

> He had killed himself—but how? Always her body went through it first, when she was told, suddenly, of an accident; her dress flamed, her body burnt. He had thrown himself from a window. Up had flashed the ground; through him, blundering, bruising, went the rusty spikes. There he lay with a thud, thud, thud in his brain, and then a suffocation of blackness. So she saw it. But why had he done it? And the Bradshaws talked of it at her party!

This is Clarissa whom Peter had described as the "perfect hostess" and whom he had remembered as a girl, "timid, hard; something arrogant; unimaginative; prudish." There was a "coldness," a "woodenness," an "impenetrability" in her. But we know better; we know also that this façade of the perfect hostess submerges the Clarissa who has intuitions and feelings which she can never fully face. It is on the ground of the failure to feel that Clarissa and Septimus are each other's double. Septimus had choked feeling when his friend Evans was killed at his side during the war. He goes through life utterly numbed by this experience.

> He could reason; he could read, Dante, for example, quite easily . . . he could add up his bill; his brain was perfect; it must be the fault of the world then—that he could not feel.

And so these two principal characters dissociate experience constantly from themselves. Both are incapable of establishing a meaningful relationship with the emotional texture of life: Clarissa escapes by giving some slight play to her insights and intuitions, "If you put her in a room with someone, up went her back like a cat's; or she purred," but the façade of the perfect hostess is untouched, the feeling submerged. Septimus escapes by throttling feeling and creating a new world within, filled with private demons and private terrors, from which he can only seek, in the end, the swift obliteration of consciousness.

The whole of the novel conveys poignantly Virginia Woolf's response to Joyce's success in reflecting how, in a big city, people's paths cross and dramas go on within range of dramas, and yet in spite of innumerable points of superficial contact and relation, each drama is isolated and each individual remains locked within walls of private experience. The book's brilliance, as writing and as poetry, lies in the skill with which Mrs. Woolf weaves from one mind into another. Septimus, in the park, sees a man walking towards him and suddenly invests him with the aspect of another man and the trauma of his war experience; and suddenly we are in the mind of the other man, Peter, who sees only a rather disturbed-looking Septimus and his anxious wife Rezia, without beginning to know what violent images have been flickering in Septimus's consciousness. This complex inner material could be rendered only by the use of brilliantly evocative prose-poetry. And this novel, like those which Virginia Woolf wrote after it, illustrates admirably the worth of the symbolist method in fiction. We have only to think of a Zola or a George Moore creating Clarissa after the manner of their naturalist doctrines to understand the difference. Clarissa would emerge as a commonplace woman, the façade described in detail, but no hint of the fascinating and troubled and mysterious personality behind her exterior. Mrs. Woolf extended with remarkable skill and literary virtuosity the creation of a novel that conveys inner experience. She was capable of finding the words that would show the world through her protagonists' minds: and she participated fully in the significant shift of emphasis, inaugurated by Henry James, from the outer social world—as explored by Balzac or the naturalists—to the sensibility with which that outer world is appreciated and felt.

If the general plan, the painting of the environment, is a scaling down of Joycean architectonics, the painting of the sensibility tends to be Proustian. And yet there is a significant difference. In Proust the odour of the lilacs is directly felt and explored with subtlety; his feelings well up out of the page and are carefully communicated. In Mrs. Woolf the odour bounces off the flowers and reaches the reader as a sharp, distinct but refracted sensation. One has indeed an effect of the bouncing-off of light and sound throughout the novel from people and objects and against the receiving mind. Proust touches experience directly. Mrs. Woolf's method is refraction, through a kind of high, tense awareness. The poetry is there on every page and always a synthesis—a pulling together of objects and impressions. In addition to Big Ben heard by London and the people immediately around or near Mrs. Dalloway, they watch an aeroplane sky-writing. The aeroplane serves to unify the city and the people as the vice-regal cavalcade did in *Ulysses*:

> Ah, but that aeroplane! Hadn't Mrs. Dempster always longed to see foreign parts? She had a nephew, a missionary. It soared and shot. She always went on the sea at Margate, not out o' sight of land, but she had

no patience with women who were afraid of water. It swept and fell. Her stomach was in her mouth. Up again. There's a fine young fellow aboard of it, Mrs. Dempster wagered, and away and away it went, fast and fading, away and away the aeroplane shot; soaring over Greenwich and all the masts; over the little island of grey churches, St. Paul's and the rest, till, on either side of London, fields spread out and dark brown woods where adventurous thrushes, hopping boldly, glancing quickly, snatched the snail and tapped him on a stone, once, twice, thrice.

This is stream-of-consciousness writing after the manner of Joyce and a fascinating dissociation of experience which Mrs. Woolf always conveys to us, a matching of incongruities. From the broad skies we are swept across a vast city—and fixed on a pin-point. The world is blotted out; the eye leaves the plane to catch a predatory thrush bouncing a snail on a rock. The world can be reduced to a snail— but a snail can also become a pin-point of experience from which the mind moves out into the world. In *The Mark on the Wall* Virginia Woolf seeks to explain involuntary association and always with a sense that memory is an invoking of the incongruous. She sees a mark on the wall. It seems to jut out. It is not entirely circular. It seems to cast a shadow. Then:

> If I ran my finger down that strip of the wall it would, at a certain point, mount and descend a small tumulus, a smooth tumulus like those barrows on the South Downs, which are, they say, either tombs or camps. Of the two I should prefer them to be tombs, desiring melancholy like most English people . . .

and so on, a mark on the wall, a barrow, a tomb, and her daydream continues to take wing like the aeroplane in the sky over trees, rivers, the Downs, *Whitaker's Almanack*, fields of asphodel, until someone standing beside her brings her back to the reality, the room, the newspaper, the mark on the wall, by saying: "All the same, I don't see why we should have a snail on our wall."

The Brown Stocking

by Erich Auerbach

"And even if it isn't fine to-morrow," said Mrs. Ramsay, raising her eyes to glance at William Bankes and Lily Briscoe as they passed, "it will be another day. And now," she said, thinking that Lily's charm was her Chinese eyes, aslant in her white, puckered little face, but it would take a clever man to see it, "and now stand up, and let me measure your leg," for they might go to the Lighthouse after all, and she must see if the stocking did not need to be an inch or two longer in the leg.

Smiling, for an admirable idea had flashed upon her this very second—William and Lily should marry—she took the heather mixture stocking, with its criss-cross of steel needles at the mouth of it, and measured it against James's leg.

"My dear, stand still," she said, for in his jealousy, not liking to serve as measuring-block for the Lighthouse keeper's little boy, James fidgeted purposely; and if he did that, how could she see, was it too long, was it too short? she asked.

She looked up—what demon possessed him, her youngest, her cherished?—and saw the room, saw the chairs, thought them fearfully shabby. Their entrails, as Andrew said the other day, were all over the floor; but then what was the point, she asked herself, of buying good chairs to let them spoil up here all through the winter when the house, with only one old woman to see to it, positively dripped with wet? Never mind; the rent was precisely twopence halfpenny; the children loved it; it did her husband good to be three thousand, or if she must be accurate, three hundred miles from his library and his lectures and his disciples; and there was room for visitors. Mats, camp beds, crazy ghosts of chairs and tables whose London life of service was done—they did well enough here; and a photograph or two, and books. Books, she thought, grew of themselves. She never had time to read them. Alas! even the books that had been given her, and inscribed by the hand of the poet himself: "For her whose wishes must be obeyed . . ." "The happier Helen of our days . . ." disgraceful to say, she had never read them. And Croom on the Mind and Bates on the Savage Customs of Polynesia ("My dear, stand still," she said)— neither of those could one send to the Lighthouse. At a certain moment, she supposed, the house would become so shabby that something must be done. If they could be taught to wipe their feet and not bring the beach in with them—that would be something. Crabs, she had to allow, if Andrew really wished to dissect them, or if Jasper believed that one could make soup from seaweed, one could not prevent it; or Rose's objects—shells, reeds, stones; for they were gifted, her children, but all in quite different ways. And the result of it was, she sighed, taking in the whole room from floor to ceiling, as she held the stocking against James's leg, that things got shabbier and got shabbier summer after summer. The mat was fading; the wall-paper was flapping. You couldn't tell any more that those were roses on it. Still, if every door in a house is left perpetually open, and no lock-maker in the whole of Scotland can mend a bolt, things must spoil. What was the use of flinging a green Cashmere shawl over the edge of a picture frame? In two weeks it would be the colour of pea soup. But it was the doors that annoyed her; every door was left open. She listened. The drawing-room door was open; the hall door was open; it sounded as if the bedroom doors were open; and certainly the window on the landing was open, for that she had opened herself. That windows should be open, and doors shut—simple as it was, could none of them remember it? She would go into the maids' bed-rooms at night and find them sealed like ovens, except for Marie's, the Swiss girl, who would rather go without a bath than without fresh air, but then at home, she had said, "the mountains are so beautiful." She had said that last night looking out of the window with tears in her eyes. "The mountains are so beautiful." Her father was dying there, Mrs. Ramsay knew. He was leaving them fatherless. Scolding and demonstrating (how to make a bed, how to open a window, with hands that shut and spread like a Frenchwoman's) all had folded itself quietly about her, when the girl spoke, as, after a flight through the sunshine the wings of a bird fold themselves quietly and the blue of its plumage changes from bright steel to soft purple. She had stood there silent for there was nothing to be said. He had cancer of the throat. At the recollection—how she had stood there, how the girl had said "At home the mountains are so beautiful," and there was no hope, no hope whatever, she had a spasm of irritation, and speaking sharply, said to James:

"Stand still. Don't be tiresome," so that he knew instantly that her severity was real, and straightened his leg and she measured it.

The stocking was too short by half an inch at least, making allowance for the fact that Sorley's little boy would be less well grown than James.

"It's too short," she said, "ever so much too short."

Never did anybody look so sad. Bitter and black, half-way down, in the darkness, in the shaft which ran from the sunlight to the depths, perhaps a tear formed; a tear fell; the waters swayed this way and that, received it, and were at rest. Never did anybody look so sad.

But was it nothing but looks? people said. What was there behind it—her beauty, her splendour? Had he blown his brains out, they asked, had he died the week before they were married—some other, earlier lover, of whom rumours reached one? Or was there nothing? nothing but an incomparable beauty which she lived behind, and could do nothing to disturb? For easily though she might have said at some moment of intimacy when stories of great passion, of love foiled, of ambition thwarted came her way how she too had known or felt or been through it herself, she never spoke. She was silent always. She knew then—she knew without having learnt. Her simplicity fathomed what clever people falsified. Her singleness of mind made her drop plumb like a stone, alight exact as a bird, gave her, naturally, this swoop and fall of the spirit upon truth which delighted, eased, sustained—falsely perhaps.

("Nature has but little clay," said Mr. Bankes once, hearing her voice on the telephone, and much moved by it though she was only telling him a fact about a train, "like that of which she moulded you." He saw her at the end of the line, Greek, blue-eyed, straight-nosed. How incongruous it seemed to be telephoning to a woman like that. The Graces assembling seemed to have joined hands in meadows of asphodel to compose that face. Yes, he would catch the 10:30 at Euston.

"But she's no more aware of her beauty than a child," said Mr. Bankes, replacing the receiver and crossing the room to see what progress the workmen were making with an hotel which they were building at the back of his house. And he thought of Mrs. Ramsay as he looked at that stir among the unfinished walls. For always, he thought, there was something incongruous to be worked into the harmony of her face. She clapped a deerstalker's hat on her head; she ran across the lawn in goloshes to snatch a child from mischief. So that if it was her beauty merely that one thought of, one must remember the quivering thing, the living thing [they were carrying bricks up a little plank as he watched them], and work it into the picture; or if one thought of her simply as a woman, one must endow her with some freak of idiosyncrasy; or suppose some latent desire to doff her royalty of form as if her beauty bored her and all that men say of beauty, and she wanted only to be like other people, insignificant. He did not know. He did not know. He must go to his work.)

Knitting her reddish-brown hairy stocking, with her head outlined absurdly by the gilt frame, the green shawl which she had tossed over the edge of the frame, and the authenticated masterpiece by Michael Angelo, Mrs. Ramsay smoothed out what had been harsh in her manner a moment before, raised his head, and kissed her little boy on the forehead. "Let's find another picture to cut out," she said.

This piece of narrative prose is the fifth section of part 1 in Virginia Woolf's novel, *To the Lighthouse*, which was first published in 1927. The situation in which the characters find themselves can be almost completely deduced from the text itself. Nowhere in the novel is it set forth systematically, by way of introduction or exposition, or in any other way than as it is here. I shall, however, briefly summarize what the situation is at the beginning of our passage. This will make it easier for the reader to understand the following analysis; it will also serve to bring out more clearly a number of important motifs from earlier sections which are here only alluded to. . . .

Mrs. Ramsay's very first remark is twice interrupted: first by the visual impression she receives of William Bankes and Lily Briscoe passing by together, and then, after a few intervening words serving the progress of the exterior occurrence, by the impression which the two persons passing by have left in her: the charm of Lily's Chinese eyes, which it is not for every man to see—whereupon she finishes her sentence and also allows her consciousness to dwell for a moment on the measuring of the stocking: we may yet go to the lighthouse, and so I must make sure the stocking is long enough. At this point there flashes into her mind the idea which has been prepared by her reflection on Lily's Chinese eyes (William and Lily ought to marry) —an admirable idea, she loves making matches. Smiling, she begins measuring the stocking. But the boy, in his stubborn and jealous love of her, refuses to stand still. How can she see whether the stocking is the right length if the boy keeps fidgeting about? What is the matter with James, her youngest, her darling? She looks up. Her eye falls on the room—and a long parenthesis begins. From the shabby chairs of which Andrew, her eldest son, said the other day that their entrails were all over the floor, her thoughts wander on, probing the objects and the people of her environment. The shabby furniture . . . but still good enough for up here; the advantages of the summer place; so cheap, so good for the children, for her husband; easily fitted up with a few old pieces of furniture, some pictures and books. Books —it is ages since she has had time to read books, even the books which have been dedicated to her (here the lighthouse flashes in for a second, as a place where one can't send such erudite volumes as some of those lying about the room). Then the house again: if the family would only be a little more careful. But of course, Andrew brings in crabs he wants to dissect; the other children gather seaweed, shells, stones; and she has to let them. All the children are gifted, each in a different way. But naturally, the house gets shabbier as a result (here the parenthesis is interrupted for a moment; she holds the stocking against James's leg); everything goes to ruin. If only the doors weren't always left open. See, everything is getting spoiled, even that Cashmere shawl on the picture frame. The doors are always left open; they are open again now. She listens: Yes, they are all open. The window on the landing is open too; she opened it herself. Windows must be open, doors closed. Why is it that no one can get that into his head? If you go to the maids' rooms at night, you will find all the windows closed. Only the Swiss maid always keeps her window open. She needs fresh air. Yesterday she looked out of the window with tears in her eyes and said: At home the mountains are so beautiful. Mrs. Ramsay knew that "at home" the girl's father was dying. Mrs. Ramsay had just been trying to teach her how to make beds, how to open windows. She had been talking away and had scolded the girl too. But then she had stopped talking (comparison with a bird folding its wings after flying in sunlight). She had stopped talking, for there was nothing one could say; he has cancer of the throat. At this point, remembering how she had stood there, how the girl had said at home the mountains were so beautiful—and there was no hope left—a sudden tense exasperation arises in her (exasperation with the cruel meaninglessness of a life whose continuance she is nevertheless striving with all her powers to abet, support, and secure). Her exasperation flows out into the exterior action. The parenthesis suddenly closes (it cannot have taken up more than a few seconds; just now she was still smiling over the thought of a marriage between Mr. Bankes and Lily Briscoe), and she says sharply to James: Stand still. Don't be so tiresome.

This is the first major parenthesis. The second starts a little later, after the stocking has been measured and found to be still much too short. It starts with the paragraph which begins and ends with the motif, "never did anybody look so sad."

Who is speaking in this paragraph? Who is looking at Mrs. Ramsay here, who concludes that never did anybody look so sad? Who is expressing these doubtful, obscure suppositions?—about the tear which —perhaps—forms and falls in the dark, about the water swaying this way and that, receiving it, and then returning to rest? There is no one near the window in the room but Mrs. Ramsay and James. It cannot be either of them, nor the "people" who begin to speak in the next paragraph. Perhaps it is the author. However, if that be so, the author certainly does not speak like one who has a knowledge of his

characters—in this case, of Mrs. Ramsay—and who, out of his knowledge, can describe their personality and momentary state of mind
objectively and with certainty. Virginia Woolf wrote this paragraph.
She did not identify it through grammatical and typographical devices
as the speech or thought of a third person. One is obliged to assume
that it contains direct statements of her own. But she does not seem
to bear in mind that she is the author and hence ought to know how
matters stand with her characters. The person speaking here, whoever
it is, acts the part of one who has only an impression of Mrs. Ramsay,
who looks at her face and renders the impression received, but is
doubtful of its proper interpretation. "Never did anybody look so
sad" is not an objective statement. In rendering the shock received
by one looking at Mrs. Ramsay's face, it verges upon a realm beyond
reality. And in the ensuing passage the speakers no longer seem to be
human beings at all but spirits between heaven and earth, nameless
spirits capable of penetrating the depths of the human soul, capable
too of knowing something about it, but not of attaining clarity as to
what is in process there, with the result that what they report has a
doubtful ring, comparable in a way to those "certain airs, detached
from the body of the wind," which in a later passage (2, 2) move about
the house at night, "questioning and wondering." However that may
be, here too we are not dealing with objective utterances on the part
of the author in respect to one of the characters. No one is certain
of anything here: it is all mere supposition, glances cast by one person
upon another whose enigma he cannot solve.

This continues in the following paragraph. Suppositions as to the
meaning of Mrs. Ramsay's expression are made and discussed. But the
level of tone descends slightly, from the poetic and non-real to the
practical and earthly; and now a speaker is introduced: "People said."
People wonder whether some recollection of an unhappy occurrence
in her earlier life is hidden behind her radiant beauty. There have
been rumors to that effect. But perhaps the rumors are wrong: nothing
of this is to be learned directly from her; she is silent when such
things come up in conversation. But supposing she has never experienced anything of the sort herself, she yet knows everything even without experience. The simplicity and genuineness of her being unfail-
ingly light upon the truth of things, and, falsely perhaps, delight, ease,
sustain.

Is it still "people" who are speaking here? We might almost be
tempted to doubt it, for the last words sound almost too personal
and thoughtful for the gossip of "people." And immediately after-
ward, suddenly and unexpectedly, an entirely new speaker, a new
scene, and a new time are introduced. We find Mr. Bankes at the
telephone talking to Mrs. Ramsay, who has called him to tell him
about a train connection, evidently with reference to a journey they

are planning to make together. The paragraph about the tear had already taken us out of the room where Mrs. Ramsay and James are sitting by the window; it had transported us to an undefinable scene beyond the realm of reality. The paragraph in which the rumors are discussed has a concretely earthly but not clearly identified scene. Now we find ourselves in a precisely determined place, but far away from the summer house—in London, in Mr. Bankes's house. The time is not stated ("once"), but apparently the telephone conversation took place long (perhaps as much as several years) before this particular sojourn in the house on the island. But what Mr. Bankes says over the telephone is in perfect continuity with the preceding paragraph. Again not objectively but in the form of the impression received by a specific person at a specific moment, it as it were sums up all that precedes—the scene with the Swiss maid, the hidden sadness in Mrs. Ramsay's beautiful face, what people think about her, and the impression she makes: Nature has but little clay like that of which she molded her. Did Mr. Bankes really say that to her over the telephone? Or did he only want to say it when he heard her voice, which moved him deeply, and it came into his mind how strange it was to be talking over the telephone with this wonderful woman, so like a Greek goddess? The sentence is enclosed in quotation marks, so one would suppose that he really spoke it. But this is not certain, for the first words of his soliloquy, which follows, are likewise enclosed in quotation marks. In any case, he quickly gets hold of himself, for he answers in a matter-of-fact way that he will catch the 10:30 at Euston.

But his emotion does not die away so quickly. As he puts down the receiver and walks across the room to the window in order to watch the work on a new building across the way—apparently his usual and characteristic procedure when he wants to relax and let his thoughts wander freely—he continues to be preoccupied with Mrs. Ramsay. There is always something strange about her, something that does not quite go with her beauty (as for instance telephoning); she has no awareness of her beauty, or at most only a childish awareness; her dress and her actions show that at times. She is constantly getting involved in everyday realities which are hard to reconcile with the harmony of her face. In his methodical way he tries to explain her incongruities to himself. He puts forward some conjectures but cannot make up his mind. Meanwhile his momentary impressions of the work on the new building keep crowding in. Finally he gives it up. With the somewhat impatient, determined matter-of-factness of a methodical and scientific worker (which he is) he shakes off the insoluble problem "Mrs. Ramsay." He knows no solution (the repetition of "he did not know" symbolizes his impatient shaking it off). He has to get back to his work.

Here the second long interruption comes to an end and we are taken back to the room where Mrs. Ramsay and James are. The exterior occurrence is brought to a close with the kiss on James's forehead and the resumption of the cutting out of pictures. But here too we have only an exterior change. A scene previously abandoned reappears, suddenly and with as little transition as if it had never been left, as though the long interruption were only a glance which someone (who?) has cast from it into the depths of time. But the theme (Mrs. Ramsay, her beauty, the enigma of her character, her absoluteness, which nevertheless always exercises itself in the relativity and ambiguity of life, in what does not become her beauty) carries over directly from the last phase of the interruption (that is, Mr. Bankes's fruitless reflections) into the situation in which we now find Mrs. Ramsay: "with her head outlined absurdly by the gilt frame" etc.—for once again what is around her is not suited to her, is "something incongruous." And the kiss she gives her little boy, the words she speaks to him, although they are a genuine gift of life, which James accepts as the most natural and simple truth, are yet heavy with unsolved mystery.

Our analysis of the passage yields a number of distinguishing stylistic characteristics, which we shall now attempt to formulate.

The writer as narrator of objective facts has almost completely vanished; almost everything stated appears by way of reflection in the consciousness of the dramatis personae. When it is a question of the house, for example, or of the Swiss maid, we are not given the objective information which Virginia Woolf possesses regarding these objects of her creative imagination but what Mrs. Ramsay thinks or feels about them at a particular moment. Similarly we are not taken into Virginia Woolf's confidence and allowed to share her knowledge of Mrs. Ramsay's character; we are given her character as it is reflected in and as it affects various figures in the novel: the nameless spirits which assume certain things about a tear, the people who wonder about her, and Mr. Bankes. In our passage this goes so far that there actually seems to be no viewpoint at all outside the novel from which the people and events within it are observed, any more than there seems to be an objective reality apart from what is in the consciousness of the characters. Remnants of such a reality survive at best in brief references to the exterior frame of the action, such as "said Mrs. Ramsay, raising her eyes . . ." or "said Mr. Bankes once, hearing her voice." The last paragraph ("Knitting her reddish-brown hairy stocking . . .") might perhaps also be mentioned in this connection. But this is already somewhat doubtful. The occurrence is described objectively, but as for its interpretation, the tone indicates that the author looks at Mrs. Ramsay not with knowing but with doubting

and questioning eyes—even as some character in the novel would see
her in the situation in which she is described, would hear her speak
the words given.

The devices employed in this instance (and by a number of contemporary writers as well) to express the contents of the consciousness
of the dramatis personae have been analyzed and described syntacti-
cally. Some of them have been named (*erlebte Rede,* stream of consciousness, *monologue intérieur* are examples). Yet these stylistic forms,
especially the *erlebte Rede,* were used in literature much earlier too,
but not for the same aesthetic purpose. And in addition to them there
are other possibilities—hardly definable in terms of syntax—of obscuring and even obliterating the impression of an objective reality
completely known to the author; possibilities, that is, dependent not
on form but on intonation and context. A case in point is the passage
under discussion, where the author at times achieves the intended
effect by representing herself to be someone who doubts, wonders,
hesitates, as though the truth about her characters were not better
known to her than it is to them or to the reader. It is all, then, a
matter of the author's attitude toward the reality of the world he
represents. And this attitude differs entirely from that of authors who
interpret the actions, situations, and characters of their personages
with objective assurance, as was the general practice in earlier times.
Goethe or Keller, Dickens or Meredith, Balzac or Zola told us out of
their certain knowledge what their characters did, what they felt and
thought while doing it, and how their actions and thoughts were to
be interpreted. They knew everything about their characters. To be
sure, in past periods too we were frequently told about the subjective
reactions of the characters in a novel or story; at times even in the
form of *erlebte Rede,* although more frequently as a monologue, and
of course in most instances with an introductory phrase something
like "it seemed to him that . . ." or "at this moment he felt that . . ."
or the like. Yet in such cases there was hardly ever any attempt to
render the flow and the play of consciousness adrift in the current of
changing impressions (as is done in our text both for Mrs. Ramsay
and for Mr. Bankes); instead, the content of the individual's consciousness was rationally limited to things connected with the particular
incident being related or the particular situation being described. . . .
And what is still more important: the author, with his knowledge of an
objective truth, never abdicated his position as the final and govern-
ing authority. Again, earlier writers, especially from the end of the
nineteenth century on, had produced narrative works which on the
whole undertook to give us an extremely subjective, individualistic,
and often eccentrically aberrant impression of reality, and which
neither sought nor were able to ascertain anything objective or generally valid in regard to it. Sometimes such works took the form of first-

person novels; sometimes they did not. As an example of the latter case I mention Huysmans's novel *A rebours*. But all that too is basically different from the modern procedure here described on the basis of Virginia Woolf's text, although the latter, it is true, evolved from the former. The essential characteristic of the technique represented by Virginia Woolf is that we are given not merely one person whose consciousness (that is, the impressions it receives) is rendered, but many persons, with frequent shifts from one to the other—in our text, Mrs. Ramsay, "people," Mr. Bankes, in brief interludes James, the Swiss maid in a flash-back, and the nameless ones who speculate over a tear. The multiplicity of persons suggests that we are here after all confronted with an endeavor to investigate an objective reality, that is, specifically, the "real" Mrs. Ramsay. She is, to be sure, an enigma and such she basically remains, but she is as it were encircled by the content of all the various consciousnesses directed upon her (including her own); there is an attempt to approach her from many sides as closely as human possibilities of perception and expression can succeed in doing. The design of a close approach to objective reality by means of numerous subjective impressions received by various individuals (and at various times) is important in the modern technique which we are here examining. It basically differentiates it from the unipersonal subjectivism which allows only a single and generally a very unusual person to make himself heard and admits only that one person's way of looking at reality. In terms of literary history, to be sure, there are close connections between the two methods of representing consciousness—the unipersonal subjective method and the multipersonal method with synthesis as its aim. The latter developed from the former, and there are works in which the two overlap, so that we can watch the development. This is especially the case in Marcel Proust's great novel. We shall return to it later.

Another stylistic peculiarity to be observed in our text—though one that is closely and necessarily connected with the "multipersonal representation of consciousness" just discussed—has to do with the treatment of time. That there is something peculiar about the treatment of time in modern narrative literature is nothing new; several studies have been published on the subject. These were primarily attempts to establish a connection between the pertinent phenomena and contemporary philosophical doctrines or trends—undoubtedly a justifiable undertaking and useful for an appreciation of the community of interests and inner purposes shown in the activity of many of our contemporaries. We shall begin by describing the procedure with reference to our present example. We remarked earlier that the act of measuring the length of the stocking and the speaking of the words related to it must have taken much less time than an attentive reader who tries not to miss anything will require to read the passage—even

if we assume that a brief pause intervened between the measuring
and the kiss of reconciliation on James's forehead. However, the time
the narration takes is not devoted to the occurrence itself (which is
rendered rather tersely) but to interludes. Two long excursuses are
inserted, whose relations in time to the occurrence which frames them
seem to be entirely different. The first excursus, a representation of
what goes on in Mrs. Ramsay's mind while she measures the stocking
(more precisely, between the first absent-minded and the second sharp
order to James to hold his leg still) belongs in time to the framing
occurrence, and it is only the representation of it which takes a greater
number of seconds and even minutes than the measuring—the reason
being that the road taken by consciousness is sometimes traversed far
more quickly than language is able to render it, if we want to make
ourselves intelligible to a third person, and that is the intention here.
What goes on in Mrs. Ramsay's mind in itself contains nothing
enigmatic; these are ideas which arise from her daily life and may
well be called normal—her secret lies deeper, and it is only when the
switch from the open windows to the Swiss maid's words comes, that
something happens which lifts the veil a little. On the whole, however,
the mirroring of Mrs. Ramsay's consciousness is much more easily
comprehensible than the sort of thing we get in such cases from other
authors (James Joyce, for example). But simple and trivial as are the
ideas which arise one after the other in Mrs. Ramsay's consciousness,
they are at the same time essential and significant. They amount to
a synthesis of the intricacies of life in which her incomparable beauty
has been caught, in which it at once manifests and conceals itself. Of
course, writers of earlier periods too occasionally devoted some time
and a few sentences to telling the reader what at a specific moment
passed through their characters' minds—but for such a purpose they
would hardly have chosen so accidental an occasion as Mrs. Ramsay's
looking up, so that, quite involuntarily, her eyes fall on the furniture.
Nor would it have occurred to them to render the continuous rumina-
tion of consciousness in its natural and purposeless freedom. And
finally they would not have inserted the entire process between two
exterior occurrences so close together in time as the two warnings to
James to keep still (both of which, after all, take place while she is
on the point of holding the unfinished stocking to his leg); so that,
in a surprising fashion unknown to earlier periods, a sharp contrast
results between the brief span of time occupied by the exterior event
and the dreamlike wealth of a process of consciousness which traverses
a whole subjective universe. These are the characteristic and distinctively new features of the technique: a chance occasion releasing
processes of consciousness; a natural and even, if you will, a naturalistic rendering of those processes in their peculiar freedom, which is
neither restrained by a purpose nor directed by a specific subject of

thought; elaboration of the contrast between "exterior" and "interior" time. The three have in common what they reveal of the author's attitude: he submits, much more than was done in earlier realistic works, to the random contingency of real phenomena; and even though he winnows and stylizes the material of the real world—as of course he cannot help doing—he does not proceed rationalistically, nor with a view to bringing a continuity of exterior events to a planned conclusion. In Virginia Woolf's case the exterior events have actually lost their hegemony, they serve to release and interpret inner events, whereas before her time (and still today in many instances) inner movements preponderantly function to prepare and motivate significant exterior happenings. This too is apparent in the random-ness and contingency of the exterior occasion (looking up because James does not keep his foot still), which releases the much more significant inner process.

The temporal relation between the second excursus and the framing occurrence is of a different sort: its content (the passage on the tear, the things people think about Mrs. Ramsay, the telephone conversa-tion with Mr. Bankes and his reflections while watching the building of the new hotel) is not a part of the framing occurrence either in terms of time or of place. Other times and places are in question; it is an excursus of the same type as the story of the origin of Odysseus' scar. . . . Even from that, however, it is different in structure. In the Homer passage the excursus was linked to the scar which Euryclea touches with her hands, and although the moment in which the touch-ing of the scar occurs is one of high and dramatic tension, the scene nevertheless immediately shifts to another clear and luminous present, and this present seems actually designed to cut off the dramatic ten-sion and cause the entire footwashing scene to be temporarily forgot-ten. In Virginia Woolf's passage, there is no question of any tension. Nothing of importance in a dramatic sense takes place; the problem is the length of the stocking. The point of departure for the excursus is Mrs. Ramsay's facial expression: "never did anybody look so sad." In fact several excursuses start from here; three, to be exact. And all three differ in time and place, differ too in definiteness of time and place, the first being situated quite vaguely, the second somewhat more definitely, and the third with comparative precision. Yet none of them is so exactly situated in time as the successive episodes of the story of Odysseus' youth, for even in the case of the telephone scene we have only an inexact indication of when it occurred. As a result it becomes possible to accomplish the shifting of the scene away from the windownook much more unnoticeably and smoothly than the changing of scene and time in the episode of the scar. In the passage on the tear the reader may still be in doubt as to whether there has been any shift at all. The nameless speakers may have entered the room and be looking at Mrs. Ramsay. In the second paragraph this interpretation is no longer possible, but the "people" whose gossip is reproduced are still looking at Mrs. Ramsay's face—not here and now, at the summer-house window, but it is still the same face and has the same expression. And even in the third part, where the face is no longer physically seen (for Mr. Bankes is talking to Mrs. Ramsay over the telephone), it is nonetheless present to his inner vision; so that not for an instant does the theme (the solution of the enigma Mrs. Ramsay), and even the moment when the problem is formulated (the expression of her face while she measures the length of the stocking), vanish from the reader's memory. In terms of the exterior event the three parts of the excursus have nothing to do with one another. They have no common and externally coherent development, as have the episodes of Odysseus' youth which are related with reference to the origin of the scar; they are connected only by the one thing they have in common—looking at Mrs. Ramsay, and more specifically at the Mrs. Ramsay who, with an unfathomable expression of sadness behind her radiant beauty, concludes that the stocking is still much too short. It is only this common focus which connects the otherwise totally different parts of the excursus; but the connection is strong enough to deprive them of the independent "present" which the episode of the scar possesses. They are nothing but attempts to interpret "never did anybody look so sad"; they carry on this theme, which itself carries on after they conclude: there has been no change of theme at all. In contrast, the scene in which Euryclea recognizes Odysseus is interrupted and divided into two parts by the excursus on the origin of the scar. In our passage, there is no such clear distinction between two exterior occurrences and between two presents. However insignificant as an exterior event the framing occurrence (the measuring of the stocking) may be, the picture of Mrs. Ramsay's face which arises from it remains present throughout the excursus; the excursus itself is nothing but a background for that picture, which seems as it were to open into the depths of time—just as the first excursus, released by Mrs. Ramsay's unintentional glance at the furniture, was an opening of the picture into the depths of consciousness.

The two excursuses, then, are not as different as they at first appeared. It is not so very important that the first, so far as time is concerned (and place too), runs its course within the framing occurrence, while the second conjures up other times and places. The times and places of the second are not independent; they serve only the polyphonic treatment of the image which releases it; as a matter of fact, they impress us (as does the interior time of the first excursus) like an occurrence in the consciousness of some observer (to be sure, he is not identified) who might see Mrs. Ramsay at the described moment and whose meditation upon the unsolved enigma of her personality might contain memories of what others (people, Mr. Bankes) say and think about her. In both excursuses we are dealing with attempts to fathom a more genuine, a deeper, and indeed a more real reality; in both cases the incident which releases the excursus appears accidental and is poor in content; in both cases it makes little difference whether the excursuses employ only the consciousness-content, and hence only interior time, or whether they also employ exterior shifts of time. After all, the process of consciousness in the first excursus likewise includes shifts of time and scene, especially the episode with the Swiss maid. The important point is that an insignificant exterior occurrence releases ideas and chains of ideas which cut loose from the present of the exterior occurrence and range freely through the depths of time. It is as though an apparently simple text revealed its proper content only in the commentary on it, a simple musical theme only in the development-section. This enables us also to understand the close relation between the treatment of time and the "multipersonal representation of consciousness" discussed earlier. The ideas arising in consciousness are not tied to the present of the exterior occurrence which releases them. Virginia Woolf's peculiar technique, as exemplified in our text, consists in the fact that the exterior objective reality of the momentary present which the author directly reports and which appears as established fact—in our instance the measuring of the stocking—is nothing but an occasion (although perhaps not an entirely accidental one). The stress is placed entirely on what the occasion releases, things which are not seen directly but by reflection, which are not tied to the present of the framing occurrence which releases them.

Here it is only natural that we should recall Proust's work. He was the first to carry this sort of thing through consistently; and his entire technique is bound up with a recovery of lost realities in remembrance, a recovery released by some externally insignificant and apparently accidental occurrence. Proust describes the procedure more than once. We have to wait until volume two of *Le Temps retrouvé* for a full description embracing the corresponding theory of art; but the first description, which occurs as early as section 1 of *Du Côté de chez Swann,* is impressive enough. Here, one unpleasant winter evening, the taste of a cake (*petite Madeleine*) dipped in tea arouses in the narrator an overwhelming though at first indefinite delight. By intense and repeated effort he attempts to fathom its nature and cause, and it develops that the delight is based on a recovery: the recovery of the taste of the *petite Madeleine* dipped in tea which his aunt would give him on Sundays when, still a little boy, he went into her room to wish her good morning, in the house in the old provincial town of Combray where she lived, hardly ever leaving her bed, and where he used to spend the summer months with his parents. And from this recovered remembrance, the world of his childhood emerges into light, becomes depictable, as more genuine and more real than any experienced present—and he begins to narrate. Now with Proust a narrating "I" is preserved throughout. It is not, to be sure, an author observing from without but a person involved in the action and pervading it with the distinctive flavor of his being, so that one might feel tempted to class Proust's novel among the products of the unipersonal subjectivism which we discussed earlier. So to class it would not be wrong but it would be inadequate. It would fail to account completely for the structure of Proust's novel. . . . Proust aims at objectivity, he wants to bring out the essence of events: he strives to attain this goal by accepting the guidance of his own consciousness—not, however, of his consciousness as it happens to be at any particular moment but as it remembers things. A consciousness in which remembrance causes past realities to arise, which has long since left behind the states in which it found itself when those realities occurred as a present, sees and arranges that content in a way very different from the purely individual and subjective. Freed from its various earlier involvements, consciousness views its own past layers and their content in perspective; it keeps confronting them with one another, emancipating them from their exterior temporal continuity as well as from the narrow meanings they seemed to have when they were bound to a particular present. There is to be noted in this a fusion of the modern concept of interior time with the neo-Platonic idea that the true prototype of a given subject is to be found in the soul of the artist; in this case, of an artist who, present in the subject itself, has detached himself from it as observer and thus comes face to face with his own past. . . .

The distinctive characteristics of the realistic novel of the era between the two great wars . . . —multipersonal representation of consciousness, time strata, disintegration of the continuity of exterior events, shifting of the narrative viewpoint (all of which are interrelated and difficult to separate)—seem to us indicative of a striving for certain objectives, of certain tendencies and needs on the part of both authors and public. These objectives, tendencies, and needs are numerous; they seem in part to be mutually contradictory; yet they form so much one whole that when we undertake to describe them analytically, we are in constant danger of unwittingly passing from one to another.

Let us begin with a tendency which is particularly striking in our text from Virginia Woolf. She holds to minor, unimpressive, random events: measuring the stocking, a fragment of a conversation with the maid, a telephone call. Great changes, exterior turning points, let alone catastrophes, do not occur; and though elsewhere in *To the Lighthouse* such things are mentioned, it is hastily, without preparation or context, incidentally, and as it were only for the sake of information. The same tendency is to be observed in other and very different writers, such as Proust or Hamsun. In Thomas Mann's *Buddenbrooks* we still have a novel structure consisting of the chronological sequence of important exterior events which affect the Buddenbrook family; and if Flaubert—in many respects a precursor—lingers as a matter of principle over insignificant events and everyday circumstances which hardly advance the action, there is nevertheless to be sensed throughout *Madame Bovary* (though we may wonder how this would have worked out in *Bouvard et Pécuchet*) a constant slow-moving chronological approach first to partial crises and finally to the concluding catastrophe, and it is this approach which dominates the plan of the work as a whole. But a shift in emphasis followed; and now many writers present minor happenings, which are insignificant as exterior factors in a person's destiny, for their own sake or rather as points of departure for the development of motifs, for a penetration which opens up new perspectives into a milieu or a consciousness or the given historical setting. They have discarded presenting the story of their characters with any claim to exterior completeness, in chronological order, and with the emphasis on important exterior turning points of destiny. James Joyce's tremendous novel—an encyclopedic work, a mirror of Dublin, of Ireland, a mirror too of Europe and its millennia—has for its frame the externally insignificant course of a day in the lives of a schoolteacher and an advertising broker. It takes up less than twenty-four hours in their lives—just as *To the Lighthouse* describes portions of two days widely separated in time. (There is here also, as we must not fail to observe, a similarity to Dante's Comedy.) Proust presents individual days and hours from different periods, but the exterior events which are the determining factors in the destinies of the novel's characters during the intervening lapses of time are mentioned only incidentally, in retrospect or anticipation. The ends the narrator has in mind are not to be seen in them; often the reader has to supplement them. The way in which the father's death is brought up in the passage cited above [omitted here—Ed.]—incidentally, allusively, and in anticipation—offers a good example. This shift of emphasis expresses something that we might call a transfer of confidence: the great exterior turning points and blows of fate are granted less importance; they are credited with less power of yielding decisive information concerning the subject; on the other hand there is confidence that in any random fragment plucked from the course of a life at any time the totality of its fate is contained and can be portrayed. There is greater confidence in syntheses gained through full exploitation of an everyday occurrence than in a chronologically well-ordered total treatment which accompanies the subject from beginning to end, attempts not to omit anything externally important, and emphasizes the great turning points of destiny. . . .

Those modern writers who prefer the exploitation of random everyday events, contained within a few hours and days, to the complete and chronological representation of a total exterior continuum—they too (more or less consciously) are guided by the consideration that it is a hopeless venture to try to be really complete within the total exterior continuum and yet to make what is essential stand out. Then too they hesitate to impose upon life, which is their subject, an order which it does not possess in itself. He who represents the course of a human life, or a sequence of events extending over a prolonged period of time, and represents it from beginning to end, must prune and isolate arbitrarily. Life has always long since begun, and it is always still going on. And the people whose story the author is telling experience much more than he can ever hope to tell. But the things that happen to a few individuals in the course of a few minutes, hours, or possibly even days—these one can hope to report with reasonable completeness. . . . We are constantly endeavoring to give meaning and order to our lives in the past, the present, and the future, to our surroundings, the world in which we live; with the result that our lives appear in our own conception as total entities—which to be sure are always changing, more or less radically, more or less rapidly, depending on the extent to which we are obliged, inclined, and able to assimilate the onrush of new experience. These are the forms of order and interpretation which the modern writers here under discussion attempt to grasp in the random moment—not one order and one interpretation, but many, which may either be those of different persons or of the same person at different times; so that overlapping, complementing, and contradiction yield something that we might call a synthesized cosmic view or at least a challenge to the reader's will to interpretive synthesis.

Here we have returned once again to the reflection of multiple consciousnesses. It is easy to understand that such a technique had to develop gradually and that it did so precisely during the decades of the first World War period and after. The widening of man's horizon, and the increase of his experiences, knowledge, ideas, and possible forms of existence, which began in the sixteenth century, continued through the nineteenth at an ever faster tempo—with such a tremendous acceleration since the beginning of the twentieth that synthetic and objective attempts at interpretation are produced and demolished every instant. The tremendous tempo of the changes proved the more confusing because they could not be surveyed as a whole. They occurred simultaneously in many separate departments of science, technology, and economics, with the result that no one—not even those who were leaders in the separate departments—could foresee or evaluate the resulting overall situations. . . .

As recently as the nineteenth century, and even at the beginning of the twentieth, so much clearly formulable and recognized community of thought and feeling remained in [most European] countries that a writer engaged in representing reality had reliable criteria at hand by which to organize it. At least, within the range of contemporary movements, he could discern certain specific trends; he could delimit opposing attitudes and ways of life with a certain degree of clarity. To be sure, this had long since begun to grow increasingly difficult. Flaubert (to confine ourselves to realistic writers) already suffered from the lack of valid foundations for his work; and the subsequent increasing predilection for ruthlessly subjectivistic perspectives is another symptom. At the time of the first World War and after—in a Europe unsure of itself, overflowing with unsettled ideologies and ways of life, and pregnant with disaster—certain writers distinguished by instinct and insight find a method which dissolves reality into multiple and multivalent reflections of consciousness. That this method should have been developed at this time is not hard to understand.

But the method is not only a symptom of the confusion and helplessness, not only a mirror of the decline of our world. There is, to be sure, a good deal to be said for such a view. There is in all these works a certain atmosphere of universal doom: especially in *Ulysses,* with its mocking *odi-et-amo* hodgepodge of the European tradition, with its blatant and painful cynicism, and its uninterpretable symbolism—for even the most painstaking analysis can hardly emerge with anything more than an appreciation of the multiple enmeshment of the motifs but with nothing of the purpose and meaning of the work itself. And most of the other novels which employ multiple reflection of consciousness also leave the reader with an impression of hopelessness. There is often something confusing, something hazy about them, something hostile to the reality which they represent. We not infrequently find a turning away from the practical will to live, or delight in portraying it under its most brutal forms. There is hatred of culture and civilization, brought out by means of the subtlest stylistic devices which culture and civilization have developed, and often a radical and fanatical urge to destroy. Common to almost all of these novels is haziness, vague indefinability of meaning: precisely the kind of uninterpretable symbolism which is also to be encountered in other forms of art of the same period.

But something entirely different takes place here too. Let us turn again to the text which was our starting-point. It breathes an air of vague and hopeless sadness. We never come to learn what Mrs. Ramsay's situation really is. Only the sadness, the vanity of her beauty and vital force emerge from the depths of secrecy. Even when we have read the whole novel, the meaning of the relationship between the planned trip to the lighthouse and the actual trip many years later remains unexpressed, enigmatic, only dimly to be conjectured, as does the content of Lily Briscoe's concluding vision which enables her to finish her painting with one stroke of the brush. It is one of the few books of this type which are filled with good and genuine love but also, in its feminine way, with irony, amorphous sadness, and doubt of life. Yet what realistic depth is achieved in every individual occurrence, for example the measuring of the stocking! Aspects of the occurrence come to the fore, and links to other occurrences, which, before this time, had hardly been sensed, which had never been clearly seen and attended to, and yet they are determining factors in our real lives. What takes place here in Virginia Woolf's novel is precisely what was attempted everywhere in works of this kind (although not everywhere with the same insight and mastery)—that is, to put the emphasis on the random occurrence, to exploit it not in the service of a planned continuity of action but in itself. And in the process something new and elemental appeared: nothing less than the wealth of reality and depth of life in every moment to which we surrender ourselves without prejudice. To be sure, what happens in that moment—be it outer or inner processes—concerns in a very personal way the individuals who live in it, but it also (and for that very reason) concerns the elementary things which men in general have in common. It is precisely the random moment which is comparatively independent of the controversial and unstable orders over which men fight and despair; it passes unaffected by them, as daily life. The more it is exploited, the more the elementary things which our lives have in common come to light. The more numerous, varied, and simple the people are who appear as subjects of such random moments, the more effectively must what they have in common shine forth. In this unprejudiced and exploratory type of representation we cannot but see to what an extent—below the surface conflicts—the differences between men's ways of life and forms of thought have already lessened. The strata of societies and their different ways of life have become inextricably mingled. There are no longer even exotic peoples. A century ago (in Mérimée for example), Corsicans or Spaniards were still exotic; today the term would be quite unsuitable for Pearl Buck's Chinese peasants. Beneath the conflicts, and also through them, an economic and cultural leveling process is taking place. It is still a long way to a common life of mankind on earth, but the goal begins to be visible. And it is most concretely visible now in the unprejudiced, precise, interior and exterior representation of the random moment in the lives of different people. So the complicated process of dissolution which led to fragmentation of the exterior action, to reflection of consciousness, and to stratification of time seems to be tending toward a very simple solution. Perhaps it will be too simple to please those who, despite all its dangers and catastrophes, admire and love our epoch for the sake of its abundance of life and the incomparable historical vantage point which it affords. But they are few in number, and probably they will not live to see much more than the first forewarnings of the approaching unification and simplification.

Never Say "I": *To the Lighthouse* as Vision and Confession

by Ruth Z. Temple

"You can tell anything, but on condition that you never say 'I'."
Thus Proust to Gide about the latter's *Corydon,* which, for its personal revelations, Proust deplored. A curious remark, one might think,
from the author of possibly the longest "I" novel ever published. The
"I" of *Remembrance of Things Past* is, of course, not merely Proust,
nor is the book merely a confession. "Are not all novels," Virginia
Woolf asks, "about the writer's self? It it only as he sees people
that we can see them; his fortunes colour and his oddities shape his
vision until what we see is not the thing itself, but the thing seen and
the seer inextricably mixed." [1] Though this is not, as she concludes,
true of all novels, it is an apt description of her own and Proust's,
and it will suggest the direction of my argument that *To the Lighthouse* is at once her most confessional and her most Proustian novel. [2]

The parallels between these two novelists are striking. Though
Proust is analytical and impressionistic and Virginia Woolf only impressionistic, they have the same concern with the contrast of chronological time to *durée* or inner time, with the relativity of character,
with involuntary memory as a key to the truth of experience and to
art, and with art as the only bulwark against time. [3] Both contrive to
situate their characters firmly in space as well as time by selected detail
and metaphor rather than by naturalistic enumeration. In the use of
metaphor, the surface dissimilarity in form (Proust's are extended,
Virgina Woolf's compressed) conceals a similar effect: widening the

---

[1] "George Moore," *The Death of the Moth* (1942; Penguin, 1961), pp. 135–36.

[2] Though Joyce is of this family of novelists too, Virginia Woolf's art is far
more closely related to Proust's, which she admired without reservation, than to
Joyce's, which she did not.

[3] Floris Delattre, in one of the earliest studies of Virginia Woolf, which remains
one of the most perceptive, documents these analogies (*Le Roman psychologique
de Virginia Woolf* [Paris: Vrin, 1932; 2nd ed., 1967]).

context. History and art unfold behind a familiar scene, the primitive looms behind the most civilized appearance; meadows, forests, and the sea—for Virginia Woolf especially the sea—are adjacent to the city pavement. In this respect both are of Shakespearian not Racinian kind. For both, the eye is an instrument of finest accuity at the service of the "I." Finally, both are elegiac: they celebrate the beloved dead, their own dead selves, the immortality of love and of the moment in memory and in art. Writing *To the Lighthouse,* Virginia Woolf wonders what to call it: "A new—by Virginia Woolf. But what? Elegy?" [4]

To go beyond parallels to influence is always dubious, but I think a case may be made out for that, too, and especially in *To the Lighthouse.*[5] In April, 1925, a little more than a month before she records the first idea for that novel, she writes in her journal, wondering whether she has in *Mrs. Dalloway* achieved anything:

> Well, nothing anyhow compared with Proust, in whom I am embedded now. The thing about Proust is his combination of the utmost sensibility with the utmost tenacity. He searches out those butterfly shades to the last grain. He is as tough as catgut and as evanescent as a butterfly's bloom. And he will, I suppose, both influence me and make me out of temper with every sentence of my own. (*AWD,* p. 71)

In Part III of *To the Lighthouse,* Lily thinks about her picture:

> Beautiful and bright it should be on the surface, feathery and evanescent, one colour melting into another like the colours on a butterfly's wing; but beneath the fabric must be clamped together with bolts of iron.[6]

At the end of June Virginia Woolf has not finished Proust, and in July she speculates: "I think I might do something in *To the Lighthouse* to split up emotions more completely. I think I'm working in that direction." (*AWD,* p. 80.) This is obviously a Proustian direction —though here it may be argued that Virginia Woolf has gone farther than Proust and taken a lead not followed until Nathalie Sarraute began in *Tropisms* to reveal those apparently unmotivated advances and recoils of the preconscious which emerge in emotion.[7] Two years after *To the Lighthouse* has been published, she writes, of a scene in Proust, "There we live along a thread of observation which is always

---

[4] June 27, 1925, *A Writer's Diary,* ed. Leonard Woolf (New York: Harcourt, Brace and World, 1953), p. 78.

[5] Jean Guiguet, mistakenly I believe, writes off Proust as an influence (*Virginia Woolf and Her Works,* Jean Stewart trans., 1962; New York: Harcourt, Brace and World, 1965; see especially p. 396).

[6] *To the Lighthouse* (New York: Harcourt, Brace, and World, 1927), p. 255.

[7] Though Lawrence did this too, it is doubtful that Virginia Woolf read him in this way, the device having been only recently recognized by critics though it is noted in his letters.

going in and out of this mind and that mind . . . so that the imagination is being stimulated on all sides to close slowly, gradually, . . .
completely around the subject." [8] In the many other references to
Proust, all admiring, we note, as here, that she selects for comment
elements of technique common to their work. Must we not then conclude that Proust on the one hand made her more conscious of her
own technique (for the most part present even in her earliest novel,
The Voyage Out), and, on the other, gave her two new themes: the
contrast of inner and outer time and the use of involuntary memory
in the creation of a work of art. The former appears in *Mrs. Dalloway;*[9] both are crucial in *To the Lighthouse,* so crucial, indeed, that
they will serve to solve the problem of that novel. For it is a "problem"
novel.

Judging by Leonard Woolf's figures in *Downhill All the Way* and
The Journey Not the Arrival Matters, To the Lighthouse has been
for some years the most popular of Virginia Woolf's novels. I suspect
it is also the most written about. The two facts may have no connection. *To the Lighthouse* has probably attracted the common reader
(56,000 in 1967) because it has a universal subject, the family, behaving
in plausible and revealing ways, surrounded by a setting of nearly
universal appeal—the sea, which, as Virginia Woolf meant it to be, is
heard throughout (*AWD,* p. 78); because it has a theme of universal
appeal—in the midst of life there is death—and a happy ending, for
Mrs. Ramsay, though dead, is touchingly remembered. And upon the
story the manner of telling—timeless except for Andrew's death in
the War—confers an atmosphere of myth or legend. One does wonder
what the common reader makes of the symbols of the lighthouse and
Lily's painting, because what the critics have made of these is marvelously diverse. Norman Friedman in 1955 lists some six different interpretations of the last section of the book and others have been
offered since then.[10] The lighthouse is on the one hand the flux and
on the other the permanence of time; it is Mr. Ramsay's symbol or
Mrs. Ramsay's or it is the contest between their two conflicting kinds
of truth. Lily's completion of her picture as the book ends means that
life has triumphed over art or that art has triumphed over life. Lily's
painting is of the Madonna and Child (Virginia Stephen, child of a
conscientiously agnostic father, displays "the near hysteria of the
doubtful atheist") and the whole novel should be read as a sustained
exercise in Christian symbolism.[11] One critic has even found it possible
to believe that Mr. Ramsay is the real hero—or victim, a good man

---

[8] "Phases of Fiction," *Granite and Rainbow* (London: Hogarth Press, 1958), p.
128. The article appeared in *The Bookman* for April/May/June, 1929.

[9] Involuntary memory is, of course, a motif here, but not a theme.

[10] *English Literary History* (March 1955), pp. 61–79.

[11] F. L. Overcarsh, "The Lighthouse, Face to Face," *Accent* (Winter, 1950), pp.
107–23.

kept down by a tyrannical wife.[12] And yet the critical consensus is that this is the best of the novels of Virginia Woolf. The existence of so many irreconcilable interpretations suggests that the novel is radically ambiguous or that the critics are more ingenious explicators than painstaking readers. It would be tedious, though by no means impossible, to prove the latter hypothesis. What seems more profitable is to re-examine the text for its meaning, pursuing the Proustian analogy and drawing upon *A Writer's Diary* for elucidation of debated matters, and so, finally, to test the critical consensus.

A Writer's Diary confirms the conjecture made by most perceptive critics even before its publication that Mr. Ramsay is drawn from the author's father, Leslie Stephen.[13] At the outset all the elements of story are present:

> This is going to be fairly short; to have father's character done complete in it; and mother's; and St. Ives; and childhood; and all the usual things I try to put in—life, death, etc. But the centre is father's character, sitting in a boat, reciting We perished, each alone, while he crushes a dying mackerel. (May 14, 1925, *AWD*, p. 75)

By June 14, Virginia Woolf has it all thought out, "perhaps too clearly" (p. 77) and on July 20 the framework is outlined:

> But this theme may be sentimental; father and mother and child in the garden; the death; the sail to the Lighthouse. . . . It might contain all characters boiled down; and childhood; and then this impersonal thing, which I'm dared to do by my friends, the flight of time and the consequent break in my design. That passage (I conceive the book in 3 parts. 1. at the drawing room window; 2. seven years passed; 3. the voyage) interests me very much. A new problem like that breaks fresh ground in one's mind; prevents the regular ruts. (p. 79)

But she is not after all quite sure: "The thing is I vacillate between a single and intense character of father; and a far wider slower book—." (July 30, pp. 79–80) (It is on this day that she speaks of splitting up emotions more completely.)

In these passages are many clues to the book as pattern and confession, but one is especially notable. Unlike all the other novels whose genesis is recorded in *A Writer's Diary*, only this one has for germ a *subject*—and an autobiographical subject—not an idea for technical innovation, which is Virginia Woolf's usual "fin passing far out" (September 20, 1926, p. 100). When the novelty of form appears

[12] Glenn Pedersen, "Vision in *To the Lighthouse*," PMLA, LXXIII (Dec. 1958), pp. 585–600.

[13] Frank Baldanza was the first to document the composition of *To the Lighthouse* from *AWD*, supplementing with material on Leslie Stephen and his wife from Noel Annan's biography of Stephen. He argues the case for the novel as indicative of the author's revolt against her parents. ("*To the Lighthouse* Again," PMLA XX [June 1955], pp. 548–52.)

here—the passage of time done impersonally—it attracts her especially, and when she comes to write Part II the composition goes extraordinarily fast, even for this book which is almost all written at great speed and with an ease that astounds her, after the anguish of *Mrs. Dalloway* (April 30, 1926, p. 87). The *Diary* reference which most clearly reveals the relation of the book to its author occurs only after *To the Lighthouse* has been out a year and a half:

> Father's birthday. He would have been 96, 96, yes, today; and could have been 96, like other people one has known; but mercifully was not. His life would have entirely ended mine. What would have happened? No writing, no books;—inconceivable.
> I used to think of him and mother daily; but writing the Lighthouse laid them in my mind. And now he comes back sometimes, but differently. (I believe this to be true—that I was obsessed by them both, unhealthily; and writing of them was a necessary act.) He comes back now more as a contemporary. I must read him some day. I wonder if I can feel again, I hear his voice, I know this by heart? (Nov. 28, 1928, p. 135)

Here in what is said and what is not said is a clue to the meaning of Lily Briscoe, whose function is never mentioned in the *Diary* though her name occurs there.

As early as 1928 a French reviewer—French criticism of Virginia Woolf has from the beginning been favorable and enlightened—recognized Lily's use in *To the Lighthouse*: Lily is Virginia Woolf and the two of them are making a work of art with the substance of Mrs. Ramsay; Lily is Virginia Woolf who observes her father (Mr. Ramsay) in Part III from the perspective of time transposed to space as the boat carries him into the distance (of memory after death); and the originality of Part III is the "ironical antiphony" of Cam and Lily, both masks for Leslie Stephen's daughter.[14] M. Mayoux has hit upon three of the Proustian devices of the book: the revelation of the author's attitudes through a variety of personae, the incorporation into the work of art of the author making that work of art; the overwhelming concern with the phases of memory, which may be conveyed through a metaphor of space. What he has not pointed out is the Proustian contrast of voluntary with involuntary memory.

Only Philip Toynbee, I think, who is on the whole an admirer of Virginia Woolf and even sometimes called a disciple, finds *To the Lighthouse* disturbing because of its three-part structure and goes so far as to wish Part I had been published separately.[15] Had this been done, the book would have lost its Proustian themes, the design would have been lost together with the vision Lily finally claims to have had.

[14] J. J. Mayoux, "Sur un livre de Virginia Woolf," *Revue anglo-américaine,* V (juin 1928), p. 438.
[15] "Virginia Woolf: A Study of Three Experimental Novels," *Horizon* XIV (November 1946), pp. 290–304.

Yet there is merit in his contention that Part I is superior to the rest and reason for his dissatisfaction with the three-part structure.

Part I, "The Window," is various but unified; character is created through the most economical of means (we know more of Mrs. Ramsay from these few hours in one day than of many a heroine whom we follow through three hundred pages); and through all is heard the sound of the sea, suggesting the fullness of life and the imminence of death. Three of Virginia Woolf's recurrent symbols provide resonance as well as structure. First, the window, which is the point of view, the dividing or connecting point between the inviolable self which Virginia Woolf so cherished and society which she loved equally and which is conveyed through, second, the party.[16] In Part I the window divides and connects Lily and Mrs. Ramsay, framing for Lily her portrait and for Mrs. Ramsay the lighthouse, instrument of her moment of solitary vision.[17] Her second "moment" is at the dinner party: "Of such moments, she thought, the thing is made that endures." (pp. 157–58) Itself a symbol, the dinner is symbolized by three "works of art": the perfectly successful *boeuf en daube*, the bowl of fruit exquisitely arranged by Rose, and the poem recited, whose words and rhythm provide a kind of music to support and universalize the mood visually created, while it brings together Mr. Ramsay and the guest who had earlier enraged him, Mrs. Ramsay and the same guest who, she usually felt, disliked her.[18]

The third major symbol is the lighthouse. Its reality in Virginia Woolf's childhood years at St. Ives was, Leonard Woolf tells us, the Godrevy light. No one who has grown up looking at a lighthouse will confuse its operation or meaning with that of the sea. The lighthouse is not flux but stability, not time passing but something permanently, inexorably—usefully—fixed above the waste of waters. To be sure, as what is seen depends upon the seer, the lighthouse, like truth or fate, is variously seen by various characters or by the same character at various times. So in Part III James and Cam, growing up, learn

---

[16] Window, party and garden are studied by Howard Moss as three dominant symbols in Proust (*The Magic Lantern of Marcel Proust* [New York: Macmillan, 1962]). In *To the Lighthouse*, though not often in Virginia Woolf's novels, garden is more important as setting than as symbol.

[17] An example, I think, of borrowing from Virginia Woolf's own experience (see *AWD*, p. 85) which is not, as transferred to a character so different—this active, sympathetic, managing woman—perfectly convincing.

[18] The identity of this poem, which has baffled investigators, has now been established by Elizabeth Boyd, who had the excellent idea of asking Leonard Woolf. An anachronism in the novel, it remained unpublished until collected in V. Sackville West's and Harold Nicolson's compilation, *Another World Than This* (London: Michael Josephson, 1945). Leonard Woolf who had had a copy in ms. from Lytton Strachey at Cambridge had memorized it and his memory was Virginia Woolf's source. The author of "Luriana, Lurilee" is Charles Isaac Elton, Q. C. 1839–1900). See *Notes and Queries* (October 1963), pp. 380–81.

that the lighthouse may be this *and* that, a far-off romantic ideal (their mother's kind of truth) and a plain, uncompromising, stark fact (their father's kind).[19] Discovering this, they prove themselves the children of their mother, with her gift of intuition and their father, whose austere integrity they have at last come to recognize and value in him and in themselves. There is indeed one sense in which lighthouse and wave are assimilated and that is in their opposition to life: the flux of life (the wave) bears within it the necessity of death (fate). So in a note on the manuscript of *To the Lighthouse* Virginia Woolf writes: "There should be children undifferentiated to bring out the sense of life in opposition to fate—i.e. waves, lighthouse." [20] But more often (and not in this novel only) the lighthouse by its intermittent radiance represents the achievements of civilized man in the surrounding darkness of eternal nature.

In the novels of Virginia Woolf the questions are often asked: What is truth? What is reality? There is never any answer, except in symbols like that of the lighthouse. Lily Briscoe, prosing in Part III, tells us what is implicit in the whole book (a rare case and not perhaps fortunate of direct statement of theme):

> What is the meaning of life? That was all—a simple question; one that tended to close in on one with years. The great revelation had never come. The great revelation perhaps never did come. Instead there were little daily miracles, illuminations, matches struck unexpectedly in the dark. . . . Mrs. Ramsay saying, "Life stand still here"; Mrs. Ramsay making of the moment something permanent (as in another sphere Lily herself tried to make of the moment something permanent)—this was of the nature of a revelation. (pp. 240–41)

The intermittent lighthouse beam represents those moments of life out of time—the intermittences of the heart—which are central to Proust's experience of reality and to Virginia Woolf's.

The three symbols—window, party, and lighthouse—with the sea and the wave, are as it were permanent symbols in the work of Virginia Woolf, enriching metaphor if not creating structure in all her novels. Here, of course, they are structural and used with perfect

---

[19] Though Mr. Ramsay may be a lighthouse, *the* lighthouse is least of all a symbol for him. He does not see it; his mind does not work by intuitive flashes but finds its way through the intricacies of the hedge or up the ladder of the alphabet. In the latter "symbol" Virginia Woolf is perhaps having a little joke. Leslie Stephen in her childhood was toiling his way through the alphabet of the *Dictionary of National Biography* of which he was initiator and first editor, though by 1891 he was only a contributor. In its early days he had feared that it would never get beyond C (*The Life and Letters of Leslie Stephen,* ed. Frederic William Maitland [London: Duckworth, 1906], p. 396).

[20] (Jan. 15, 1926) The Henry W. and Albert A. Berg Collection, New York Public Library, Astor, Lenox, and Tilden Foundations. Quoted by permission.

mastery. There is another symbol operative for the structure of this novel, one just glanced at in Lily's parenthesis above—her painting. And here we enter upon the perplexed question of the relation of parts to whole in *To the Lighthouse*.

The very brief second part (25 pages to 93 for Part III and 177 for Part I), "Time Passes," is a tour de force, an answer to a dare. It succeeds as a prose poem and anticipates the remarkable lyric prefaces of *The Waves*. Some sort of interlude was required by the design—time must elapse, Mrs. Ramsay die, the children of Part I grow up—so that the new point of view on the author's childhood, on her father and mother, might emerge. Reducing to essentials, simplifying in the classic manner, Virginia Woolf omits all the trivia of the interval and paints "pure" time, showing it by its effects on human possessions —the house gradually decays—recording human events in their unimportance relative to the natural process (the deaths of Mrs. Ramsay, Prue and Andrew are recorded in parentheses). In Part III *durée,* time experienced—and especially recaptured in memory—replaces outer time. This part is composed of two separate actions not fused but yoked by ingenuity together.

In the first recorded idea for the book, Virginia Woolf had set down as central "father's character in a boat." Now, finally, this obviously remembered scene vitalizes all the passages in which the voyage to the lighthouse is described. No memories are so vivid as those of childhood (". . . children never forget," said Mrs. Ramsay) and the boat scenes have all the immediacy and conviction of Part I. Moreover, episodes in the childhood of James and Cam, now adolescent—episodes which recall to us Part I—are skilfully evoked through involuntary memory and show how Mrs. Ramsay, who had wondered about immortality, is alive in them. The inference is that she has somehow influenced Mr. Ramsay to undertake the voyage, but this inference depends upon the active, indeed generous, collaboration of the reader. Mr. Ramsay in the boat is not different from his earlier self, and the author, who rarely ventures to intrude upon the privacy of Mr. Ramsay's consciousness, refrains from suggesting that the voyage is in any way definitive for him. "He sat and looked at the island and he might be thinking, I have reached it. I have found it; but he said nothing." (p. 308) What was to have been the central figure in the design of the book remains inscrutable, the cause of action, the source of emotion in others, himself dimly apprehended. Two notes in the manuscript reinforce the suspicion that the author had to remind herself of his centrality. "The dominating impression is to be of Mr. R's character." "Theme of first part shall *really* contribute to W R's [*sic:* evidently referring to Mr. Ramsay] character at least Mrs. R's character shall be displayed but finally in conjunction with his so that one gets an impression of their relationship." [21] What has come to occupy Virginia Woolf in Part III is not, of course, Mr. Ramsay or even Mrs. Ramsay as remembered but rather the process of recovering the past and the shaping of memory into art, the two central themes of Proust's *A la recherche du temps perdu* (the English title is misleading). What was one incident among many in Part I, Lily's picture, has become in Part III, "The Lighthouse," a salient figure in the design. It is even Lily's lighthouse ("She saw her canvas as if it had floated up and placed itself white and uncompromising directly before her." p. 234), a rival of the other, which it survives, for the other disappears but Lily's picture is there as the book ends.

In Part I Lily was painting a portrait of Mrs. Ramsay and James, a nonrepresentational portrait. As she explains to William Bankes, in a passage that constitutes an apologia for the book, it is possible without irreverence to do Mrs. Ramsay as a triangular purple shape. So the daughter writing of her parents pleads the case for a biographical book in which design represents instead of reproducing subject. In Part III Lily is painting a new picture (not completing the first, as some critics have affirmed). This time it is of Mrs. Ramsay only, though it is still nonrepresentational. But the process of recapturing the past in art fills, one cannot help feeling, too many pages. The soliloquy in solitude (for the attempt to include the inert figure of the old poet, Mr. Carmichael, surely fails) becomes tedious, and Lily, lacking the contacts with other people which in Part I gave her characterizing color, becomes a bore. Too much of her narrated monologue[22] just misses, as she thinks of Mr. or of Mrs. Ramsay, the confessional "I." The hostility toward Mrs. Ramsay that in Part I complicated Lily's admiration and love for this different kind of woman here emerges into rivalry and Lily has her triumphs: the Rayleys' marriage that Mrs. Ramsay engineered has not turned out well, Lily has not married William Bankes as Mrs. Ramsay hoped she would. (Lily almost deteriorates into a ficelle for conveying the content of the conventional last chapter of a Victorian novel: what became of everyone.) Most important, Lily is creating "moments" in a medium more permanent than Mrs. Ramsay's

[21] After the date August 6, 1925, the first of these on page two of fore-material, the second separated from the first. The Berg Collection, New York Public Library. Quoted by permission.

[22] This term I have adopted from Dorrit Cohn whose article distinguishing among modes of rendering consciousness is the best brief discussion in English of a subject already thoroughly investigated by French and German scholars. ("Narrated Monologue: Definition of a Fictional Style," *Comparative Literature* XVIII [Spring 1966], pp. 97–112.) Virginia Woolf does not, of course, ever use stream of consciousness. Her special distinction is in the third person, past tense rendering of interior monologue—a highly selective version of the flow of mind—but always in her own idiom so that the total effect of a book is unified. She is especially skilfull in making transitions from impressions of the outer world as they impinge on consciousness to the continuum of thought where past, present and future are in solution.

time (". . . 'you' and 'I' and 'she' pass and vanish; nothing stays; all changes; but not words, not paint." [p. 267]). Even the description of the process of creation disappoints, for the transmutation of novel into painting does not quite come off:

> And she wanted to say not one thing, but everything. Little words that broke up the thought and dismembered it said nothing. . . . Words fluttered sideways and struck the object inches too low. (p. 265)

> Phrases came. Visions came. Beautiful pictures. Beautiful phrases. But what she wished to get hold of was that very jar on the nerves, the thing itself before it has been made anything. (p. 287)

What we do have in the Lily passages is the clearest demonstration of that contrast between voluntary and involuntary memory which Virginia Woolf must have appreciated in Proust's work. The "thing in itself" Lily knows she cannot get by thinking in the manner of Mr. Ramsay (the hedge) or by "soliciting urgently," so she lets associative memory range freely for some twelve pages which only *tell* what has already been admirably *shown* in Part I. Suddenly a wave of white goes over the window and by this sensory perception involuntary memory is stimulated, the anguish of the loss of Mrs. Ramsay floods Lily's consciousness (one thinks of Marcel's sudden experience, long after the event, of grief for the loss of his grandmother), and Mrs. Ramsay again sits at the window knitting the reddish-brown stocking.[23] It seems the moment for Lily to put brush to canvas, but instead she wanders off to look out to sea for Mr. Ramsay. Once more *A Writer's Diary* glosses a difficulty in the text:

> The novel is now easily within sight of the end, but this, mysteriously, comes no nearer. I am doing Lily on the lawn; but whether it's her last lap, I don't know. Nor am I sure of the quality. . . . At this moment I'm casting about for an end. The problem is how to bring Lily and Mr. R. together and make a combination of interest at the end. I am feathering about with various ideas. The last chapter . . . is In the Boat: I had meant to end with R. climbing on to the rock. If so, what becomes of Lily and her picture? Should there be a final page about her and Carmichael looking at the picture and summing up R.'s character? In that case I lose the intensity of the moment. If this intervenes between R. and the lighthouse, there's too much chop and change, I think. Could I do it in a parenthesis? So that one had the sense of reading the two things at the same time. (p. 98)

The manuscript, too, bears witness to the artist's indecision. This section has many more false starts, unfinished sentences, than any

---

[23] I believe the text refutes Josephine O'Brien Schaefer's contention in her brilliant book on Virginia Woolf that Lily creates Mrs. Ramsay by her questions in this long passage (*The Three-Fold Nature of Reality in the Novels of Virginia Woolf* [The Hague: Mouton, 1965], p. 135).

other. And the author's final verdict was quite rightly against Lily on the lawn.

> Dear me, how lovely some parts of the Lighthouse are! Soft and pliable, and I think deep, and never a word wrong for a page at a time. This I feel about the dinner party and the children in the boat; but not of Lily on the lawn. That I do not much like. But I like the end. (March 21, 1927, p. 105)

It is not that Virginia Woolf has meant to end the book ambiguously. She has attempted here a conclusive ending. (The endings are often the weakest parts of her novels, which should be open-ended.) But how provide a conclusive ending for a novel lacking unity? What began as a book about Virginia Woolf's father and mother has gradually assumed a more complex—and Proustian—subject: the truth of her memory of her parents and of her relations with them in childhood and in memory, and the way in which the making of this novel has illuminated or even created that truth. The artist's rôle, properly subsidiary in Part I, has come in Part III to take on such importance that Lily's final brushstroke ends the book. Lily has triumphed over Mrs. Ramsay even in completing her portait, Virginia Woolf has triumphed over Leslie Stephen ("His life would have entirely ended mine. . . . No writing, no books. . . .") to whom she has made a final ironic offering, this book. That is why *To the Lighthouse* cured Virginia Woolf of her "obsession" with her parents as earlier studies of them had not done (Mr. and Mrs. Ambrose in *The Voyage Out,* Mr. and Mrs. Hilbery in *Night and Day*). And it is the Proustian use of memory that has made this book possible. But as the subject changed, the emphasis shifted, confession has not been fully transmuted into art and Lily's picture fails of being a satisfactory symbol for the making of the book. Design finally did not embody vision but was imposed on it. Tested by Virginia Woolf's own definition of a masterpiece, "books . . . where the vision is clear and order has been achieved" the novel falls short.[24] *To the Lighthouse,* an act of piety, of expiation, of self-vindication, her most confessional and most Proustian book, is, despite all its merits, not her best. (*Mrs. Dalloway* is that.)

[24] "Robinson Crusoe," *The Common Reader: Second Series* (London: Hogarth Press, 1948), pp. 53–54. This essay was written during the composition of *To the Lighthouse.*

The "Caricature Value" of Parody and Fantasy in *Orlando*

by John Graham

> I want (and this was serious) to give things their caricature value.
> *Diary*, 136 (Nov. 7, 1928)

In the *Diary* entry from which the epigraph to this essay is taken, Virginia Woolf paused to reflect on what she had learned from writing *Orlando*, what had prompted her to write it, and what its status was in relation to her more serious works. The phrase "caricature value" suggests, in a condensed and enigmatic fashion, a great deal about all three of these subjects. A caricature of a person selects his most salient features and throws them into relief by simplification and exaggeration, usually to mock but sometimes to make us recognize with amusement someone we love or respect. In either case, we look at this person *through* the caricature with momentary detachment, and in that moment we may go beyond recognition to the discovery of something new about his face and character. For the artist who draws it the caricature may be more exploratory than critical. The simplified and distorted treatment of many of the heads which Leonardo da Vinci scribbled in his notebooks indicates that he was testing through caricature the artistic possibilities of a certain expression or physical type, concentrating on and accentuating those features which seem to hint such possibilities. Caricature can explore because it ignores the complexity of the total object and isolates only its relevant features, thereby allowing a sharper focus of attention than is possible in a full treatment. In many ways it can function for the artist as a refined sort of doodling, in which he "feels out" the forms and designs of his more serious work.

In *Orlando*, caricature operates in both of these ways. It holds up for mocking inspection certain things which Virginia Woolf heartily disliked and certain others which she heartily admired. It also explores, in

"The 'Caricature Value' of Parody and Fantasy in *Orlando*" by John Graham. From *University of Toronto Quarterly*, XXX (July 1961), 345–66. Reprinted by permission of the author and the University of Toronto Press.

an indirect fashion, the potential features of a new kind of fiction which she was at that time increasingly eager to write. Both of these activities link *Orlando* more closely to the works preceding and following it than is the case with any other of Virginia Woolf's novels. Critics have always been struck with the prominence of literature as one of its subjects: the recurrent appearance of writers among the characters, Orlando's own struggle to write, the parody of styles, even the historical atmosphere, which is derived more from literature than from a reading of history, all indicate a preoccupation with writers and writing which is unmatched in her other novels. More is involved, however, than a survey of the literature of the past. Virginia Woolf scrutinizes her own style, and some of her distinctive themes, with a good deal of irony; and she goes beyond this veiled criticism of her own writing to explore some of the elements which appear in her later work.

On the surface, *Orlando* is simply a playful fantasy, conceived as an escape from the labour of writing "these serious poetic experimental books whose form is always so closely considered," [1] designed only to amuse, and written for fun. Nearly two-thirds of the first draft was written at top speed between October and December, 1927, but the final third was not completed until March of 1928. The "pure delight of this farce," [2] which had carried Virginia Woolf exuberantly through the first three months of composition, dwindled in the new year, and at one point she remarked gloomily that she was "hacking rather listlessly at the last chapter of *Orlando,* which was to have been the best." [3] She began to have second thoughts at this point: that it was too fantastic to write at such length; that it fell beween the comic and the serious; that it was too long for a joke and too frivolous for a serious book. After she had completed revisions which she cut off impatiently, and had given her husband the manuscript to read, she was surprised by his enthusiasm for it and expressed her suspicion that "I began it as a joke and went on with it seriously. Hence it lacks some unity." [4] In the course of writing it, therefore, she came to feel, as most critics do, that *Orlando* was a blend of comic and serious elements, the latter dominating its later chapters to its detriment as a work of art.

At present, the relevant fact about this is the way in which an irresponsible comic escapade grew uncontrollably into something else; for it suggests that in writing *Orlando* Virginia Woolf undertook something less frivolous than she had intended; that she was more profoundly engaged with serious matters than she wished; and that much

[1] *A Writer's Diary, Being Extracts from the Diary of Virginia Woolf,* ed. Leonard Woolf (London, 1953), 105 (March 14, 1927), hereafter referred to as *Diary.*

[2] *Ibid.,* 117 (Oct. 22, 1927).

[3] *Ibid.,* 123 (Feb. 11, 1928).

[4] *Ibid.,* 128 (May 31, 1928).

of this engagement sprang from unconscious pressures which she actually resisted as far as she could. Even after the book was published, her attitude to it was ambiguous, as we see from the lengthy entry in her *Diary* in which she mused over its significance. She began by noting, as she had when finishing *To the Lighthouse*, that she

> cannot think what to write next. I mean the situation is, this *Orlando* is of course a very quick brilliant book. Yes, but I did not try to explore. And must I always explore? Yes I think so still. Because my reaction is not the usual. Nor can I even after all these years run it off lightly. *Orlando* taught me how to write a direct sentence; taught me continuity and narrative and how to keep the realities at bay. But I purposely avoided of course any other difficulty. I never got down to my depths and made shapes square up, as I did in the *Lighthouse*.
>
> Well but *Orlando* was the outcome of a perfectly definite, indeed overmastering, impulse. I want fun. I want fantasy. I want (and this was serious) to give things their caricature value. . . . My notion is that there are offices to be discharged by talent for the relief of genius: meaning that one has the play side; the gift when it is mere gift, unapplied gift; and the gift when it is serious, going to business. And one relieves the other.[5]

This passage is curiously defensive, as if Virginia Woolf felt impelled to explain and justify to herself the writing of *Orlando*. It is also full of contradictions which appear when we trace the sequence of her ideas. She begins by noting that she did not try to explore in this book and that she still must explore because her reaction is not the usual. This clearly associates her "reaction" with the need to explore, and the logical conclusion to draw from this association is that, since she did not explore in *Orlando,* this reaction did not figure in its creation. But when she goes on to say that she *cannot* run off this reaction lightly "even after all these years," she seems to assume that she recently tried to do so without success; and the obvious place for the attempt was in *Orlando,* the only "light" book among her works at that time. When she proceeds to note that it taught her how to "keep the realities at bay," and describes as *serious* her desire to give things their caricature value, she seems to contradict her next assertion, that it was purely the result of talent playing idly for the relief of genius. The tone of the whole passage, ending with the magisterial divorce of talent from genius (both, however, aspects of the same gift), suggests that she wished to persuade herself that *Orlando* was not "serious." One feels that her remark about not trying to explore should be altered to read "tried not to explore," and that the attempt failed: talent yielded to genius, and the realities were not quite kept at bay.

While she was still writing it, she remarked with astonishment how "extraordinarily unwilled by me but potent in its own right, by the way, *Orlando* was! as if it shoved everything aside to come into existence." [6] The metaphor of birth used in this remark is strangely appropriate, with its overtone of helplessness before the force of a process beyond her conscious control. The office of talent in *Orlando* was not, as she tried at one point to argue it was, that of giving genius a rest; it was that of playing midwife, and the "relief" it gave genius was that of assisting at the birth of the fiction she was about to write, especially her next book, *The Waves*. In 1933, long after both books had been published, she seemed to realize and to certify this when she turned back in her *Diary* to the entry recording the original conception of *Orlando* and scribbled this marginal note: "*Orlando* leading to *The Waves*." [7]

The evidence provided by the text of *Orlando* and by the *Diary* is supported by several articles written between 1926 and 1929, in which, behind the impersonal mask of the literary critic, Virginia Woolf carried on the complex process of assessment and speculation which was figured forth in *Orlando* behind the mask of the comic fantasist. I have not the space to deal with these articles[8] closely, but they are clearly related to each other by their common dissatisfaction with the contemporary English novel and by their air of prophetically forecasting its future course of development. All of them touch some aspect of one central argument, that the novel must learn to fuse three things: its traditional power to render the texture of life closely; the freedom, detachment, and impersonality of poetry; and the concentration and strict control of drama. The personal relevance of such generalizations appears from a *Diary* entry for February 21, 1927, in which she noted her urge to write a new kind of work, something away "from facts; free; yet concentrated; prose yet poetry; a novel and a play." [9] Her irritation with the psychological novel, expressed repeatedly in three of these four articles, makes it clear that she was going beyond the strictures of "Mr. Bennett and Mrs. Brown" to include in the category of the unsatisfactory her own most recent and successful novels. The hypothetical book which appeared to her "on the rim of the horizon," [10] was to be

[6] *Ibid.*, 120 (Dec. 20, 1928).

[7] *Ibid.*, 105 (March 14, 1927).

[8] All of these articles are reprinted in *Granite and Rainbow: Essays by Virginia Woolf* (New York, 1958). They first appeared in the following journals: "Impassioned Prose" in *Times Literary Supplement* (Sept. 16, 1926), 601–2; "The Narrow Bridge of Art" (under the title "Poetry, Fiction and the Future") in *New York Herald Tribune* (Aug. 14, 1927), vol. I, 6–7 and (Aug. 21, 1927), vol. I, 6; "Women and Fiction" in *Forum* (New York, March 1929), 179–182; and "Phases of Fiction" in *Bookman* (New York, 1929), in April (123–132), May (269–79), and June (404–12).

[9] *Diary*, 104.

[10] "The Narrow Bridge of Art," *Granite and Rainbow*, 23.

a distinctly new thing, something which the famous "method" of *To the Lighthouse* had not and never would bring forth.

II

Everything mocked.   *Diary,* 105 (March 14, 1927)

This process of evaluation and exploration was continued in *Orlando,* lending it "un certain détachment critique" [11] which Floris Delattre describes as its most distinctive feature. The mode of this detachment is irony, both comic and serious; a mode which liberates an artist much as caricature does. In both, he may shut out the complexities of his subject, may abandon his full and serious involvement with it for the moment, may select any aspects of it which attract his interest, and may deal with these without being forced to commit himself to any view of them. In her first *Diary* entry about *Orlando,* Virginia Woolf stated: "Satire is to be the main note—satire and wildness. The ladies are to have Constantinople in view. Dreams of golden domes. My own lyric vein is to be satirised. Everything mocked." [12] This passage glancingly indicates the two most important elements of the special charm which marks this book—fantasy and mockery. But it is difficult to see how satire is truly the main note of the text: its mockery lacks the thrust of implicit moral judgment and the sustained critical purpose inherent in satire. "Everything mocked" is too sweeping a statement to indicate a satirical intention, which demands selective precision: it is, rather, a statement of an ironical attitude which, because it subjects all things to ridicule, liberates the author from the need to engage any of them seriously.

Irony provided her with an impregnable shield of detachment because it is in itself morally and emotionally uncommitted. This lack of commitment is manifest in the wide variety of purposes which it may serve: that of the satirist, who is anything but uncommitted; or of the cynic, who is indifferent; or of the pure ironist, who simply does not express in his irony his moral and emotional position, if any. The unsophisticated reader of a satirist like Swift testifies to this neutrality when he accuses Swift of being "insincere" or "cynical," thereby showing that he has felt the icy detachment of Swift's ironic manner without sensing the moral passion behind it. A slightly more sophisticated reader will sense that passion and will call Swift's irony a mask—something to be seen past and finally ignored in assessing Swift's satire. But the reader who truly understands irony will realize that the cold surface and the

---

[11] Floris Delattre, *Le Roman psychologique de Virginia Woolf* (Paris, 1933), 185.
[12] *Diary,* 105 (March 14, 1927).

fiery depths must be contemplated together in a tension which is never relaxed if Swift's irony is to be savoured to the full. This tension is common to all forms of irony, and springs from the fundamental act of the ironist, which is to perceive, expose, and contemplate a contradiction between two terms: between what is expected and what happens (the irony of fate), what circumstances seem to be and what they are (the irony of situation), what is known and what is not known (dramatic irony), or what is professed and what is performed (the irony of behaviour). The neutrality of irony appears in its usefulness for expressing both the comic and the tragic responses to these contradictions. The only response of irony is the refusal to respond, to get involved, to be partisan or passionate. It leaves the contradiction over which it plays exactly where it found it, more sharply exposed but in no way resolved. . . .

The lightness of the irony in *Orlando* is due chiefly to the prominence of parody among its ironic devices. Parody is the most translucent form of ironic mockery: it acts as a lens through which we look at an object familiar to us and see it, at first glance, almost as it is in fact, the pleasure of recognition being followed quickly by the realization that its characteristic features are slightly distorted. The slighter the distortion, the subtler the parody; and the subtler it is, the better, for the hallmark of good parody is its ironically straight-faced imitation of its victim. . . .

Parody, like caricature, does not necessarily judge the object ridiculed and may play with something which, in our serious moments, we regard with respect, admiration, or affection. It shrugs aside all questions of literary value, critical julgment, or fidelity to the complex truth and turns with equal glee on the genuine and the fake, the great and the shoddy, the profound and the superficial. . . .

The curiously irreducible character of parody makes it possible to use it intermittently in a larger work, to apply it to a general style of writing as well as to the styles of specific writers, to combine it with other comic devices, and to sustain it with slight touches as a vein of amusement running through a narrative, without losing or blurring the special comic effect which it provides. . . .

From all this it appears that a work dominated by parody will be "playfully" mocking in a special way, its ridicule implying an attitude of withdrawal which permits intellectual scrutiny without intellectual, moral, or emotional commitment. The prevalence of parody in *Orlando* reinforces the conclusion to be drawn, as we shall see, from the prominence of fantasy: that in this book Virginia Woolf paused to assess, by playing with them, certain themes and methods of her work thus far. She also paused to explore, by playing with them, certain themes and methods of the work to come. In neither case did the detachment afforded by parody and fantasy involve rejection—or acceptance—of these themes and methods. Having played this game, she was still free to choose the battleground and the weapons for the serious engagement with experience which marks the later novels, and, indeed, the later chapters of *Orlando* itself, in which her ironically playful detachment breaks down under the pressure of her mounting interest in the vision of her heroine.

The subtitle of this book—*A Biography*—indicates the object of its most sustained parody. Virginia Woolf's life-long fondness of reading biographies, which she frequently reviewed for periodicals, must have led her on many a weary trek through tomes more remarkable for their pretentious style and solemn pedantry than for any real insight into the lives with which they dealt. From the stereotyped flourishes of the preface to the learned uselessness of its scholarly index, *Orlando* parodies this type of biography. But the ridicule goes farther than that. The absurdities of the biographer are the absurdities of the whole approach to things which she considered typically masculine: the pompous self-importance; the childish faith in facts, dates, documents, and "evidence"; the reduction of truth to the logical conclusions deducible from such evidence; and the reluctance to deal with such nebulous aspects of life as passion, dream, and imagination. For all his learning and labour, the biographer does not understand his subject, and when understanding Orlando's life began to engross Virginia Woolf's serious attention, he became an encumbrance instead of a joke and disappeared from the book.

The parody of the biographer is most emphatic in those passages where he pauses solemnly to explain the obvious, to record with meticulous precision a trivial detail, to shake his head over the shocking state of the documents, to lament the paucity of facts, or to confess his dismay at having to deal with matters which decorum would suppress but which the dedicated scholar must record. Between these direct intrusions, the parody is sustained by the style; and here Virginia Woolf brilliantly solved a difficult technical problem. The biographer is a bore; we must know from the way he writes that he is a bore; but what he writes cannot bore us if we are to read "his" book. The style nicely blends his pretensions to formal elegance with a driving narrative energy and a ready flow of exact and fresh imagery. The following passage illustrates this blend at its best, in the chapters dealing with the Elizabethans. Orlando is waiting for Sasha to join him:

> *Many a time* did Orlando, pacing the little courtyard, *hold his heart* at the sound of some *nag's* steady footfall on the cobbles, or at the rustle of a woman's dress. But the traveller was only some merchant, making home *belated*; or some woman of the quarter whose errand was *nothing so innocent*. They passed, and the street was quieter than before. [1] Then those lights which burnt downstairs in the small, huddled quarters where the poor of the city lived moved up to the sleeping-rooms, and then, one

by one, were *extinguished*. The street lanterns in these *purlieus* were few at most; and the *negligence* of the night watchman often *suffered them to expire* long before dawn. The darkness then became even deeper than before. [2] Orlando *looked to* the wicks of his lantern, saw to the saddle girths; primed his pistols; examined his holsters; and did all these things a dozen times at least till he could find nothing more needing his attention. [3] Though it still lacked some twenty minutes to midnight, he could not bring himself to go indoors to the inn parlour, where the hostess was still serving sack and the cheaper sort of Canary wine to a few seafaring men, who would sit there trolling their ditties, and telling their stories of Drake, Hawkins, and Grenville, till they toppled off the benches and rolled asleep on the sanded floor. The darkness was *more compassionate to his swollen and violent heart.* He listened to every footfall; *speculated on* every sound. Each drunken shout and each wail from some *poor wretch* laid in the straw or in other distress *cut his heart to the quick,* as if it *boded ill omen* to his *venture*.[13]

The italicized words and phrases are removed slightly from current good usage (though not sufficiently to confuse their meaning), and sustain our sense of a style both consciously formal and "elegant." This is done by mixing genuinely archaic turns of phrase with modern *clichés*. Among the former are: *hold his heart, belated* (in the sense of "made late"), *nothing so* innocent, suffered them *to* (with reference to an inanimate object like "lights"), looked *to,* compassionate *to* (in the sense of "showing compassion towards"), and speculated *on* (of a sensation, such as "sound"). Formal diction, deriving from late eighteenth-century or early nineteenth-century prose style, is apparent in: *extinguished* (of lights), *purlieus, negligence, expire,* and *venture,* none of which is archaic. At the end of the paragraph, the stiffness of these "refined" expressions modulates into the grosser absurdity of phrases which originated in romantic prose fiction and which are still *clichés* of the pulp romance: *many a time, his swollen and violent heart, some poor wretch, cut his heart to the quick, boded ill omen.* None of these requires any knowledge of specific works parodied, and none obtrudes so violently that amusement disrupts the momentum of the narrative.

The vigour and directness of the numbered sentences counterbalance this inflated manner: the visual image of the lights going out in the quarters of the poor, the kinetic swiftness of Orlando's fidgeting as he waits, and the image of the sailors telling stories and getting drunk are all simple and vivid. Such words as "toppled" and "rolled" offset with their energy the soggy *clichés* of the sentences which follow them; and even in these sentences, phrases like "drunken shout . . . wail . . . laid in the straw" bolster up the slack words in which they are set. We are gently reminded of the biographer's stuffiness even as we enjoy the speed and energy of his narrative, which save his prose from becoming so tedious that it is unreadable.

[13] *Orlando, A Biography,* Uniform Edition (London, 1949), 55–6.

. . . Sharply defined parodies are rare in *Orlando*: the intrusions of the biographer, where he self-consciously moralizes; some passages ridiculing Virginia Woolf's lyric style; the mental sonneteering of Orlando as he thinks of Sasha, or his Jacobean meditations on death; Lieutenant Brigge's diary, the pompous testament of The Briton Abroad; the sentimental letter of Miss Penelope Hartopp, the gushing flirt; the elaborate parody of the masque, when Modesty, Chastity, and Purity rant and posture around the bed of the transformed Orlando; the snippets of Victorian Female Verse—these, and a few other short passages, strike our *conscious* attention as parodies. Without the enveloping parody of the biographer's style, they would be too sudden and brief to be effective; with it, they affect us as quick rays of wit flashing out from an ambience more diffuse than they but identical in kind.

The mocking gleam of parody is shed also by the clouds of allusion which float lightly over most of the narrative in the first four chapters. Consider, for example, the opening scene of the book, the charm of which is founded on the universal adult reaction to youthful ardour, a reaction which can range from approving indulgence to ironic sadness, depending on the control of tone. In this case, a comic tone is sustained by defining Orlando's ardour through a parody of romance, which first appears in the last sentence of the first paragraph: "Orlando's father, or perhaps his grandfather, had struck it from the shoulders of a vast Pagan who had started up under the moon in the barbarian fields of Africa; and now it swung, gently, perpetually, in the breeze which never ceased blowing through the attic rooms of the gigantic house of the lord who had slain him." [14] The uncertainty about which ancestor won this trophy is balanced by the grandiose emphasis of *vast Pagan,* which is echoed by *gigantic house* at the end of the sentence; and between these two portentous phrases the crude elements of romance are tossed before us in the picture of the Pagan *starting up under the moon in the barbarian fields of*—not Yorkshire, by any means, but the inevitably exotic Africa. In the opening sentence of the second paragraph, the allusive note is maintained: "Orlando's fathers had ridden in fields of *asphodel,* and stony fields, and fields watered by *strange* rivers . . ."; but this is balanced anticlimatically by "and they had struck *many* heads of *many* colours off *many* shoulders," [15] which reduces their heroic exertions to a kind of vague trophy collecting, very much as if they had absentmindedly been gathering a splendid array of the footballs which this particular head resembled. Then we are confronted by the grave youth who moves in the mental world which has just been parodied: "So too would Orlando, he vowed." [16] The affec-

[14] *Ibid.*, 15.
[15] *Ibid.*
[16] *Ibid.*

tionate mockery generated by this scene carries over into the whole section devoted to the Elizabethans and Jacobeans, where the parodistic treatment of courtly love, the courtier's life, and melancholy obsessions with Death, Fame, and the *vita brevis* are in effect a tribute to the abundant belief of an age in which men pursued values from which, for better or worse, we are detached.

III

I want fantasy.   *Diary*, 136 (November 7, 1928)

In Virginia Woolf's opinion, the defects of *Orlando* rose from her failure to fuse the comic and the serious, and this failure rose in turn from the fact that she began to write it as a joke and went on with it seriously. Most critics seem to agree with this view of the book's status as a work of art; and yet it is hard to see why it should be so difficult to combine serious and comic elements in a book, or why, as it was composed, its author could not change her emotional relation to it without destroying its artistic integrity. While she was still bogged down in revision of *Orlando*, Virginia Woolf vowed that she would spend no longer at it, and dismissed it irritably as a "freak." [17] The term seems a reflex of her critical acumen because it defines exactly the real failure of *Orlando*—its failure to follow to the end the laws of its literary nature, which is fantasy. In common usage, "fantasy" is associated with notions of the grotesque, the odd, the eccentric, the capricious, the whimsical, the irrational, and the arbitrary, all of which express different nuances of its central meaning, that of an extravagant and impossible deviation from nature. In the usage of literary criticism, however, the term must mean both more and less than that: more, because the literary fantasy, unlike the fantasy in life, is a work of art and must be created according to some kind of artistic laws which are not arbitrary, capricious, or irrational; and less, because other literary types, such as the utopia, the satire, the allegory, and the romance, also use extravagant and impossible deviations from nature. Some such deviation, indeed, is involved in all art; and if "fantasy" is given a wide inclusive meaning, it will end up being applied to works like the *Divine Comedy* or *King Lear*, an application of no interest to the literary critic, though it may be to the psychologist who regards all art as fantasy.

The term becomes useful for literary criticism when we compare the sort of work to which it can be applied with similar works, such as romance and allegory. In fantasy, the deviation from nature is enjoyed primarily for its own sake, for the pleasure of playing with natural law; whereas romance and allegory, while they may provide this pleasure,

---

[17] *Diary*, 126 (April 21, 1928).

subordinate it to a didactic intention. The hero of romance transcends natural law because in doing so he displays his virtues; but when a figure in fantasy does the same thing, he need not display anything except his power to do it. If he reveals his virtues, such as courage or quick wit, the revelation is accidental, not a fundamental part of the fantastic role he plays. The impossible convolutions of plot in allegory serve to articulate the structure of thought and feeling which it bodies forth, but in fantasy they satisfy us primarily because they are impossible. The satisfaction of fantasy may be comic, or it may take a more serious form of wish-fulfilment; but in either case it resembles the satisfaction of parody in its irresponsibility, its moral neutrality, and its root reliance upon our childlike urge to escape from the pressures of life.

This vague resemblance is tantalizing, for it suggests that the effect of fantasy in *Orlando* is at least congruous with, and possibly intensifies, the irony which is the mode of the whole book, and of which parody is an example. Yet at first glance the sophistication, self-consciousness, and intellectual complexity of irony seem antithetical to the naïveté, spontaneity, and simplicity of fantasy. That the antithesis is less radical than it seems is hinted by the fact that satire frequently employs both together, and that the fantastic voyage of Gulliver, for example, in no way inhibits or qualifies the play of Swift's irony.

What fantasy and irony have in common is the deliberate disengagement from life so striking in parody, which may be closer than any other form of irony to the psychic root of all ironic responses. . . . In disengaging from life, fantasy withdraws into a realm of libidal fulfilment in which the conflict between fact and desire is momentarily annihilated, our sense of the facts serving only to sharpen the pleasure of ignoring them. Irony withdraws into a realm of intellectual contemplation, in which the disparity between fact and illusion is itself the object of contemplation, so that we are not involved in reconciling them. In both cases, the pleasure is one of release from what is fated in our experience: from the frustrations of desire and the contradictions of reason which we cannot escape in life. In irony we "master" contradictions by exposing them; in fantasy we "master" frustrations by ignoring them and reconstituting experience arbitrarily, to suit desire; and in both there is something inconclusive, evasive, and improvised. We always know that a fantasy is "make-believe" in a way that *King Lear* is not; and our pleasure in it is as provisional as that produced by parody, in which we surrender momentarily to the possibility that Milton's style is laughable. It is for these reasons that the satirist so often blends fantasy and irony. . . .

In defining further the distinguishing features of fantasy, it should be noted that it is not a clear-cut literary type: like satire or allegory, it may infiltrate many genres, may provide serious or comic effects, and may serve purposes ranging from sheer escape through satiric criticism to moral instruction. Fantasies like those of Lewis Carroll and H. G. Wells are freighted with satiric or didactic ore, and, on the other hand, Gulliver's voyage to Lilliput becomes with a few snips of the censor's scissors, a children's fantasy. When we call a complete work a fantasy, therefore, we are really describing a work in which the sustaining pleasure is that created by the impossible abrogation of natural law, and in which didactic or critical material is ancillary to this pleasure.

In these terms, *Orlando* is a fantasy. In the *Diary* entry recording the original conception of the book, Virginia Woolf sketched a story of two "women, poor, solitary at the top of a house. One can see anything (for this is all fantasy) the Tower Bridge, clouds, aeroplanes. . . . Everything is to be tumbled in pell mell. . . . No attempt is to be made to realise the character." [18] The fantasist's dominating urge to cut loose from fact is certainly evident here, and in the early chapters of the text it is manifested in the glittering shower of extravagant exaggerations shed by the mockery of literary conventions, social manners, and individual foibles. But as the work proceeded, Virginia Woolf's interest in Orlando's voyage through the centuries became steadily more serious and less ironic, so that it vitiated the artistic integrity of the book, slowly undermining the fantastic frame thrown up so exuberantly at its beginning.

This vitiation can be measured only if we examine the technical principles of fantasy. The first of these is the need to preserve within the fantasy-world a human perspective: we need an Alice to take us through wonderland, for her presence in this world enables us to accept it imaginatively. At the same time it sharpens our sense of its fantastic exaggeration by reminding us, through Alice's bemused reactions, of the "normal" perspective we share with her. No fantasy can successfully omit this perspective, which is usually supplied by a human narrator, but may also be supplied by an omniscient author. The second general principle is to make the fantasy-world coherent enough to strike us as a *world* and not a chaos; to make us believe that it has laws even if we do not understand them. The narrative momentum of most fantasies is provided by the human hero's effort to fathom these laws, and in most fantasies he succeeds: after the initial astonishment, perhaps terror, of facing the incomprehensible, he gradually comprehends it, reduces it to order, "makes sense" of it. The possibility of doing this demands some element of consistency in the fantasy-world itself. This is often supplied by a scrupulous consistency of distortion, like the scales of measurement in Lilliput or Brobdignag, or like the consistent scale of the monsters which appear in fantastic movies about lost worlds. The purest fantasies, however, do not need to rely on this control of the

[18] *Ibid.*, 105 (March 14, 1927).

physical. The objects and atmosphere of Carroll's wonderland change arbitrarily; things shrink, grow large, change shape, vanish, reappear, and so on. Its status as a world is maintained by the invariable assumption of its native inhabitants that it *is* a world, and a very sensible one at that. . . .

The freakishness of *Orlando* lies in the failure to follow these two principles of fantasy throughout. In the first half, the human perspective is supplied by the biographer in his struggle to make sense of his subject's fantastic life. Although he is the butt of ridicule, we are forced to look at things through his eyes, not those of Orlando the noble lord, courtier, would-be writer, and diplomat; just as in *Gulliver's Travels* we must accept Gulliver's account of the events he experiences even when we do not credit his interpretation of them. As long as the biographer provides us with the human perspective required in fantasy, Orlando remains a fantastic figure and can support airily the tissue of hyperbolic descriptions woven around his life; but as soon as Orlando has become a woman for good, we draw steadily closer to her, and the biographer steadily diminishes in importance until, in the last chapter, he disappears.

As he shrivels, so do the distortions. In the early chapters, the fantastic career of Orlando proceeds in an environment equally extravagant, and by the time we reach the superb description of the Great Frost, we are acclimatized to a world of extremes and can relish such details as the bumboat woman frozen in the Thames or the flood which follows the Great Thaw. The burlesque of diplomatic protocol in Constantinople sustains this, and the change of sex is the boldest fantastic stroke of all; but with the onset of the eighteenth century, the fantasy begins to deflate. Orlando has no adventure that is truly fantastic; and instead of the old bumboat woman we have the usual prostitutes in Piccadilly Circus. The heroine assumes in this society the conventional role of a patroness of the arts and brings to it little of the *panache* which Orlando the courtier had brought to the London of Elizabeth. When Bonthrop Marmaduke Shelmerdine thunders out of the pages of *Jane Eyre,* he is artistically unconvincing, as the bumboat woman and Sasha were not, because we are no longer moving imaginatively in the atmosphere provided by fantasy and parody. (Addison, Swift, and Pope, for example, are quoted directly, not parodied.)

This deflation of the fantasy was caused by Virginia Woolf's growing desire to make us take her heroine seriously. To do this, it was necessary for our relation to her to change: from being a fantastic object *at* which we look, she becomes a human subject *with* whom we look; and this involved transferring to her the human perspective formerly supplied by the biographer. Beginning with the scene in Marshall & Snelgrove's and proceeding through the city and countryside to Orlando's ancestral home, the restless world of time present is described with cinematic precision, so that such dazzling sequences as the kaleidoscopic view of the city seen from a moving car impress us by their literal accuracy, not their fantastic distortion. When Sasha "reappears" to Orlando, we know that she reappears only in the mind's eye, and that the woman mistaken for her is not Sasha at all; whereas in fantasy she *would* reappear, if not in the flesh, then as a very fleshlike apparition. By the time Orlando sits down in the long gallery of her home, she has become a distinctly credible aristocrat of the present age, down to the lavender bags, ropes, and name-cards which mark the passing of her private heritage into the public domain. Along with this reduction of Orlando and her *milieu* to the proportions of actual life runs a steady transfer of their fabulous aura to the events of the past which she now recalls. Yet these events are carefully robbed of their absurdity, and the more grotesque among them, such as the Archduchess Harriet, are omitted: the helmeted warriors of the past return from such real battle-grounds as Flodden and Poitiers, not from Ariostan forays against the paynim and the Turk. Fable must become history, for we are intended to take this resurrection of the dead not in the irreverent spirit with which we took the Great Frost, but in the spirit of a solemn vision.

To effect this intention, Orlando is altered from a fantastic figure to an actual person, so that we may share her grave vision of her own past, which was anything but grave when we moved through it with her. But the paradoxical fact is that the more "believable" Orlando becomes, the less we can believe in her or her vision, because her aesthetic "believability" has resided precisely in the fantastic charm which she has now lost. Hanging uncertainly between fantasy and actuality, we are jolted back into the fantastic by Bonthrop Marmaduke Shelmerdine's return. The shock is too great, and so the wild goose flying into the night is not a successful symbol but a melodramatic stage-prop which only completes the bathos of the final scene.

IV

The comic play of parody and fantasy in *Orlando* served the end of critical detachment more directly than that of the artistic exploration to which caricature may also lead: it is obvious that they are more useful for skeptically scrutinizing past methods and themes than for laying one's artistic hand on the resources necessary to create a new fiction. The truly exploratory nature of *Orlando* must be inferred, therefore, by comparing it with the novels which precede and follow it, on the working hypothesis that Virginia Woolf was seriously committed to creating this new fiction in her artistic practice. When such a comparison is made, several revealing similarities emerge between this most frivolous of her books and the intensely serious last three novels. I shall deal only with one of them, the way in which the biographer prefigures the narrative point of view which was employed in *The Waves*.

Orlando was the first of Virginia Woolf's novels in which the narrator frankly revealed himself. The concealed narrator of *Jacob's Room, Mrs. Dalloway,* and *To the Lighthouse* controlled our point of view subtly, shifting it back and forth from the consciousness of a character to a disguised omniscient position and to a vantage point between these two, in which we hover beside the consciousness of a character without entering it. In all of these novels, the decision to eliminate the omniscient author made it impossible to detach ourselves from consciousness for very long; and the boldest attempt to do so, "Time Passes," never satisfied Virginia Woolf. She was probably aware that this interlude was the piece of *trompe l'œil* which William Empson has analysed so tellingly[19]—a bit of trickery which her artistic conscience could never quite accept.

Intervening awkwardly between us and the narrative, the mind of the biographer who "writes" *Orlando* is a caricature of the mind in solitude to which Virginia Woolf had referred frequently in critical essays written at this time,[20] and with which she felt fiction must learn to deal. By mind in solitude she obviously could not have meant merely the mind of a character who is alone. She had begun to deal with that in *The Voyage Out,* had perfected in *To the Lighthouse* her method for rendering its movement, and in *Orlando* parodied this method in the meandering solitary reflections of her central character. She meant, rather, that fiction must learn to saturate a *complete work* with the essentially poetic activity of a contemplative consciousness reflecting in solitude. Such a mind could never be that of a character in the action because we are bound to look *at* such a character as well as through him. The biographer is a rudimentary model for this containing consciousness, which can stand a little back from the characters and look past them at a larger reality of which they need not be aware. The artistic possibilities of a containing mind are various, but two are especially striking. If the characters do perceive what it perceives, then we will accept their perception more fully, because we have perceived the same thing ourselves and it has an imaginative objectivity lacking if we are forced to rely entirely on the reactions of the characters. If they do not perceive it, this objectivity serves the purpose of dramatic irony, for their impercipience is then measured by our superior knowledge. Both reinforce the impersonal and detached character of the reality so perceived.

Although the biographer is the butt of ridicule, his self-conscious fussiness does reflect his genuine desire to discover the truth and his fret-

[19] See his essay, "Virginia Woolf," *Scrutinies,* ed. E. Rickword (London, 1931), 204–16.

[20] See *Granite and Rainbow,* 13, 34, 119, 130, *passim.*

ful suspicion that the "facts" are not revealing it; and here he serves
to intensify our sense of the elusive nature of his subject, Orlando's life.
His reflections on Time, on the multiple self, and on the Meaning of
Life allow Virginia Woolf to mock her own lyric style and her preoccupation with these themes, and at the same time allow her to test the
possibility of handling them from a position clearly outside and above
the characters. The brilliant clarity of the events he narrates becomes
coloured, as his account rushes on, with a curiously mysterious tint, as
if they must mean more than the nervously applied dull tools of his
scholarship can reveal. We always look *at* these events, never surrender-
ing to them as participants; and this detachment rises from the biographer's baffled air as much as from their fantastic impossibility. If
anything rises consistently from the pages of *Orlando*, it is this faint
wraith of mystery, which becomes more sharply defined in Orlando's
meditations in the last chapter and which assumes a dark symbolic
shape at the end when the wild goose flies off into the night.

In "The Narrow Bridge of Art," *Tristram Shandy* served to illus-
trate the successful attainment of poetic detachment and freedom in
fiction through the use of a narrator. In many ways, the biographer
resembles Tristram. The speed of his narrative, his long loose-knit
sentences, his frequent use of the parenthetical aside, his tendency to
digress, his lyric meditations, and his habit of juxtaposing passages
widely differing in tone—all remind us of Sterne's inimitable mask.
But there is a crucial difference: Tristram is in complete command
of his narrative from beginning to end; and if we succumb to the
eccentric charm of his approach to his subject, we finish the book
with the realization that the title does after all describe it exactly—
that Tristram, not the marvellous *ménage* of which he incessantly
talks, *is* the book. In all of this Sterne's mask never slips: Tristram
is always obtrusively present, confident, loquacious, utterly absorbed
in his task. The biographer of *Orlando* neither charms nor commands
us to believe in him in this way; and since he is not the subject of
his own book, he fades out of sight when the true subject, the meaning of Orlando's life, rises into serious prominence in the last chapter.
Virginia Woolf's mask is never firmly in place, and her tentative use
of it is characteristic of this exploratory uncommitted book.

The Waves was originally intended to be a first person narrative in
which the narrator is so firmly in command that he is presented as
omniscient, and the gradual diffusion of this narrator into the uniform
style continues to control our relation to the entire book with a sure-
ness worthy of Sterne or Proust. The biographer in *Orlando* is the
tentative sketch for this figure, and his ingenuous incompetence is the
caricature of the other's brooding omniscience.

"Death Among the Apple Trees":
The Waves and the World of Things

by *Frank D. McConnell*

And what were thou, and earth, and stars, and sea,
If to the human mind's imaginings
Silence and solitude were vacancy?

Mont Blanc

Shelley's final question in the Vale of Chamouni, like the apparent cliché which concludes the *Ode to the West Wind,* is not so triumphantly rhetorical as a simple reading suggests. In context, both questions reveal an uncertainty about the relative primacy, in this world, of the human imagination, with its endless train of rich and apparently holy impressions, on the one hand, and the "everlasting universe of things" which, as inhuman and possibly mindless power, presents a chillingly negative version of the Intellectual Beauty in which the mind craves to believe, on the other hand. If the apocalyptic wind of change and revolution, like the "Necessity" of Shelley's tutor Godwin, is in fact *not* a power benign to and consonant with the mind's imaginings, then a humane Spring may be very far indeed behind the Winter it brings on. The questions reverberate in the silence they impose with that curious and profound self-criticism which is characteristic of Shelley's best poetry.[1] But of course they are only an extreme manifestation of one of the most permanent dilemmas of the romantic imagination: the terrible ambiguity, Coleridgean in origin, implied by the autonomy of the creative mind, the fear that what seems an imaginative transfiguration of the world of matter may in the end be only the vaudeville trick Edward Bostetter calls it: ventriloquism.[2]

" 'Death Among the Apple Trees': *The Waves* and the World of Things" by Frank D. McConnell. From *Bucknell Review*, XVI (December 1968), 23–39. Reprinted by permission of the author and *Bucknell Review*.

[1] James Rieger, *The Mutiny Within* (New York, 1967), pp. 200 ff., refers to this quality as Shelley's "polysemism."

[2] *The Romantic Ventriloquists* (Seattle, Wash., 1963), pp. 3–7.

Virginia Woolf, writing about Shelley in 1927, at about the time she envisioned the novel that was to become *The Waves,* seems to have been aware of this distinctively romantic problem:

> He loved the clouds and the mountains and the rivers more passionately than any other man loved them; but at the foot of the mountain he always saw a ruined cottage; there were criminals in chains, hoeing up the weeds in the pavement of St. Peter's Square; there was an old woman shaking with ague on the banks of the lovely Thames. . . . The most ethereal of poets was the most practical of men.[3]

It is an odd conflation of Shelley with Wordsworth and with Virginia Woolf herself; for certainly the "ruined cottage" is an unconscious reminiscence of *The Excursion,* and the old woman on the banks of the Thames seems remarkably like the grimly prophetic figure, "a tall quivering shape, like a funnel, like a rusty pump, like a wind-beaten tree for ever barren of leaves," Peter Walsh encounters in *Mrs. Dalloway.*[4] But as an evaluation of Shelley it is enlightened, accurate, and, for the era of the "New Criticism," courageously generous. And by one of those tricks which literary history seems delighted to play on authors, it ironically anticipates the critical fate of Virginia Woolf's own work, particularly her strangest and richest novel, *The Waves.* For while criticism, both enthusiastic and dyslogistic, of Virginia Woolf has taken it more or less for granted that she is "the most ethereal of novelists," indications have been rare—if indeed there have been any—that she is also "the most practical of women": that the aestheticism of her "stream of consciousness" includes the qualifying and fulfilling countermovement toward things in their blind phenomenalism, a countermovement which is an essential energy of the profoundest romantic and modern literature.

The reasons for Virginia Woolf's reputation as ethereal are, of course, both apparent and inevitable, with a perverse kind of inevitability. The very violence with which she inveighed against a double critical standard for women writers, and her vast scorn for the characterization of herself as "lady novelist," have insured for her an enduring attractiveness to people who hold precisely the values she contemned: a hypersensitive feminist apartheid, a concern for the obsessively "mystical" element in literature, and a kind of narrative introspectionism which has less to do with the mainstream of twentieth-century fiction than with the neurasthenia of the suffragette who insists on the vote but swoons at the editorial page. The inaccuracy of such a view finally results in the domesticated "Mrs. Woolf" of a book like Dorothy Brewster's *Virginia Woolf,*[5] a mixture of the tough-

---

[3] *The Death of the Moth* (New York, 1942), p. 125. Later citations refer to this edition.

[4] New York, 1925, p. 122.

[5] New York, 1962.

minded narrator with her own heroines, a book much like one that would result if one were to take as the final authoritative voice in *The Rape of the Lock* Belinda rather than Pope; or the Virginia Woolf-guru of N. C. Thakur's *The Symbolism of Virginia Woolf,* which in an access of mystagogy identifies as analogues for *The Waves* the Persian mystic Malauna Rumi, the Christian Trinity, the Hindu Trimurti, a misreading of Shelley's "Hymn to Intellectual Beauty," and the sayings of Buddha—in a single page.[6]

It is finally "mysticism," as a kind of exalted subjectivity, which is the *ignis fatuus* for Virginia Woolf's commentators, and particularly for commentators on *The Waves.* For *The Waves,* as both Miss Brewster and Mr. Thakur inform us, was the novel which the author called her "abstract mystical eyeless book," her "playpoem." The reference is to a 1928 entry in Virginia Woolf's diary, one of the earliest pertaining to *The Waves,* at that time still to be called *The Moths.* But the passage, read more fully, puts a significant bias on the aura of "mysticism." Virginia Woolf writes:

> Yes, but *The Moths*? That was to be an abstract mystical eyeless book: a playpoem. And there may be affectation in being too mystical, too abstract; saying Nessa and Roger and Duncan and Ethel Sands admire that: it is the uncompromising side of me; therefore I had better win their approval. . . . I rather think the upshot will be books that relieve other books: a variety of styles and subjects: for after all, that is my temperament, I think, to be very little persuaded of the truth of anything —what I say, what people say—always to follow, blindly, instinctively with a sense of leaping over a precipice—the call of—the call of—now, if I write *The Moths* I must come to terms with these mystical feelings.[7]

It was, in fact, in one sense precisely the "coming to terms" with the mystical feelings that accounted for the long and complex growth of the book and its transformation from *The Moths* to *The Waves.* An earlier entry, from 1927, in Virginia Woolf's diary explains the relevance of the first title as she again mentions "the play-poem idea; the idea of some continuous stream, not solely of human thought, but of the ship, the night, etc., all flowing together: intersected by the arrival of the bright moths." [8] She obviously thought of this book as the *chef d'oeuvre* of her distinctive fictional talents, and · obviously identified the initial impulse of its writing as a quasi-mystical revelation of what the completed whole would be like—the prophetic "fin in a waste of waters" which finds its way into Bernard's Roman vision. But in the very writing of the book, in the "coming to terms" with its subjectivist origin, it seems to have grown into something which Virginia Woolf herself could not have recognized at the beginning, something both

[6] London, 1965, p. 105.
[7] *A Writer's Diary* (London, 1953), p. 137.
[8] *Ibid.,* p. 108.

tougher and more profoundly relevant to her own best gifts than the
triumph of affectiveness the book has often been thought to be—something whose insignia is in fact the difference between the bright and
evanescent moths who were first to "intersect" the book's plot and the
inhuman, terrifying neutral waves which have the last inarticulate
"word" in the final novel and give their ambiguous benediction to the
human sense of a personal immortality.

"Coming to terms" with mysticism—at least in the English imaginative mainstream—is precisely a matter of translation, which implies
necessarily eradication of the full subjective flower of mysticism, of
writing it down, turning contemplation into verbalization, vision into
version. From Walter Hilton's medieval *Scale of Perfection,* which in
making the mystic's way a ladder refuses to leave out the lower rungs
of unrefined experience, to Wesley's "methodizing" of the Evangelical
Inner Light; and from the Red Cross knight's descent from the mount
of vision to the self-conscious and quizzical apocalypse of *Prometheus
Unbound,* the massive common-placing bias of the English mainstream
is clear: a mainstream to which Virginia Woolf irrevocably belongs,
as her earliest diary entries indicate, with their unflattering comparison
of Christina Rossetti to the Byron of *Don Juan.*[9]

One of the most important "translations" of the mystic into the
fictive is the passage already referred to, describing Bernard's experience in Rome:

> These moments of escape are not to be despised. They come too seldom.
> Tahiti becomes possible. Leaning over this parapet I see far out a waste of
> water. A fin turns. This bare visual impression is unattached to any line
> of reason, it springs up as one might see the fin of a porpoise on the
> horizon. Visual impressions often communicate thus briefly statements
> that we shall in time to come uncover and coax into words. I note under
> F., therefore, "Fin in a waste of waters." I, who am perpetually making
> notes in the margin of my mind for some final statement, make this mark,
> waiting for some winter's evening.[10]

There is something remarkably Wordsworthian about this passage, not
only in the gratuitousness with which the vision, the moment of escape,
comes, but also in its spareness, the deliberate and nearly abstract
simplicity of it. What gives it its peculiar force, however, is the deter-
mination of Bernard to "coax into words" the phenomenon whose
irrational, unawaited appearance defeats his present effort at description. The fin, he says, springs up suddenly, like a fin in a waste of
waters.[11] And with the romantic phrasemaker's characteristic faith in

---

[9] *Ibid.,* pp. 1–4.

[10] *Jacob's Rooms and The Waves* (New York, 1959), p. 307. This edition is cited
throughout.

[11] This is remarkably like W. K. Wimsatt's famous definition of Romantic metaphor as the "tenor" generating its own "vehicle" in *The Verbal Icon* (New York,
1963).

his own failures, he duly notes the phenomenon in his mental chap-book for later working into the story he is trying to make of his life and the lives of his friends.

It is, in fact, precisely the befuddlement of the vision which makes it important to Bernard. For if the vision of the fin in a waste of waters is a "moment of escape," the escape is *from* words themselves, with their implicit "plotting" of human life and with their pretensions to causality and coherence. Bernard simultaneously welcomes and fore-stalls the defeat of his language since this defeat, by revealing a tension between word and world, insures his liberation from the possible "mysticism," or absolute subjectivity, of his perpetual storytelling. He is the most pretentious and self-conscious of catalogers, noting this purely phenomenological and non-human revelation under "F" for "fin"; but it is just this pretension, anxious to take risks with experi-ence yet willing to be made absurd by the experience itself, which is his imaginative salvation.

Is there a story to tell at all? asks Bernard a moment before he has the vision of the fin. Confronted with the teeming and massively un-differentiated sight of a Roman street, he realizes that he could isolate any figure or grouping within range and "make it a story":

> Again, I could invent stories about that girl coming up the steps. She met him under the dark archway. . . . "It is over," he said, turning from the cage where the china parrot hangs. Or simply, "That was all." But why impose my arbitrary design? Why stress this and shape that and twist up little figures like the toys men sell in trays in the street? Why select this, out of all that,—one detail? (p. 306)

It is a question directly relevant, not only to the internal coherence of *The Waves* and, indeed, of all fiction, but to the specific situation in which Bernard finds himself. For his Roman monologue is, among other things, his first speech after the death of Percival, the strange, mute seventh figure about whom the other six characters of *The Waves* weave so much of their discourse. And whatever the similarity between Percival and Virginia Woolf's brother Thoby Stephen, his importance for the novel cannot be mistaken.

If Percival's death is a rupture in the hopes and sensibilities of the other characters, it is equally a rupture in the serial organization of their monologues: a delicate and highly subtle instance of imitative form. In the manner of serial music, each set of monologues by the six characters begins with a speech by Bernard and runs through the speeches of the other five before Bernard initiates a new "movement." But at the beginning of the fifth large section of the novel, the section introducing the news of Percival's death, Bernard for the first and only time does not begin the series: the first speaker is Neville, the closest of the six to Percival: " 'He is dead,' " said Neville. 'He fell. His horse tripped. He was thrown. The sails of the world have swung round and caught me on the head. All is over. The lights of the world have gone out. There stands the tree which I cannot pass' " (p. 280). Throughout the fifth and sixth sections, Bernard does not appear, and the order of speakers is Neville—Rhoda—Louis—Susan—Jinny—and again Neville. Six speakers, but no Bernard. With that kind of mathematical aesthetic puzzlement which is common to *The Waves* and serial music, we can ask whether Bernard when he begins section six with his Italian monologue is initiating a new series or ending the previous one; whether he is reacting to Percival's death or continuing (subsisting) in Percival's absence; whether, in fact, this most articulate of the six has overcome or been overcome by the sheer datum of the body's end. The narrative placement of his voyage to Rome imposes on the reader the same kind of casuistry he imposes upon himself in his crucial vision of the fin. And in forcing us to ask, with and about Bernard and his friends, Is there a story?—or, Does the form hold?— the book also forces us to question, again with Bernard, the subjectivity which is its own inmost structure.

All this, of course, depends upon Percival, the silent, physically impressive character whose nearly Sartrean role in *The Waves* is *to be present* and *to be seen* by the others. "But look," says Neville, seeing Percival in the school chapel, "he flicks his hand to the back of his neck. For such gestures one falls hopelessly in love for a lifetime" (p. 199). And the lonely Louis, in his vision of fields and grass and sky, sees that "Percival destroys it, as he blunders off, crushing the grasses, with the small fry trotting subservient after him. Yet it is Percival I need; for it is Percival who inspires poetry" (p. 202). As the figure who is, resplendently, *there,* both conscious and yet definitely the object of all the other consciousnesses in the book, Percival is necessarily the inspirer of poetry as transaction between the inner and outer worlds. He is also necessarily mute since the fullness of his presence in his own body is a plenum of self-consciousness which does not require the kind of speech the others constantly perform: their continual effort at pontification, or bridge-building between consciousness and experience.[12] Neville notes this essential "in-himselfness" of Percival at the crucial dinner party in section four of *The Waves.* "Without Percival," he says, "there is no solidity. We are silhouettes, hollow

---

[12] Sartre, in speaking of the incompatibility of conscious and "phenomenal" being, makes the following point:

> If we suppose an affirmative in which the affirmed comes to fulfill the affirming and is confused with it, this affirmation cannot be affirmed—owing to too much of plenitude and the immediate inherence of the noema in the noesis. It is there that we find being . . . in connection with consciousness. It is the noema in the noesis; that is, the inherence in itself without the least distance.

(*Being and Nothingness,* trans. Hazel Barnes [New York, 1966], p. lxv.) It can be readily seen how Percival in *The Waves,* as both "hero" of consciousness and full objective corporeality, is precisely this self-creating and therefore "silent" affirmation.

phantoms moving mistily without a background" (p. 259). And Bernard, least affected yet most perceptive about Percival, puts the matter in the precise terms, not only of the characters' experience but of the book's own highly self-conscious structure:

> "Here is Percival," said Bernard, "smoothing his hair, not from vanity (he does not look in the glass), but to propitiate the god of decency. He is conventional; he is a hero. The little boys trooped after him across the playing-fields. They blew their noses as he blew his nose, but unsuccessfully, for he is Percival. Now, when he is about to leave us, to go to India, all these trifles come together. He is a hero." (p. 260)

Much in the manner of the window-turned-mirror in the first chapter of *To the Lighthouse*, Percival by his presence organizes the other six into a "party" in the fourth section of *The Waves*, and again organizes them—this time by his absence—in the final gathering in section eight. For the unity he represents, the impossible—for the six and for the book itself—full transaction between subject and object, is a unity no less primary in its negation than in its assertion. Susan realizes this when she addresses the dead Percival: "You have gone across the court, further and further, drawing finer and finer the thread between us. But you exist somewhere. Something of you remains. A judge. That is, if I discover a new vein in myself I shall submit it to you privately. I shall ask, 'What is your verdict?' You shall remain the arbiter" (p. 283).

Percival is a "hero" of acclimatization, of that at-homeness in both the world of things and the world of self-awareness whose loss is the creative trauma of the Romantic imagination. He represents in his self-containment, his absolute visibility, the sense which the other characters can never quite attain or resign themselves to, the sense that "I am (rather than I have) this body" which implies that "I am of (as well as in) this world." Bernard's summing-up of the final gathering of the six at Hampton Court is, in this context, an immensely poignant coda to the book's career: "We saw for a moment laid out among us the body of the complete human being whom we have failed to be, but at the same time, cannot forget" (p. 369). For the body is at once the body of the dead Percival, impossible of attainment for these modern children, the stunted corpses of each one's potential self, and of course the shattered and diminishing continuity of the six sensibilities taken as a single *gestalt*.

That the six speaking characters do form a kind of *gestalt*, not only in their common relationship to Percival, but in their sustained effort to see clearly the world around them and each other, has long been a commonplace of commentary on *The Waves*. But we must not confuse the *gestalt*-narrative with either lyricism or allegory; we must not assume, with Jean Guiguet, that the monologues of *The Waves* are a sustained single voice only factitiously differentiated by character names,[13] or, with Dorothy Brewster, that the six characters are a code for different aspects of a single massive human personality. Both interpretations, which end by more or less totally "subjectivizing" the book, fail to take account of the range of complexity and phenomenological subtlety of the grouping of the six.

Perhaps the most useful commentary on the organization of *The Waves* is Virginia Woolf's brief sketch, "Evening Over Sussex: Reflections in a Motor Car," published posthumously in *The Death of the Moth*. In this remarkable performance, Virginia Woolf not only projects a set of six "personalities"—six separate yet complementary reactions to the world of things—but explicitly links them to the central Romantic and modern problem of breaking out of the subjective into a real resonance with the phenomenal: the selves are "six little pocket knives with which to cut up the body of a whale" (p. 8); and although she may not have had Melville in mind at the time, the "whale" involved is obviously of the same mysterious and absolute objectivity, terrible in its purity, as Moby Dick. Driving through Sussex at evening, when incipient darkness has obliterated all but the most permanent rock-face of the landscape, Virginia Woolf notes (again in noticeably Wordsworthian terms) that: "One is overcome by beauty extravagantly greater than one could expect . . . one's perceptions blow out rapidly like air balls expanded by some rush of air, and then, when all seems blown to its fullest and tautest, with beauty and beauty and beauty, a pin pricks; it collapses" (p. 7).

The pin prick, the sense of despair at the fecund exuberance of the world, introduces the first of the "selves": for "it was allied with the idea that one's nature demands mastery over all that it receives; and mastery here meant the power to convey . . . so that another person could share it" (p. 8). Such despair, however, generates the second self whose counsel is to "relinquish . . . be content . . . believe me when I tell you that it is best to sit and soak; to be passive; to accept . . ." (p. 8). As these two selves hold colloquy, a third self is detached, and observing the other two aloofly, reflects that: "While they are thus busied, I said to myself: Gone, gone; over, over; past and done with, past and done with. I feel life left behind even as the road is left behind. We have been over that stretch, and are already forgotten. . . . Others come behind us" (p. 9). The first three selves seem to have reached a point of exhaustion in each other's counsel and in the melancholy at imminent death which the third self articulates. But suddenly a fourth self, which "jumps upon one unawares . . . often disconnected with what has been happening," says, " 'Look at that.' It was a light; brilliant, freakish; inexplicable" (p. 9). It is a star; and as soon as the star is named as such, a new self attempts to find the "meaning" of the star in its prospects for human progress: "I think of Sussex in five hundred years to come. I think much grossness will have evaporated. Things will have been scorched up, eliminated. There will be magic gates. Draughts fan-blown by electric power will cleanse houses. Lights intense and firmly directed will go over the earth, doing the work" (p. 9).

With this, the sunset is complete, and a sixth self, presumably dormant all the time, arises to coordinate the other five:

> Now we have got to collect ourselves. . . . Now I, who preside over the company, am going to arrange in order the trophies which we have all brought in. Let me see; there was a great deal of beauty brought in today: farmhouses; cliffs standing out to sea; marbled fields; mottled fields; red feathered skies; all that. Also there was disappearance and the death of the individual. . . . Look, I will make a little figure for your satisfaction; here he comes. (p. 10)

The "bringing in" of beauty, with its homey touch of "bringing in" produce at the end of the day, strikes precisely the right note: for this extended *gestalt* activity of assimilation, energetic as it is, is still a kind of factitious "bringing in" whose origin is the insuperable otherness of the phenomenal and whose end-product is the deliberately ambiguous *placebo* of the "little figure." [14]

Working back from the sixth "self" of "Evening Over Sussex," it is a fairly simple matter to see in each of the selves a close parallel to the six speaking characters of *The Waves*. The sixth, making his little figure against the onset of night, is obviously very like Bernard, the inveterate phrasemaker who "sums up," or attempts to, in the last section of the novel. The fourth self, with its quick and inarticulate cry of "Look!" resembles Jinny, who says of herself, "Every time the door opens I cry 'More!' But my imagination is the bodies. I can imagine nothing beyond the circle cast by my body" (p. 264). And the fifth, who in reaction to the fourth attempts to describe and to project into the future the world of appearances, is like Louis, the man of business, ashamed of his past and his father, the banker in Brisbane, who imagines himself forging in iron rings the world to come. Rhoda, the most ethereal of the characters, for whom life is "the emerging monster" (p. 219) and whose career is a calculated disappearing act, is the full-blown version of the third self, in love with death and the approaching dark. The second self, with its counsel to resign and accept, is like the country-bred, self-contained Susan, probably the most chthonic of Virginia Woolf's characters. And the first self, whose

[14] Jean Piaget in Chapter One of *Play, Dreams and Imitation in Childhood* (New York, 1962) notes that the child's imitative accommodation *to* the external world arises from the growing impossibility of his assimilation *of* the external world; these are exactly the dichotomies of "Evening Over Sussex" and *The Waves*.

need to master and to articulate sets off the procession of the other selves, is like Neville, the poet and precisian whose terrible need for communication seems almost to skirt a desperate homosexuality.

But more important than these striking parallels of mood is the light thrown by "Evening Over Sussex" on the basic phenomenological impulse of *The Waves,* which, as I have tried to indicate, is a compelling effort to subvert the subjective or the comfortably "mystical." For as it is the discomfort—highly Wordsworthian or Shelleyan—of the first self at the *intransigence* of the non-human world which necessitates the procession of "selves," so Neville's crucial version in the first chapter of the man with his throat cut seems to "begin" the movement of the novel. The version must be quoted at length:

> His blood gurgled down the gutter. His jowl was white as a dead codfish. I shall call this structure, this rigidity, "death among the apple trees" for ever. There were the floating, pale-grey clouds; and the immitigable tree; the implacable tree with its greaved silver bark. The ripple of my life was unavailing. I was unable to pass by. There was an obstacle. "I cannot surmount this unintelligible obstacle," I said. And the others passed on. But we are doomed, all of us by the apple trees, by the immitigable tree which we cannot pass. (p. 191)

The tone of this passage is inescapably related to one of the most important apprehensions of things in the English language, Wordsworth's despairing sight of the *Intimations Ode:*

> —But there's a Tree, of many one,
> A single Field which I have looked upon,
> Both of them speak of something that is gone:
>   The Pansy at my feet
>   Doth the same tale repeat:
> Whither is fled the visionary gleam?
> Where is it now, the glory and the dream?   (ll. 51–57)

The doom is, of course, the doom of consciousness-in-the-body, the "dying animal" of Yeats or the "ghost in the machine" of Gilbert Ryle. And this is the essential context for the italicized passages describing the waves, the house, and the birds at the beginning of each chapter. For these passages are not simply, as Joan Bennett and others have described them, compelling prose-poems paralleling human life with the cycle of the day and of nature. They are, on the other hand, deliberate and highly effective attempts to present a phenomenal world without the intervention of human consciousness, a world of blind things which stands as a perpetual challenge to the attempts of the six monologists to seize, translate, and "realize" their world. And although full of lyrical and "anthropomorphic" metaphors, it is difficult not to see in these passages an anticipation of the concerns and predispositions of contemporary novelists like Alain Robbe-Grillet and Nathalie Sarraute:

> *The sun fell in sharp wedges inside the room. Whatever the light touched became dowered with a fanatical existence. A plate was like a white lake. A knife looked like a dagger of ice. Suddenly tumblers revealed themselves upheld by streaks of light. . . . The veins on the glaze of the china, the grain of the wood, the fibres of the matting became more and more finely engraved. Everything was without shadow.* (p. 251)

The sense of preternatural (or preconscious) clarity, the way in which the precision with which things appear actually jeopardizes their stability as "this" thing—everything Robbe-Grillet most desires for the so-called "new novel" is there, and profoundly assimilated to the central theme of *The Waves*. In fact, the obvious parallel between the "day" of these descriptions and the lives of the characters may well be quite too obvious. The connection is such a ready commonplace that the ease with which we adopt it may be a deliberately planted instance of our own willingness to assume an overeasy mastery of the universe of things. Certainly the very end of the book is disturbingly ambiguous: Bernard's final ecstatic resolve to assert the human, to fling himself, "unvanquished and unyielding" against death itself is followed by the chilling line: "*The waves broke on the shore*" (p. 383). To ask whether this is an affirmation or a denial of Bernard's resolve is nugatory: it is simply and sublimely irrelevant to Bernard, as Bernard to it, and therein lies its enormous power. For the "nature" of the italicized passages is neither the anthropomorphic and sympathetic nature of the pastoral nor its malevolent but equally anthropomorphic contrary in a view like Gloucester's: "As flies to wanton boys, are we to th' Gods;/ They kill us for their sport." It is rather the nature of sublime and self-sufficient *un*humanity which finds articulation in the dirge from *Cymbeline* (an important "hidden theme" for both *Mrs. Dalloway* and *The Waves*), in Shelley's confrontation with Mont Blanc, or in Sartre's conception of the forbidding and impenetrable *être en-soi*.

Each of the characters, in lifelong quest of a fully articulate existence, reflects in one way or another the inherent tension between the words of subjective consciousness and the irrecoverable otherness of both things and other people. Only Bernard, in a moment of vision near the end of his final summing-up, achieves a perception which "redeems" him and his five friends precisely by bringing the terms of their failure to full consciousness: "For one day as I leant over a gate that led into a field, the rhythm stopped: the rhymes and the hummings, the nonsense and the poetry. A space was cleared in my mind. I saw through the thick leaves of habit. Leaning over the gate I regretted so much litter, so much accomplishment and separation, for one cannot cross London to see a friend, life being so full of engagements" (p. 373). As the life of intrasubjectivity, "so full of engagements," grows finally to the proportions where it chokes off the possibility of even the most minimal actions, Bernard momentarily shunts off personality and sees "the world without a self":

> But how describe the world seen without a self? There are no words. Blue, red—even they distract, even they hide with thickness instead of letting the light through. How describe or say anything in articulate words again?—save that it fades, save that it undergoes a gradual transformation, becomes, even in the course of one short walk, habitual—this scene also. Blindness returns as one moves and one leaf repeats another. Loveliness returns. . . . But for a moment I had set on the turf somewhere high above the flow of the sea and the sounds of the woods, had seen the house, the garden, and the waves breaking. The old nurse who turns the pages of the picture-book had stopped and had said, "Look. This is the truth." (p. 376)[15]

It is a vision of absolute phenomenality, where "there are no words" or, in Bernard's earlier terms, "there is no story." [16] And as such it is not an absolutely beautiful vision, since "beauty" is a product of the affective consciousness.[17] "Loveliness" and "blindness" return together as the vision fades and becomes habitual—literally as it again becomes a vision subject to the *use* of language. But what is most startling about this passage is what Bernard does see in his moment of enlightenment. What "the old nurse" (who may very well be a reminiscence of the foster-mother Nature of the *Intimations Ode*) *shows* Bernard is precisely the world of the italicized chapter-heads, "the house, the garden, and the waves breaking"—precisely, that is, the world of unobserved, nonconscious things in the full ambivalence of its relationship to the characters of *The Waves* so that in a moment of almost perfect representative form, Bernard simultaneously breaks out of subjectivity into a phenomenological perception, and breaks into *The Waves* in its inmost narrative structure. Her lyrical tough-mindedness will not allow Virginia Woolf to take the way either of aestheticism or of "objectivism," but insists even here that narrative form and form-

[15] Interestingly, one anticipation of this oceanic world-without-human-consciousness may well be the last vision of the Time Traveller, of the final disappearance of man eons in the future, in H. G. Wells' *The Time Machine*.

[16] One of the earliest essays on *The Waves* is that of Floris Delattre, *Le roman psychologique de Virginia Woolf* (Paris, 1932), containing the following comment:

> The successive monologues are long asides which the actors pronounce before the stage-set, without distinguishing themselves from each other, and in which we see only far-off reflections of the drama playing itself out. (p. 199, my translation)

It is interesting to compare this with Robbe-Grillet's ideas of eliminating "the illusion of depth" from the novel in *For a New Novel* (New York, 1965).

[17] This is much like the purely "phenomenal" and hence terrifying vision of the Marabar Caves in *A Passage to India*.

less world mutually condition each other. The way out and the way in, like the way up and the way down, are one and the same.

Finally, what *The Waves* gives us is something very like the world of Jorge Luis Borges' fable, "Tlön, Uqbar, Orbis Tertius," where an attempt to project a fictive, totally Berkeleyan and subjective world ends by taking over and transforming the "real" world. Virginia Woolf's mystical and eyeless book achieves a subjectivity so total and so self-conscious that it finally becomes a radical criticism of "mysticism" and of the subjective eye itself in the face of sheer phenomenalism. It is a kind of Hegelian paradox of "purity" whereby the subjective carries itself through a mirror reversal, entering a new and strange style of the insuperably nonhuman and "other":

> People go on passing; they go on passing against the spires of the church and the plates of ham sandwiches. The streamers of my consciousness waver out and are perpetually torn and distressed by their disorder. I cannot therefore concentrate on my dinner. "I would take a tenner. The case is handsome; but it blocks up the hall." They dive and plunge like guillemots whose feathers are slippery with oil. (*The Waves*, p. 240)

> Soon unfortunately time will no longer be master. Wrapped in their aura of doubt and error, this day's events, however insignificant they may be, will in a few seconds begin their task, gradually encroaching upon the ideal order, cunningly introducing an occasional inversion, a discrepancy, a confusion, a warp, in order to accomplish their work: a day in early winter without plan, without direction, incomprehensible and monstrous.[18]

The first passage is Louis's monologue in a London restaurant; the second is Robbe-Grillet's description of a day in a French café. The remarkable resemblance between these passages, from novels normally assumed to represent polar schools of contemporary literature,[19] is an index not only of the substantiality of a "modern tradition" of narrative but also of the profound contemporaneity of Virginia Woolf's greatest novel. Far from being the *sui generis* masterpiece of a hyper-aesthetic "lady novelist," *The Waves* is a tough-minded and sobering examination of the chances for the shaping intellect to shape meaningfully at all. And far from being a "dead end" for fiction,[20] it is a novel whose penetration to the roots of a distinctly modern and crucially humanistic problem is human and humanizing as few other books can claim to be.

[18] Alain Robbe-Grillet, *The Erasers*, trans. Richard Howard (New York, 1964), p. 7.

[19] See R. M. Adams, "Down Among the Phenomena," *Hudson Review*, XX (1967), 255–267.

[20] See Arthur Koestler, "The Novelist's Temptations," in *The Yogi and the Commissar* (London, 1965); and John Edward Hardy, *Man in the Modern Novel* (New York, 1966).

The Vision Falters:
The Years, 1937

by Josephine O'Brien Schaefer

The Years marks an unmistakable break in Virginia Woolf's novels. Although the threefold reality of social conventions, natural phenomena, and individual experience remains, Virginia Woolf quite consciously moves away from the inner life that chiefly concerned her in *The Waves*.[1] She felt that in *The Waves* she had slighted the conventional pattern of human existence, the dull routine of ten to six that continues in spite of the advance of the seasons and the tides, in spite of the secret life, the subjective communings of a Rhoda or a Bernard.[2] *The Waves* treats the surface texture of experience as merely a means of getting at the emotions and thoughts, the inner life, it initiates.[3] What Louis sees from the restaurant window, what Jinny sees in a London ballroom exist only in terms of Louis and Jinny as perceivers, not in terms of any larger, more objective reality.

Yet of all English novelists, Virginia Woolf is, perhaps, the least apt to relegate the outer world to such indirect importance. The surface of things is a source of delight to her.[4] The shop windows on Bond Street, beef and wine sauce steaming in a casserole, fresh print on the white sheets of a newspaper, a deserted street late at night, are all immensely enjoyable in their own right. But this world of phenomena, what is "observed and collected," "things seen," "the external," was not given proper notice and proportion in *The Waves*.[5] At least, so Virginia Woolf thought as she turned from that novel to *The Years*.

"The Vision Falters: *The Years*, 1937" by Josephine O'Brien Schaefer. From *The Three-Fold Nature of Reality in the Novels of Virginia Woolf*, Studies in English Literature, no. 7 (The Hague: Mouton & Co. n.v., Publishers, 1966), pp. 167–85. Reprinted by permission of the author.

[1] Cf. Roger Fry's discussion of the need for experiment in art, the danger of a "strong personal rhythm" (*Reflections on British Painting*, p. 77).

[2] *A Writer's Diary*, October 16, 1935.

[3] See Joan Bennett, *Virginia Woolf*, p. 123.

[4] Cf. Virginia Woolf's comment in a review of *An Apology for Old Maids*, "The best artistic work is done by people who mix easily with their fellows" (*TLS.*, February 8, 1917, p. 67).

[5] *A Writer's Diary*, December 19, 1932.

As she began working on her new novel in 1932, she felt exultantly surprised by the rich residue life had deposited inside her, marvelling at the rush and tumble of memories and observations that continually heaped themselves up as new material for the day's writing.[6] But the old commitment made itself felt again. Much as she respected the world of objects and bare events, she soon began to note in her diary how difficult it was to resist the tug to "vision." [7] What she means by "vision" Virginia Woolf never adequately explained, but it seems to refer to the submerged side of reality, to the poetry rather than the facts of existence.[8] E. M. Forster, in discussing the unique qualities of Virginia Woolf as a writer, describes her as beginning with the poetry:

> Holding on with one hand to poetry, she stretches and stretches to grasp things which are best gained by letting go of poetry. She would not let go, and I think she was quite right, though critics who like a novel to be a novel will disagree.[9]

This is certainly her technique in *Jacob's Room, Mrs. Dalloway, To the Lighthouse* and *The Waves.* But in *The Years,* as earlier in *Night and Day,* Virginia Woolf let go of poetry.[10] Moving from the topography of the inner life back to the local geography of social situation, she was finally returning to the challenge she had incompletely met in *Night and Day.*[11] She did not, however, intend to abandon "vision" entirely.[12] As she writes in her diary, "I want to give the whole of the present society—nothing less: facts as well as the vision. And to combine them both. I mean, *The Waves* going on simultaneously with *Night and Day.*" [13]

Unfortunately *The Years* fails to achieve that goal.[14] Granville Hicks' remark that Virginia Woolf talks here very brilliantly about the weather is perhaps unfair, but it reflects an actual weakness in the novel.[15] Only the world of nature has the ring of authenticity. Rain, wind, snow, sun are described with the same accuracy and richness

[6] *Ibid.*

[7] *Ibid.,* November 2, 1932.

[8] Cf. Karin Stephen's use of the word "facts" to mean "the external object," "sense data," "phenomena" (*The Misuse of Mind,* p. 20).

[9] "Virginia Woolf," *Two Cheers for Democracy,* p. 258.

[10] *The Years* and *Night and Day* are the only novels by Virginia Woolf in which one does not hear the sound of the sea. The poetry of life was always connected with the summer days of her childhood spent in Cornwall.

[11] *A Writer's Diary,* November 2, 1932.

[12] In writing the final section to the novel, she wonders "how to make the transition from the colloquial to the lyrical, from the particular to the general?" (*Ibid.,* August 7, 1934).

[13] *Ibid.,* April 25, 1933.

[14] See, however, James Hafley's praise of this book as "the most persuasive of Virginia Woolf's novels" (*The Glass Roof,* pp. 132–39).

[15] "Weather Report," *New Republic,* April 28, 1937, p. 363.

that make the italicized portions of *The Waves* and the middle section of *To the Lighthouse* so remarkable. The facts of the season and the weather with which she begins each "chapter," each year, *are* facts, perhaps the most prosaic in man's existence, yet they carry a weight of associations with history and place that makes them immensely significant and highly evocative:

> It was a summer evening; the sun was setting; the sky was blue still, but tinged with gold, as if a thin veil of gauze hung over it, and here and there in the gold-blue amplitude an island of cloud lay suspended. In the fields the trees stood majestically caparisoned, with their innumerable leaves gilt. Sheep and cows, pearl white and particolored, lay recumbent or munched their way through the half transparent grass. An edge of light surrounded everything. A red-gold fume rose from the dust on the roads. Even the little red brick villas on the high roads had become porous, incandescent with light, and the flowers in cottage gardens, lilac and pink like cotton dresses, shone veined as if lit from within. Faces of people standing at cottage doors or padding along pavements showed the same red glow as they fronted the slowly sinking sun. (329)

This mingling of the transitory and the eternal, this constant motion and the suspended stillness are almost a hallmark of Virginia Woolf.

These "facts," however, are not the ones Virginia Woolf had ignored in *The Waves* where references to the natural world abound. What is unrepresented, what is lacking (despite Louis, the man of business) in that novel is the conventional world of men, the "march of events." [16] In contrast *The Years* presents a chronicle of the Pargiter family from 1880 to 1936 which is replete with "facts": the details of traffic in High Street, a court in session, an evening of cards. When she describes these facts, Virginia Woolf avoids that heaviness, that repetition and redundancy which mar *Night and Day*. Never bogged down by the events, the reader fairly skims along the chronological "plot" line as the years come and go for different members of the Pargiter family.

The novel opens in the spring of 1880 as the Pargiter family—the Colonel, Eleanor, Milly, Delia, Martin, and Rose—and their servant Crosby await the death of Mrs. Pargiter. Another son, Edward, is away at college; still another, Morris, is studying law. The mother has been ill a long time and is perversely slow in dying. At the end of the chapter, she dies. Virginia Woolf then moves on to 1891, supplying a panorama of England in the fall, with a description of the doings of the now scattered members of the family. Kitty, the cousin Edward loved but did not marry, is now living in the north of England as Lady Lasswade; Milly is married and living in Devonshire; Edward is a don at Oxford; Morris is a married man and a barrister; Delia has taken political causes to heart and is working for Irish independ-

[16] *A Writer's Diary*, April 25, 1933.

ence; Eleanor lives on with her old father, doing committee work to improve the plight of the poor. On the occasion of his niece Maggie's birthday, the central incident in this chapter, Colonel Pargiter visits his sister-in-law Eugenie and his brother Digby. In the summer of 1907 Maggie goes to a party while her crippled sister, Sara, remains at home in bed. In 1908 it is spring; Digby is dead, and Rose and Martin visit the family home again where old Crosby, grown slower and weaker, and the efficient Eleanor look after the now sluggish and gloomy Colonel. In the spring of 1910 Rose visits her cousins Maggie and Sara in their run-down apartment on the south side of the river. She takes Sara with her to one of Eleanor's committee meetings. Kitty, who is there also, goes on to the opera afterwards. In the summer of 1911 Eleanor returns to England from a trip to Greece and Spain. She visits her brother Morris and enjoys her young niece Peggy and her nephew North. The winter of 1913 brings the sale of the dead Colonel's home and the end of Crosby's many years of service for the Pargiters. The spring of 1914 finds Martin lunching with his cousin Sara, talking about Rose's imprisonment for her woman's suffrage work. They then go to the park to meet Maggie, who has married a Frenchman and is minding the baby in his pram. Martin then goes to a party at Kitty's in the evening. Kitty rushes off to the country by night train after her party. In 1917 we meet a new character, Nicholas, the homosexual friend of Maggie's husband Renny. Eleanor and Sara join them for dinner at Renny's and talk through an air raid. In the winter of 1918 Crosby mutters to herself on the street as the war ends. Virginia Woolf then ends her year chapters and turns to the "Present Day." Some of the incidents are very well drawn, but they fall short of the vivid representation of the surface look of things in Mann's *Buddenbrooks,* Butler's *Way of All Flesh,* Galsworthy's *Forsythe Saga* or even Bennett's *Old Wives' Tale.*[17]

But Virginia Woolf was not attempting to imitate, to fall back on the Bennett-Galsworthy tradition which she had once parodied.[18] Between *To the Lighthouse* and *The Waves,* in 1928, Virginia Woolf had begun as a joke and completed in earnest one of her most delightful books. *Orlando,* that fantastic biography of the Sackville-West family which yet manages to be a history of English literature and society, convinced her that she could contribute an entirely new sort of family chronicle. She writes in her diary that *The Years,* which she first thought of as *The Pargiters,*

> releases such a torrent of fact as I did not know I had in me. . . . What I must do is to keep control; and not be too sarcastic; and keep the right degree of freedom and reserve. But oh how easy this writing is compared

[17] She notes that she wants to give "ordinary waking Arnold Bennett life the form of art" (*A Writer's Diary,* May 31, 1933).

[18] See "Mr. Bennett and Mrs. Brown," *The Captain's Death Bed,* pp. 90–111.

with *The Waves!* I wonder what the degree of carat-gold is in the two books. Of course this is external: but there's a good deal of gold—more than I'd thought—in externality. Anyhow, "What care I for my goose feather bed? I'm off to join the raggle taggle gipsies oh!" The gipsies, I say: not Hugh Walpole and Priestley—no. In truth *The Pargiters* is first cousin to *Orlando,* though the cousin is the flesh: *Orlando* taught me the trick of it.[19]

In *Orlando* Virginia Woolf makes facts caper and cavort as they never had before. History gives her book an undeniable shape as it progresses from the 16th century to the 17th to the 18th and on to the 20th. The personal voice of Virginia Woolf, the voice of *The Common Reader* and her journals, creates a unity that holds the whole together, gives to Orlando whatever reality that figure has. But Orlando's reality is not the important thing. The ice floating on the Thames, the peacocks in the garden, the damp of the nineteenth century constitute the fantastic reality of *Orlando.* The verve, the vigor, the charm of the book spring from Virginia Woolf's own peculiar awareness of the vitality of objects. The tables and chairs, the oak tree, certainly the great house at Knole, become the characters of *Orlando.* Physical "facts" seen in this light, vividly real and living, yet vaguely nightmarish in their animated existence, are Virginia Woolf's kind of "facts." She takes on a swashbuckling attitude toward this world, as well she might, since it is largely her own creation. No one could see Priestley or Walpole as the forerunners of *Orlando.* The mind has turned gipsy and the historical and literary world dances at its command. True, there are chairs at Knole and London did have a great frost in the 16th century—but never such chairs as these! Never such a frost!

This freedom to make facts, things observed, immensely suggestive was what *Orlando* had taught Virginia Woolf. If she could handle fictive facts with this same ease, she could make *The Years* a new sort of novel, an essay-novel. Just as *Orlando* capaciously held Virginia Woolf's many ideas about history and literature, *The Years* would

> take in everything, sex, education, life, etc.; and come with the most powerful and agile leap, like a chamois across precipices from 1880 to here and now.[20]

Such an endeavor would require tremendous resilience. But the gusto and humor that enlivened *Orlando* and might have sustained the prosaic material of *The Years* are not present. Some of the life of the facts went out of them when they changed their abode. In *Orlando* the rich associations of history make almost all the objects and places mentioned—the signet ring of Queen Elisabeth, the coffee houses fre-

[19] *A Writer's Diary,* December 19, 1932.
[20] *Ibid.,* November 2, 1932.

quented by Pope and Addison—a signal to which the reader's imagination and memory immediately respond. The more he knows of English literature and history, the more the reader enjoys *Orlando.* In *The Years,* however, the old walrus brush that Eleanor claims will outlast them all hasn't that power. Perhaps Bernard Blackstone hit it right: "The masculine world is a pasteboard construction surrounding the feminine world in which the author is really interested." [21] Unfortunately since the "facts" of *The Years* come out of that masculine world, they simply cannot perform the suggestive task Virginia Woolf requires of them.

The sense of vitality and fruitfulness that Virginia Woolf thought was the peculiarity of her family chronicle is certainly not to be found in an impartial examination of the incidents.[22] Individual scenes are sometimes vivid and real but the over-all impression is one of drabness, and futility. From the opening chapter in which Colonel Pargiter visits his slatternly mistress, finds her in pin curlers, and examines her dog's ears for eczema until the final chapter in which people fall asleep, mutter, annoy others at a very lonely, "fagged out" party, the reader is oppressed by the mediocrity and dullness of this world.[23] Fires are always going out, kettles won't boil, people can't talk to each other. Childhood is a period of constraint, of tortured waiting, of unknown terror. Old age is full of a whining imperiousness. Old servants must wash bathtubs with blobs of spittle on the rim; waiters try to cheat steady customers of a few shillings. Even Leonard Woolf, her most sympathetic reader, speaks of the sadness in this novel.[24]

Perhaps one of the reasons Virginia Woolf thought *The Years* so lively is that it is full of *her* life. More of the material from the *Writer's Diary* finds its way into *The Years* than into any other of her novels. The memory of her own response to her mother's death, for example, forms the basis of the scene centering around the death of Mrs. Pargiter.

> Remember turning aside at mother's bed, when she had died, and Stella took us in, to laugh, secretly, at the nurse crying. She's pretending, I said, aged 13, and was afraid I was not feeling enough.[25]

Delia, too, notes the crying nurse and feels her father's tears are part of a hypocritical performance (48–49). At the grave she tries desperately to "feel" something.

Similarly the scene of Eleanor's visit to old Mrs. Potter (105) cor-

[21] *Virginia Woolf,* p. 202.

[22] *A Writer's Diary,* December 29, 1935.

[23] See Joseph Warren Beach, "Virginia Woolf," *English Journal,* XXVI (October, 1937), 611.

[24] *A Writer's Diary,* November 4, 1926. Leonard Woolf had also spoken of the sadness in *Night and Day:* see March 27, 1919.

[25] *Ibid.,* September 12, 1934. Cf. this guilty feeling for not feeling with the failure of Septimus to feel in *Mrs. Dalloway.*

responds in physical detail and sentiment to Virginia Woolf's description of a similar visit to take plums to old Mrs. Grey:

> She is shrunk and sits on a hard chair in the corner. The door open. She twitches and trembles. Has the wild expressionless stare of the old. L. liked her despair: "I crawls up to bed hoping for the day; and I crawls down hoping for the night. I'm an ignorant old woman—can't write or read. But I prays to God every night to take me—to go to my rest. Nobody can say what pains I suffer. Feel my shoulder," and she began shuffling with a safety pin. I felt it. . . . She repeated her misery, her list of ills, over and over; could see nothing else; could only begin all over again; and kissed my hand, thanking us for our pound. This is what we make of our lives—no reading or writing—keep her alive with * doctors when she wishes to die. Human ingenuity in torture is very great.[26]

Moreover, the schoolgirl crush that Kitty has for Lucy Craddock, her history teacher, the inarticulateness of Miss Craddock, Kitty's feelings of love and admiration, the aura of romance that surrounds even the oilcloth of the stairs that lead Kitty to Lucy's room (67–70) have their counterpart in Virginia Woolf's life. As she is preparing an obituary for Janet Case, her Greek teacher, Virginia Woolf notes,

> . . . she was oddly inarticulate. No hand for words. Her letters, save that the last began "My beloved Virginia," always cool and casual. And how I loved her, at Hyde Park Gate: and how I went hot and cold going to Windmill Hill: and how great a visionary part she has played in my life, till the visionary became a part of the fictitious, not of the real life.[27]

Even some very small details come directly out of Virginia Woolf's life. The feeling that one is the youngest person on a bus (a feeling repeated in the novel) is ascribed by Virginia Woolf in her diary to her sister Vanessa.[28] And the lovely white owl that Eleanor and Peggy see circling in a twilight sky owes its existence to an actual experience recorded in her diaries.[29]

Because the book is so full of her own life, Virginia Woolf has perhaps claimed for the novel qualities that are not there. The reader actually feels surrounded by a kind of emotional poverty in *The Years*.[30] And this too, remarkably enough, is autobiographical. In con-

---

[26] *Ibid.*, August 20, 1932. (The asterisk indicates an illegible word.)

[27] *Ibid.*, July 19, 1937.

[28] *Ibid.*, January 13, 1932.

[29] *Ibid.*, August 17, 1932.

[30] Irma Rantavaara thinks that this bleakness is only in the daughters' lives, that "The theme of *A Room of One's Own* and *Three Guineas* is woven into the novel. The Pargiter girls are in the position of the ordinary Victorian middle-class daughters: unless they marry, there is not much they can do except private charity work, or else they have to enter the camp of the rebels" (*Virginia Woolf and Bloomsbury*, p. 156). But this does not account for the drabness of Nicholas' life, North's feeling

nection with Roger Fry's death in September of 1934 Virginia Woolf notes, "I think the poverty of life now is what comes to me; and this blackish veil over everything. Hot weather; a wind blowing. The substance gone out of everything." [31] The years 1932–34 were full of death for Virginia Woolf.[32] At least three of her friends died in 1932: Lytton Strachey,[33] Dora Carrington, G. Lowes Dickinson. Her fellow writers, those she had opposed all these years, were also dying: Arnold Bennett had died in 1931; Galsworthy in 1933. A much younger writer, Stella Benson, also died in 1933. Reading the notice of her death on a news placard, Virginia Woolf thinks:

> A curious feeling, when a writer like S. B. dies, that one's response is diminished: *Here and Now* won't be lit up by her: it's life lessened. My effusion—what I send out—less porous and radiant—as if the thinking stuff were a web that were fertilized only by other people's (her that is) thinking it too: now lacks life.[34]

With Roger Fry's death Virginia Woolf experienced an even greater loss: ". . . his death is worse than Lytton's. Why I wonder? Such a blank wall. Such a silence: such a poverty. How he reverberated!" [35] As another friend, Francis Birrell, begins the unsuccessful fight for his life at the end of that year, Virginia Woolf thinks: "But I can't feel any more at the moment—not after Roger. I cannot go through that again." [36] But, of course, she does.[37]

These deaths and the sense of impoverishment they created in Virginia Woolf seem to cast a shadow over *The Years*. Death punctuates the novel. Almost every chapter up to 1914 can be remembered in terms of who died that year: 1880, Mrs. Pargiter finally dies; 1891, Parnell dies; 1908, Eugenie and Digby die; 1910, the King dies; 1911, Abel Pargiter dies; 1913, Crosby's dog, her last tie with her old life as a servant in the Pargiter home, dies. The years that follow 1913 lead to the Great War, to the destruction of a generation. After that, of course, the whole world is different. The entire social structure, the values, standards, conventions have altered. In a very real sense, a world has died.

---

of abortiveness in human relations, or Abel Pargiter's loneliness and inability to communicate. Bleakness also surrounds the masculine world.

[31] *A Writer's Diary*, September 12, 1934.

[32] In 1932 Virginia Woolf visited Greece again. She had visited it first with her brother Thoby in 1905. As a result of that trip, Thoby caught typhoid fever and died. See Aileen Pippett, *The Moth and the Star*, p. 53.

[33] Virginia Woolf wrote of Lytton Strachey to Vita Sackville-West in January, 1932, "I should mind it to the end of my days if he died." Quoted in Aileen Pippett, *The Moth and the Star*, p. 322. In her diary, Virginia Woolf speaks of "a longing to speak to him; all that cut away, gone . . ." (May 25, 1932).

[34] *A Writer's Diary*, December 7, 1933.

[35] *Ibid.*, October 16, 1934.

[36] *Ibid.*, December 2, 1934.

[37] *Ibid.*, December 2, December 18, December 30, 1934, and January 19, 1935.

The next generation, the adults of the "Present Day" who were the children of 1911, have crossed a frontier they can never recross. A lack of reticence, the freedom to speak of homosexuality and sanitary napkins are only superficial signs of the emergence of a new world, the death of an old. Eleanor's niece, Peggy, now a young doctor, perceives the profundity of the change as she comments on Eleanor's tearing a newspaper carrying the picture of Mussolini.

> . . . when Eleanor, who used English so reticently, said "damned" and then "bully," it meant much more than the words she and her friends used. And her gesture, tearing the paper. . . . So she had seen her father crumple *The Times* and sit trembling with rage because somebody had said something in a newspaper. How odd!
>
> And the way she tore it! she thought, half laughing, and she flung out her hand as Eleanor had flung hers. Eleanor's figure still seemed erect with indignation. It would be simple, she thought, it would be satisfactory, she thought, following her down flight after flight of stone steps, to be like that. (356)

The world of such integrated beings, people who could express by a physical response their personal indignation with a public fact conveyed through an impersonal form of communication, no longer exists. If the first part of the novel reiterates the fact of personal death, the last part plays upon the anonymous demise of an age.

The death of the individual, however, is not a forgotten theme. Physical extinction is not the only form of death; by changing man dies, by not changing he dies. North and Peggy who were so close in childhood find only hostility and distance in their adult relations with each other. The children they were have not flowered into the the adults they are; those childish figures died as quite different adults were born from the old selves. After reverting to childhood memories, Peggy and North stand silent, unable to carry the old selves into the present. It is now a source of amazement to North to remember "he used to read her his poetry in the apple-loft" (426).

Though this death by change can be painful to behold, the death that results from an inability to change is much commoner, more deplorable. Nicholas reappears in "Present Day" still talking, this time to North, of "dictators; Napoleon; the psychology of great men." His mind seems to have atrophied at some point in 1917. Rose and Martin reveal a similar stagnation as they banter each other for the hundredth time about their childhood experiences. Their repetitions lead Peggy to think:

> Each person had a certain line laid down in their minds . . . and along it came the same old sayings. One's mind must be crisscrossed like the palm of her hand. (386)

This substitution of another kind of death for the literal ones in the first portion reflects Virginia Woolf's over-all intention. She speaks of *The Years* as composed of two parts: the first portion of the book is narrative; the second is the submerged side of the narrative.[38] Thus the literal fact of personal death carries the submerged implication of a more symbolic, more general death. Similarly the deformities of the first part, Abel Partiger's hand with its two missing fingers, Sara's one shoulder slightly higher than the other, become mental and emotional deformities. "I" and "my" are the deformed hand and the contorted shoulder of the second part of *The Years.* The physical deformities were on the surface, easily discernible, limited to a few characters. The "I" and "my" deformity issues from each self-enclosed mind. North records a conversation between his Aunt Milly and cousin Maggie:

> *my* boy—*my* girl . . . they were saying. But they're not interested in other people's children, he observed. Only in their own; their own property; their own flesh and blood, which they would protect with the unsheathed claws of the primeval swamp, he thought looking at Milly's fat little paws, even Maggie, even she. For she too was talking about my boy, my girl. How then can we be civilized, he asked himself? (407–08)

Later North again looks at Maggie's hands.

> They were strong hands; fine hands; but if it were a question, he thought, watching the fingers curl slightly of "my" children, of "my" possessions, it would be one rip down the belly; or teeth in the soft fur of the throat. We cannot help each other, he thought, we are all deformed. (409–10)

This sort of deformity is not limited to a Sara or an Abel; it is a universal deformity.

Like death and deformity which are first presented as facts of individual occurrence and later transformed into themes of universal significance, communication in the first part of *The Years* takes the shape of abortive attempts of individuals to speak to one another, and in the second part of the failure of formal speeches to get themselves said, of songs to make themselves understood. If communication fails on the personal level in part one, it fails on the public level in part two. Abel and his daughter Eleanor live together silently, never speaking to each other of their thoughts and feelings. In 1891 Abel realized he could not tell Eleanor about himself, for she has "her own affairs to think about" (110). The years 1907, 1908, 1910 pass and still nothing gets said to his daughter. When he visits his sister-in-law Eugenie, he wants to talk about his mistress, but again he fails. "He went downstairs rather slowly. He felt depressed and disappointed. He had not seen her alone; he had not told her anything. Perhaps he never would tell anybody anything" (136). Maggie and Rose, Kitty and Eleanor similarly experience this lack of communication, this silence instead of

[38] *Ibid.,* May 22, 1934.

talk when for them talk is "the only way we have of knowing each other" (184).

In the second part of the novel Nicholas tries again and again to deliver a speech to express the general appreciation of the guests at the party. The speech is never given. It is interrupted so often that Nicholas finally abandons the attempt altogether. The only formal public performance is given by a group of children who sing:

> Etho passo tanno hai
> Fai donk to tu do,
> Mai to, kai to, lai to see
> Toh dom to tuh do—(463)

The words and tune remain unrecognizable to the guests. "There was something horrible in the noise they made. It was so shrill, so discordant, and so meaningless" (464). What was an individual inadequacy in part one has become a common inadequacy in part two.

The relation between the narrative and the submerged reflection of the narrative takes still another form. In her diary Virginia Woolf refers to the narrative section as "upper air scenes." [39] The things which happen in these upper air scenes of the first part of the novel, people remember in the second half. Thus experience and memory, as well as literal and symbolic death and deformity, and the particular and universal inability to communicate, are really two aspects of the same thing: the fact and the vision.

By making certain events which occur in the children's lives in the first part of the book recur in their imaginations in the later section, Virginia Woolf is returning to a technique she had used brilliantly in *Jacob's Room.* Although she discarded it for a more immediate description of the coexistence of past and present in *Mrs. Dalloway,* she now resumes the longer formula. For example, Rose's visit to Lamley's shop, her first experience with real danger and evil, serves as an incident in the early part of the novel. The ugly face, the menacing sexuality of the man who emerges from the darkness, linger in the child's memory and emerge in Rose's mature mind. Similarly the moment when the vivacious Eugenie dances in Sara's bedroom to the delight of her daughters is revived when Sara speaks of it later; and the name Antigone in the second part of the novel sets off a series of associations that recall an important evening in Sara's early girlhood. The kettle that won't boil, the flowers hardly discernible in a painting under its accumulation of dust, two figures stepping out of a cab in the house across from the Pargiters', the Oxford boy with chips in his hair, the owl flying in the summer sky—all are first introduced as facts in the

---

[39] *Ibid.,* October 16, 1935. Elsewhere, she calls the narrative the representational part of the novel (September 30, 1934).

narrative and later rise up out of the memory of Eleanor, Sara, Martin, Kitty.

This rebirth of experience after years of submerged existence should expand and deepen the present. The whole last section, "Present Day," is a single evening which should form a sonorous vault that echoes and reechoes with the past.[40] The present has distilled the past until only the essence of all those years from 1880 to 1926 remains. But the essence of those years is never made clear to the reader. When Eleanor is asked to talk about her life, a period that encompasses the years of the novel, she finds that she has only the present moment (395). Looking for a pattern, she finds none (398). Eleanor's inability to find a pattern reflects Virginia Woolf's aesthetic complacency in making "Present Day" a series of echoes that have no significance beyond the fact that they refer back to the years preceding the evening of the party. Like Eleanor the reader wonders, "Does everything then come over again a little differently?" (398).[41]

If this last chapter fails to make the book meaningful, then Virginia Woolf has failed to do what the reader has every right to expect her to do: give the vision that the facts support. She notes in her diary:

> The last chapters must be so rich, so resuming, so weaving together that I can only go on by letting my mind brood every morning on the whole book. There's no longer any need to forge ahead, as the narrative part is over. What I want is to enrich and stabilize. This last chapter must equal in length and importance and volume the first book: and must in fact give the other side, the submerged side of that. I shan't I think, re-read; I shall summon it back—the tea-party, the death, Oxford and so on, from my memory. And as the whole book depends on bringing this off, I must be very leisurely and patient . . .[42]

The moment of Peter Walsh's apprehension of Clarissa in *Mrs. Dalloway,* the great dinner of *To the Lighthouse,* the grand soliloquy that closes *The Waves* all were the sort of moments that Virginia Woolf seems to be describing in the diary. But the stabilizing aim is never achieved in *The Years.* Instead of enrichment, there is almost a parody, a belittlement of the great moments of stasis in her preceding novels. Like Peter Walsh in *Mrs. Dalloway,* North in *The Years* goes to a party after his years away from England in India. At that party he finds instead of Clarissa's carefully selected group, a motley assembly, an unblendable assortment of people whose angles and humors hurt and

---

[40] Compare "Time Remembered," the last book of Marcel Proust's *Remembrance of Things Past.*

[41] Virginia Woolf declares, "I want to keep the individual and the sense of things coming over and over again and yet changing. That's what's so difficult, to combine the two" (*A Writer's Diary,* November 21, 1935).

[42] *Ibid.,* May 22, 1934.

annoy each other.[43] Delia looks at her guests and delights in their
variety.

> All sorts of people were there, she noted. That had always been her aim;
> to mix people; to do away with the absurd conventions of English life.
> And she had done it tonight, she thought. There were nobles and com-
> moners; people dressed and people not dressed; people drinking out of
> mugs, and people waiting with their soup getting cold for a spoon to be
> brought to them. (429–30)

The party lacks not only shape but content. Whereas Mrs. Dalloway's
party gave Peter Walsh that moment of joy in which he felt the presence of Clarissa, North unsuccessfully seeks in the party a moment
with his cousin Maggie. The party so completely fails to give him any
individual sense of Maggie that he ends by feeling that she is like all
the other domestic animals in the room.

The fullest failure of human relations, however, comes in the scene
that parodies the lit-up dinner of *To the Lighthouse*. North goes to
dinner with Sara before attending the party. The underdone mutton
trickling red juice (392), the cabbage oozing green water (393), the fly-
blown fruit bring to mind the steaming casserole at Mrs. Ramsay's table,
the succulent pieces she fishes out for her guests, the beautiful bowl of
fruit so harmoniously arranged that it is a delight to look at. The two
lonely figures of Sara and North seated before that dismal meal in the
ugly surroundings seem a monstrous parody of the family and friends
gathered in the pleasant and communal setting of the Ramsay dining
room. E. M. Forster, in analysing the importance of the goodness, the
deliciousness of that dinner in *To the Lighthouse*, has, as it were, indicated the sense of human emptiness the contrasting meal in *The Years*
must convey. He refers to

> the great dish of Boeuf en Daube which forms the centre of the dinner of
> union in *To the Lighthouse*, the dinner round which all that section of
> the book coheres, the dinner which exhales affection and poetry and love-
> liness, so that all the characters see the best in one another at last and
> for a moment, and one of them, Lily Briscoe, carries away a recollection
> of reality. Such a dinner cannot be built on a statement beneath a dish-
> cover which the novelist is too indifferent or incompetent to remove.
> Real food is necessary and this . . . she knew how to provide. The
> Boeuf en Daube, which had taken the cook three days to make and had
> worried Mrs. Ramsay as she did her hair, stands before us with its con-
> fusion of savoury brown and yellow meats and its bay leaves and its wine;
> we peer down the shining walls of the great casserole and get one of the

---

[43] William Troy remarks in this connection, ". . . no expansion of scale, no experimentation with method can lend meaning and significance where neither is
implicit in the experience" ("Variations on a Theme," *Nation*, CXLIV [April 24,
1937], 474).

best bits, and like Wm. Bankes, generally so hard to please, we are satisfied.[44]

The final contrast, between the abortiveness of all attempts to sum things up in *The Years* and Bernard's full soliloquy in *The Waves,* seems to grow naturally out of the differences in these two scenes. *The Waves* ends on a note of struggle, a resumption of the old hostility between man and nature as Bernard prepares to face the enemy, Death. *The Years* ends with the laurel given to nature:

> The sun had risen, and the sky above the houses wore an air of extraordinary beauty, simplicity and peace. (469)

Simplicity and peace were the very things Bernard found in oblivion; complexity and struggle returned with his return to the world of man.

But in 1936 perhaps oblivion seemed preferable to the struggle.[45] It was not her personal life alone that made death, ugliness, and destruction rather than love, beauty, and art the chief themes of *The Years.* While she was writing and revising this novel, Hitler and Mussolini were making preparations for war in Germany and Italy. In the last months of 1934 Leonard Woolf finished *Quack, Quack!* his careful examination of the intellectual and emotional fraudulence of fascism.[46] Early the next year Virginia Woolf expressed in her diary a desire to write an anti-fascist pamphlet of her own.[47] During May, 1935, she paused in her revisions to take a holiday with her husband in Holland, Germany, Italy, and France and recorded in her diary the swastikas seen on cars in Germany.[48] In her talks with Maynard Keynes, Aldous Huxley, Leonard Woolf, she could not forget the threat of Hitler who "has his army on the Rhine." [49] The private and the public lives touch as Virginia Woolf notes: ". . . it's odd, how near the guns have got to our private life again. I can quite distinctly see them and hear a roar, even though I go on like a doomed mouse, nibbling at my daily page." [50]

With death so large a part of her personal life, with the consolidation of fascism occupying the public sphere, Virginia Woolf was led to describe the surface of life as both empty and ugly.[51] The blob of spittle,

---

[44] "Virginia Woolf," *Two Cheers for Democracy*, p. 260.

[45] Virginia Woolf had even begun to doubt herself as a writer. "Can I still 'write'? That is the question, you see. And now I will try to prove if the gift is dead, or dormant." (*A Writer's Diary*, October 30, 1936).

[46] *Ibid.*, December 30, 1934.

[47] *Ibid.*, February 26, 1935.

[48] *Ibid.*, May 6 through May 26, 1935. See particularly May 9, 1935.

[49] *Ibid.*, August 7, 1934; March 13, 1936.

[50] *Ibid.*

[51] Discussing Virginia Woolf among other writers, Mark Schorer notes, "The motive that impels men to write at all is the conviction that man and his experience

the leering face, the cold slab of sausage, the noseless flower vendor, the line of grease around the bathtub indicate an almost Swiftean revulsion from the human flesh. In *The Years* Sara tried to describe for Maggie what men in the future would say of their world of 1910.

> . . . people looking into this room—this cave, this little antre, scooped out of mud and dung, will hold their fingers to their noses"—and she held her fingers to her nose—"and say, 'Pah! They stink!'" (203)

The echo of Hamlet's words to Horatio in the grave-digging scene is central to the book as well as the scene. Surrounded by death, constantly thinking of death, Hamlet describes the human condition: "And smelt so? Pah!" The view, however, is Hamlet's not Shakespeare's. Similarly encompassed by death, Virginia Woolf in *The Years* gives a picture of the futility, poverty, drabness of human life and ignores the possibility of heightened states of consciousness. Like her own creation Septimus, she has turned from the lyrical, romantic Shakespeare whose spirit embued *Night and Day* to the Shakespeare who "loathed humanity." In a way the chronicle relates what Septimus thought: that "the secret signal which one generation passes under disguise to the next is loathing, hatred, and despair." Hamlet's cry, "And smelt so? Pah!" has replaced the vision.

-----

are worth celebration; but in the modern world these writers found nothing to sustain their conviction, and the technique which they developed instead only pushed man lower than they had found him" ("The Chronicle of Doubt," *The Virginia Quarterly Review*, XVIII [Spring, 1942], 215).

A Principle of Unity in
Between the Acts

by Ann Y. Wilkinson

For a novel that contains most of Virginia Woolf's important themes and some of her most exciting—and controlled—experimentation in form and technique, *Between the Acts* has provoked a curiously mixed comment—when it has not been ignored. Readers during the war, when the book was published, apparently wanted a novel dealing directly and explicitly with the problems society was facing. A novel which still had as its focus the human consciousness and sensibility, which treated contemporary problems as part of the flow of life in which the individual consciousness is immersed, war or no, inevitably met the formidable scrutiny of F. R. Leavis, for example, who found in the novel only an "extraordinary vacancy and pointlessness" and an "absence of concern for any appearance of grasp or point," of which lapses "we can say that this is where her famous preoccupation with the essential, with the significant, with 'life' has led." [1] This point of view, which included D. S. Savage's pronouncement that the novel "was marked by a disintegration of form expressing surrender of all significance to the accidental passage of time," [2] was countered not by a consideration of the formal and thematic totality of the novel, but by insistence that Virginia Woolf was indeed writing to "epitomize England's ordeal and England's hope," her work being "more realistic and more cognizant of crucial issues than some judgments of her have acknowledged." [3]

Such criticism, which limits its discussion of a novel to the ideas or issues it deals with, is perhaps understandable given the urgencies of a war situation. But twenty and more years' perspective should suggest that we need to consider the book from the point of view of its fuller

---

"A Principle of Unity in *Between the Acts*" by Ann Y. Wilkinson. From *Criticism*, VIII (Winter 1966), 53–63. Reprinted by permission of the author and of Wayne State University Press.

[1] "After *To the Lighthouse*," *Scrutiny*, X (1942), 295–297.
[2] "Virginia Woolf: The Last Phase," *Kenyon Review*, IV (1942), 381–87.
[3] Warren Beck, "For Virginia Woolf," in *Forms of Modern Fiction*, ed. William Van O'Connor (Minneapolis, 1948), pp. 246–248.

artistic achievement. Nor is this to ignore Virginia Woolf's concern for making some statements about contemporary problems. The truth is that in *Between the Acts* Virginia Woolf succeeded in making form part of the statement and statement part of the form. Indeed, apart from other considerations, this novel would be interesting in this respect alone, that it expanded even further the possibilities of development in a form which had almost been given over as exhausted after *Ulysses*. Yet Mr. Melvin Friedman, who has more recently given attention to Virginia Woolf's technique and form, has written of *Between the Acts* that "a unifying principle is nowhere to be found." He sees in it a series of "purple patches which fail to conform to the intended structure of her book," [4] unaware, perhaps, of Virginia Woolf's own observation on the purple patch that it is not the purpleness but the patchiness which is objectionable in a novel.[5] One may, of course object to purpleness entirely, but that is a matter of taste which does not admit of critical rejoinder. Once it is granted, however, that a novelist has every right to work into the structure and texture of his novel "lyrical" and "poetic" passages, the business of the critic is judging whether or not these passages do indeed conform to the intended structure of the book. The question of a principle of unity is the point of departure for this essay. That principle is to be found in the simultaneity, the identity, of form and statement.

Between the Acts is "the novel to come" (arriving on schedule in 1941) that Virginia Woolf wrote of in 1927.[6] She proposed then that "in ten or fifteen years' time prose will be used for purposes for which prose has never been used before. That cannibal, the novel, which has devoured so many forms of art will by then have devoured even more." Among the new forms the medium would take would be a novel (so called, but in reality hard to christen) "written in prose, but in prose which has many of the characteristics of poetry. It will have something of the exaltation of poetry, but much of the ordinariness of prose. It will be dramatic, and yet not a play. It will be read, not acted." This new form would "serve to express some of those feelings which seem at the moment to be balked by poetry pure and simple and to find the drama equally inhospitable to them." The position of the novelist would be further back from life, so that a larger view of its important features would be possible. The novel would give, as poetry does, the outline instead of the detail, making little use of its "fact-recording power" but within its limitations (not being a sociological novel or a novel of environment) expressing the feelings and ideas of its characters

---

[4] *Stream of Consciousness: A Study in Literary Method* (New Haven, 1955), p. 208.
[5] "The Narrow Bridge of Art," in *Granite and Rainbow*, Essays by Virginia Woolf (New York, 1958), p. 20.
[6] In "The Narrow Bridge of Art," which appeared in the *New York Herald Tribune*, August 14, 1927.

closely and vividly. It would do this from a different angle; like poetry, it would give not only people's relations to each other and their activities together, but also the relation of the mind to general ideas and its "soliloquy in solitude," give not only a character's relations to nature, his imagination, and his dreams, but also "the sneer, the contrast, the question, the closeness and complexity of life."

The prose of this novel, freed from the "beast-of-burden work . . . of carrying loads of details, bushels of fact," would show itself capable of rising from the ground "in sweeps and circles," at the same time keeping touch with the amusements and idiosyncrasies of daily life. Most important, this prose would be dramatic: the writer will have extended his scope as to dramatize those influences which play so large a part in life: "the power of music, the stimulus of sight, the effect on us of the shape of trees or the play of colour . . . the delight of movement. . . ." But the novelist must "bring to bear upon his tumultuous and contradictory emotions the generalizing and simplifying power of a strict and logical imagination. Tumult is vile; confusion is hateful; everything in a world of art should be mastered and ordered. His effort will be to generalize and split up."

Virginia Woolf thus enlarged the possibilities of the novel in *Between the Acts,* which was published posthumously and without her usual last revisions. She had put into effect some of these ideas in *To the Lighthouse* and *The Waves.* Indeed, they were part of her method even in *Mrs. Dalloway* and *Jacob's Room.* But in none of these novels does the author stand back far enough to see the outline rather than the detail; to get the larger view of some of the important features of life; to shift attention from the crocus and the moment to society and the larger, historic flow of time, or to grasp experience not through the limitations of The Window but from the expanse of the countryside.[7] And none of these novels is informed by a sense of the really dramatic uses of juxtaposed and interacting prose and poetry—and of the poetic uses of drama—as *Between the Acts* is, so much so that it seems almost as if the writer had her own fifteen-year-old prescription in front of her as she wrote.

So long a gestation period, between the idea and the writing, was not without value. By this time, Virginia Woolf had come to a clear realization of the essential problems she treats. She had made both prose and prose-poetry instruments of particular skill and scope. (I use the words "poetry" and "poetic" of course in her sense of writing that is "intense," "lyrical" and even "purple.") She had worked for order

[7] J. K. Johnstone in *The Bloomsbury Group* (London, 1954) writes that part of Virginia Woolf's difficulty in this novel is that she was "not strongly attached to the countryside by deep emotions . . . and she does not understand its people" (p. 372). It seems to me that the large, open setting was meant to have a significance more symbolic than literal, giving a larger scope to the ideas the novel expresses.

and pattern in her novels and was ready to seek the larger possibilities of a new form.

She wrote on the day she finished *Between the Acts* that she was "a little triumphant" about it, thinking it "an interesting attempt in a new method," a method "more quintessential than the others." [8] I should call this new method the novel-drama, more quintessential because the form itself, the ordering of experience and idea into a kind of drama, becomes statement and is able by its nature to deal with an enormously complex group of relationships. The form of the drama itself does away with the beast-of-burden work of arranging, explaining and describing these relationships: they all occur within the pattern of the dramatic conflict, worked out as the "play" proceeds. Because of this, the author is able to stand back further, see the outline, give more attention to the larger elements.

The difficulty, and the danger, in attempting to give the larger view, with its sneer and its contrast as well as its crocus, is that the fragmentation of society, and necessarily of the author's view of society, can become a fragmented statement. But this novel-drama is able to express in itself, *by* itself, the conflict of fragmentation and continuity, flux and stability, chaos and order. Moreover, when the large drama of life in *Between the Acts* faces the formalized drama of art, drama takes on the significance of symbol, as well as treatment, and its various forms stand in the book for these basic oppositions, for art itself and for life itself.

The framework organization seems simple enough: a group of people meets to watch the annual Village Pageant, held to raise money for the illumination of the church (a note not without its symbolic significance as a kind of traditional repository of order now darkened). But within this framework there is a quite complex interworking of relationships. There is the drama of the pageant itself, the "Acts." There is the drama of the relationships of the people watching the pageant, the "between the acts" (which also goes on before and after the acts).[9] Most important, perhaps, is the drama of the interrelationships of the two dramas themselves, for it is here that the problems of order and chaos, art and society, stasis and flux are given expression.

The pageant is a series of scenes from the history of England. It becomes obvious that part of the pageant's purpose is the illustration of the external changes time makes: in conventions, in "moralities," in clothes even; the cleverly parodied literary styles themselves become

[8] *A Writer's Diary* (London, 1954), p. 359.

[9] Like everything about the novel, the question of which is the more important of the two dramas has evoked opposing comment: John Graham, "Time in the Novels of Virginia Woolf," *UTQ*, XVIII (1949), calls the pageant microcosmic, and the story of the audience macrocosmic (196). David Daiches, *Virginia Woolf* (Norfolk, 1942), calls this latter element a "minor drama" (p. 125).

a symbol of the change from age to age.[10] But it is true, too, though not so obvious, that there is a basis of permanence beneath the flux, that though there are outward signs of change, people still dig and delve, as the chorus of villagers do, still make love and die, whether in eighteenth century boudoirs or Victorian fourposters, still feel the need for some unifying elements. "We act different parts; but are the same" (192).[11] Lady Harpy Harradan was once a Canterbury pilgrim; Mr. Hardcastle was a Viking.

And in the audience the same drama is going on, but in terms not so formalized, not so pulled together (that is the business of art). Old Lucy Swithin looks for unity between "mind time" and "clock time," reads the *Outline of History,* sees a harmony of the past with the present, of the seen with the unseen, "for she belonged to the unifiers. . . ." (118). Isa, caught in the chaos of flux and change, seeks instinct as she is with the artist's vision, a place of stasis: "Unblowing, ungrowing are the roses there. Change is not; nor the mutable, nor the lovable . . ." (155). But she is trapped by the webs of the mutable: her love, which is sometimes hate, for Giles, her husband; Giles' passion for her, which turns into lust for Mrs. Manresa, that "wild child of nature" whose consciousness is only aware of or responsive to the impulse of the moment; the inversion of William Dodge, who is made whole by Lucy's vision and disintegrates without it; the indifference, selfishness, and fear of the middle-class society which the audience represents and which we catch glimpses of as the members of it talk to and about each other. Everything is so varied, so changeable, so fragmented, so liquid: "Above the air rushed; beneath was water. Lucy stood between two fluidities, caressing her cross" (204).[12] But, paradoxically, change is always the same. Looking at the play, Isa asks if the Victorians were like that: "The Victorians . . . I don't

---

[10] Marilyn Zorn, "The Pageant in *Between the Acts*" *MFS*, II (Spring, 1965), believes that the purpose of the pageant is to convey "all of English literature from the nursery rhyme to a passage of Isa's which rings clearly of T. S. Eliot." (34). This is only partly true, and undoubtedly incidental to the purpose of this un-Joycean novel.

[11] All references in the text are to *Between the Acts* (New York, 1941).

[12] The cross here is a strange symbol for Virginia Woolf to use. Usually the staunch advocate of a clear-cut agnosticism, she blurs the outline a little in this novel, making the cross a symbol of that unified and harmonic vision which Lucy, alone in the novel, perceives. Yet there are signs of Christian symbol in *To the Lighthouse* as well. It may be that its use is a "literary" one in the sense that the writer appropriates a traditional public symbol in the interests of economy. That is, it is not Lucy's religious beliefs *per se* that are important for the novel but her finding in them a way to order, harmony, and continuity. A traditional symbol expresses all this much more economically than would a private one, which would necessarily entail an examination of the religion itself, something irrelevant to the main oppositions set up in this novel.

believe . . . that there ever were such people. Only you and me and
William dressed differently" (175).

The pageant treats of history, the passage of time. The past impinges
upon the present and Isa is burdened by it, by "memories; possessions.
This is the burden that the past laid on me, last little donkey in the
long caravanserai crossing the desert. 'Kneel down,' said the past. 'Fill
your pannier from our tree. Rise up, donkey. Go your way till your
heels blister and your hoofs crack' " (155). The pageant thus crystal-
lizes, gives stasis to the flow of time which the members of the audience
sense but cannot make stand still.

Such reactions to the pageant by members of the audience remind us
constantly of the continuing drama outside the formalized play because
they are conflicting in nature, representing the conflicts which make
the drama of life. Giles thinks the play is nonsense: he is a stock-broker
and his mind is on the darkening events of Europe. His concern is not
for the historical and continuing life of man but for the present, the
tangible. He wants action, not stasis; action relieves him. The
"natural," the rollicking appeals to Mrs. Manresa, who flaunts her
voluptuousness to excite Giles' lust; eighteenth century bawdy moves
"the indigenous, the pre-historic" old lady to laughter: her age is
beyond the change of convention; the conflict of love and hate is seized
upon by Isa, caught in the chaos of her own love and hate. For Lucy,
who belongs to the unifiers and who seeks a harmony with the past,
the play stirs in her "unacted part": "What a small part I've had to
play! But you've made me feel I could have played . . . Cleopatra!"
(153).

And to all of the audience the spectacle, the color appeals. Here
Virginia Woolf suggests the question of appearance and reality: the
audience moved by spectacle, the spectacle in reality consisting in
bedspread gowns, dish-towel turbans, scouring-swab silver cloaks. How
much do we know of anything? And how much can we bear of what we
know as reality? When, during a ten-minute interval in the pageant,
the audience unawares acts out "Present Time: Ourselves," Miss
La Trobe had wanted to expose them, "to douche them, with present-
time reality," and something went wrong with the experiment. "Reality
too strong" (179). And when the pageant continues, and the players
present "Ourselves" by holding up bits of mirror and reflecting objects,
reality is too cruel "to snap us as we are, before we've had time to
assume . . . And only, too, in parts . . ." (184).

The pageant is formalized, unified, progressive in movement. The
members of the audience are isolated or only momentarily connected.
What relationship can there be between the two? As in *To the Lighthouse* art—the painting—brings together, orders, unifies, so here the
pageant does. It shows society that it, society, is only "scraps, orts,
fragments." Having shown this, having made people aware of their

isolation and distressed by it, art pulls them together again. Miss La Trobe is an artist, "one who seethes wandering bodies and floating voices in a cauldron, and makes rise up from its amorphous mass a recreated world" (153). And after the shattering experience of seeing reality, themselves, reflected as the latest act in the drama of history, music—was it Bach, Handel, Beethoven, Mozart or merely a traditional tune?—pulls the chaotic into order: "Like quicksilver sliding, filings magnetized, the distracted united. The tune began; the first note meant a second; the second a third. Then down beneath a force was born in opposition; then another. On different levels they diverged. On different levels ourselves went forward; flower gathering some on the surface; others descending to wrestle with the meaning; but all comprehending; all enlisted" (189). So the drama becomes part of life; and life enters into the drama. Art and society become complementary; the orderly and the chaotic, the permanent and the mutable.[13] Both must live in the world: the shower of rain descends on them both, "all people's tears, weeping for all people" (180). The mooing of the cows and the flight of the swallows bring the countryside and its people, the audience, into the pageant, reinforcing the connection of art to society, showing that art does not function without life-lines to nature and man. Both face the problem of survival: the airplanes swoop over audience and pageant both, threaten both. Both must find a workable relationship to the machine, represented by the gramophone which disperses the audience and calls it together as it begins and ends the acts.

The interworking of these dramas is constantly highlighted and counterpointed by Virginia Woolf's manipulation of technique: much of the ordinariness of prose surrounds and describes players, audience and setting. But there is the exaltation of poetry too: this not so much in the formalized, stylized verse of the pageant, which as art is stasis and has no need of the poetry of moments of perception and sensation; but more in the lyricising of the mind's "soliloquy in solitude," like Isa's: "The words made two rings, perfect rings, that floated them . . . like two swans down stream. But his snow-white breast was circled with a tangle of dirty duckweed; and she too, in her webbed feet was entangled, by her husband, the stockbroker" (5). There is drama in these carefully-plotted interplays of "ordinariness" and "exaltation"; drama also in the expression of the power of music and sight and

---

[13] In Bergsonian terms James Hafley, "A Reading of *Between the Acts*," *Accent*, XIII (1953), sees Virginia Woolf's purpose in the novel: "denying the One, denying the Many, she affirms the Manyness beneath the Many . . . It is the unity of the separateness beneath separate individuals which constitutes the One . . . the One is, therefore, Manyness. It is precisely the interruption which is the unity." Yet the novel is "first and foremost a novel about free will" (178–184). It appears to me that this philosophical and theological problem of free will is not one of Virginia Woolf's major preoccupations in this book.

colour: "The actors . . . lingered; they mingled. . . . Each still acted the unacted part conferred on them by their clothes. Beauty was on them. Beauty revealed them. Was it the light that did it? . . . 'Look,' the audience whispered, 'O look, look, look—' " (195–196).

And this prose is ordered. Like Miss La Trobe, who orders society by creating her pageant, Virginia Woolf orders society by seeing it as part of drama, informing her presentation of it by a sense of drama. The complexities of such a form are obvious: it is like holding a mirror to a mirror, seeing the reflections scale down into infinity. We watch the drama of the novel, becoming an audience for it; the audience in the novel is drama, watching drama which reflects the audience itself. The pageant presents the continuing drama of history; Queen Elizabeth commands the players to "Play out the play!" Thus does the use of this form become a symbol of a condition.

It is hard to see, then, how anyone could speak of the "extreme vacuousness" of *Between the Acts* or of its absence of any appearance of grasp or point. Twelve airplanes sweeping down to interrupt the flow of society's life on a summer afternoon are as good a suggestion to the perceptive mind of the forces which threaten survival as a Panzer division, perhaps better, because they don't take our attention away from that life, which is after all the important thing. And does not the image of the snake trying to swallow a toad, not able to swallow, the toad not able to die, give us a sense of the horror of the contemporary situation: where it is no longer possible to speak of a new age powerless to be born but of "a monstrous inversion"—"birth the wrong way round" (99)? Giles, the man of action, crushes the snake and toad, but the blood remains on his shoes, its presence representing the evil and violence that thwart the impulses of love and recalling that primeval slime from which the *Outline of History* emerges but which is still there beneath civilization, its poisoning oozing out and threatening to overwhelm the face of the earth again. The suggestions are compressed, quintessential: in them Virginia Woolf answers affirmatively the question she had asked over a decade before: if the novel can "amass details . . . can it also select? Can it symbolize? Can it give us an epitome as well as an inventory?" [14] In their quintessence every gesture, every thought, every thing, almost, functions as epitome, suggesting and standing for the resonance and density of massed detail. And of course none of these things stands alone: its relationship to every other thing is implied simply within the dramatic form by which the novelist symbolizes the continuous dramatic conflict she sees as the condition of life.

It is even harder to see how anyone could write of *Between the Acts* that "a principle of unity is nowhere to be found." The principle of

[14] "Phases of Fiction," in *Granite and Rainbow,* p. 145. (First published in *The Bookman,* June, 1929).

unity is everywhere present: drama, or art, becomes part of the way of life, ordering it; the conflicts of life, also drama, nourish the art, which like the novel itself, takes the fears and problems, the beauty and the hope—"the resolute refusal of some pimpled dirty little scrub in sandals to sell his soul" (188)—and abstracts them, shapes them into comprehendible but nonetheless real form: the drama that they are. Drama, then, is form, statement and symbol in the novel.

Having said this, however, that "life is drama," one has not yet finished. "Life is drama" in *Pride and Prejudice* and in *Bleak House* too, and it is important to get at the particular quality of Virginia Woolf's drama if we are to say anything at all. Having shown that in *Between the Acts* form has not disintegrated but has in fact been refined and made "significant" in the fullest import of this term, we must reduce an already reduced statement and ask what this fusion of content and form have to say about the "question . . . and the complexity of life."

We have, then, by way of the formal principle of dramatic arrangement, the problems of isolation and connection, permanence and mutability, stasis and flow, and appearance and reality set in opposition to each other. The dramatic principle becomes a methodology in the logic of the novel: where there is one, there must necessarily be the other part of each set. The drama must consist in revealing or, more precisely, resolving the relationship between these opposites. If the drama in *Bleak House* consists in large part in the revelation of moral connectedness between apparently isolated, idiosyncratic particles of reality, and the drama of *Pride and Prejudice* consists in the conflicts attending the systematic exclusion from the universe of discourse all irrational, foolish, or malicious elements, the drama in *Between the Acts* consists not only in the conflict of opposites but in the more startling revelation of the identity of these opposites. The course of the argument in this novel, then, is dialectical, and the statement that emerges out of the complexity of circumstances is the dialectical one that all things imply their opposites, contain them in fact.

Isolation and connection are identical, insofar as one logically "implies" the other: the isolation of each character implies the connectedness of all by virtue of their being related to the same problem. Separate particles of humanity and human consciousness they may be, but the stuff of their visions or the motives for their actions involve their connection to other characters or their wish for such a connection, even if the relationship is an entanglement. And as separate particles of consciousness they must necessarily join to make up the flux of total experience that is set down in the *Outline of History,* and that identifies them with the roles they play in the Pageant. Their awareness of uniqueness and anonymity in the flux of things imposes a sense of isolation upon them, yet all realize that though they appear to change and to be unique, they are still the same, and can thus see their identities objectified for them in the *Outline* and the Pageant.

If time is arrested in sudden perceptions and awareness, or in the Art of the Pageant, the stasis of the moment or of the form implies the unarrested flux from which the moment or the form is snatched, and which threatens and qualifies the stasis, just as the Pageant is threatened by rain and airplane and the characters on a Sunday afternoon are menaced by the rush of events in the larger world. So obviously Art implies and contains Life, as in the Pageant the characters, props, and roles are identical with their existence outside the play. And just as clearly the drama is going on outside the Pageant in the same terms, essentially, as it goes on on the stage: questions of love and lust, death, art, morality.

Formally, the logical identity of these opposites is demonstrated in the last act of the Pageant, when Art consists in Life objectified and Life is Art lived, purple passages, fragmentation and all. Each contains the other as the *Outline of History* contains the density of History and implies it, and as the density of Life and Lives—History—is known by its *Outline,* its "epitome" rather than its "inventory." The "question . . . and the complexity" of life are dialectically resolved here by means of the dramatic form through which the novelist imposes upon tumult and contradictory emotions "the generalizing and simplifying power of a strict and logical imagination." Drama becomes, then, not only a principle of unity in the novel, but a diagram for the process of unification by which Art, Life and History are created, both within the novel and without.

Virginia Woolf and the Critic as Reader

by Mark Goldman

I. Reader and Critic

Virginia Woolf's title for the two volumes of essays collected in her lifetime, *The Common Reader*,[1] has been taken for a descriptive image of the critic as impressionist or amateur reader. In the preface to her first *Common Reader*, Mrs. Woolf explains her title and epigraph, taken from Dr. Johnson's "Life of Gray," in place of a statement of purpose. Her description is deliberately casual and informal, but she provides a structure and point of view for her essays by adding that the common reader does wish to create from his reading "some kind of whole—a portrait of a man, a sketch of an age, a theory of the art of writing." [2] Though Mrs. Woolf's deceptive remarks on the function of criticism may partly account for the persistent view of her as "reader" rather than "critic," other writers have contributed to the stereotype of Virginia Woolf as an occasional essayist and impressionist, as a literary portrait painter and miniaturist; or as an antiquarian rummaging through the attics of a rather charming but peripheral past. Unsympathetic readers have carried the belletristic image further and coupled it with the conception of her fiction as a total immersion in pure subjectivity or (in Sean O'Faolain's view)[3] as an exercise in the novel as narcissism. Yet, in fairness to reviewers of Virginia Woolf's essays, it should be noted that both favorable and unfavorable com-

---

"Virginia Woolf and the Critic as Reader" by Mark Goldman. From *PMLA,* LXXX (June 1965), 275–84. Reprinted by permission of the author and the Modern Language Association of America.

[1] *The Common Reader,* first series, 1925; *The Common Reader,* second series, 1932. These have been supplemented by a series of posthumous volumes edited by her husband, Leonard Woolf (*The Death of the Moth,* 1942; *The Moment and Other Essays,* 1947; *The Captain's Death Bed,* 1950). Though Mr. Woolf announced, in the Editor's note to *The Captain's Death Bed,* that this would be the last posthumous collection of essays, another volume appeared in 1958 (with an explanatory note by Mr. Woolf) entitled *Granite and Rainbow.*

[2] "The Common Reader," in *The Common Reader,* first series, 1925 (London, 1951), p. 11.

[3] Sean O'Faolain, "Narcissa and Lucifer," in *New World Writing,* x (November 1956), 161–175.

ments seem to be based on a similar conception of her as an appreciator or impressionist rather than a serious critic . . .

It is obvious . . . that the specter of impressionism, the subjective taint of the Pater-Wilde inheritance, still haunts the modern critic's imagination. It is also this fear of impressionism or subjectivity that lies behind the modern critical ideal of scientific objectivity. Yet by this time, of course, both the fear of the disease and the fantasy of the cure should have been dispelled. As a matter of fact, if we look again at that landmark of modern criticism, T. S. Eliot's *The Sacred Wood* (1920), we can now see that Eliot is not merely reacting against the "aesthetic" or impressionistic criticism of the recent past, but is attempting to reconcile impressionism or "appreciation" and a so-called "intellectual" criticism. Almost forty years later, disturbed by the tremendous shift in the direction of objective or scientific criticism, Eliot renewed his plea for a balance or middle way between the extremes of "appreciation" and "understanding." [4]

Virginia Woolf's criticism, it will be seen, reveals a similar attempt to reach a *via media*, a creative balance between reason and emotion, sense and sensibility, the individual critic and the impersonal method. While denying the dichotomy between a so-called objective and subjective literary criticism, Mrs. Woolf's kind of impressionism achieves a critical objectivity, even a structure. . . .

My purpose is to examine Mrs. Woolf's essays on the art of reading rather than her criticism of various writers or specific works of art. This approach is necessary, in view of what has been said earlier, in order to reach some understanding of her aesthetic or critical position; to arrive at a more balanced or complex view of the common reader as literary critic. Though the essays on reading stress the need for sensibility over system, we can see Mrs. Woolf moving quickly from individual perceptions to a critical position, from the stance of a reader to the status of a critic.

As early as 1916, in an essay entitled "Hours in a Library," Mrs. Woolf celebrated the delights of reading and proclaimed the freedom of the private reader against the authority of the specialist or man of learning. . . . Her own "pure and disinterested" passion for books began at the age of fifteen, when her father, the Victorian scholar and critic, Sir Leslie Stephen, gave her the run of his large, "quite unexpurgated" library. The pains she takes to preserve her amateur standing and independent spirit as a critic are also an inheritance from her father, as she reveals in her essay "Leslie Stephen." "To read what one liked because one liked it, never to pretend to admire what one did not —that was his only lesson in the art of reading. To write in the fewest

---

[4] "The Frontiers of Criticism," in *On Poetry and Poets* (London, 1957).

possible words, as clearly as possible, exactly what one meant—that was his only lesson in the art of writing." [5]

In an essay simply called "Reading," [6] Mrs. Woolf again reflects on the strange seductive power of books, this time indulging her impressionist fancy as she rambles over the rich landscape of English literature. Here is the sense of literature as part of the English life and land, as an old house and garden and rolling downs stretching toward the sea where the Elizabethan voyagers took ship and sailed for the new world. The sense of historical tradition runs through Mrs. Woolf's essays, and she sees literary history, from the "Pastons and Chaucer" [7] to the present age, as an evolutionary process in the discovery of reality. [8] . . .

But the art of reading is also a critical matter, as Mrs. Woolf demonstrates in the essay concluding the second *Common Reader,* "How Should One Read a Book?" Originally presented as a talk, the audience must have realized that as readers they were to be created in Mrs. Woolf's image. At the outset, she again admonishes the reader to follow his own critical conscience, in the Cambridge-Bloomsbury tradition of the individual against authority and conformity. To be open-minded, to get rid of all preconceptions about the author and the work when we read, is the first step not merely toward enjoyment but understanding. . . . The reading process is intensified, then, as we turn to the familiar question of form. What is clearly revealed here, and implicit throughout her essays, is a creative tension in her criticism between the emotional response, the impression, the experience of the work, and its rational explanation and evaluation—on formal grounds and in terms of traditional standards. As a psychological novelist, Mrs. Woolf was committed to the "unconscious" self, as she describes the creative source, as well as to the equally essential tool for the writer, the critical intelligence. Though her faith in sensibility may also be part of her characteristic feminine protest against masculine, academic authority, the critic's emotional response to the work of art was integral, as we shall see, to the Bloomsbury aesthetic.

Mrs. Woolf's argument is further complicated when the idea of form is associated with feeling or emotion, a point to be explored in connec-

---

[5] "Leslie Stephen," in *The Captain's Death Bed,* p. 72. "Hours in a Library," in *Granite and Rainbow,* p. 24.

[6] In *The Captain's Death Bed.*

[7] In *The Common Reader,* first series.

[8] A discussion of Mrs. Woolf's conception of reality would require a separate essay. It would be possible, as a matter of fact, to arrange her own essays chronologically for a survey of literature seen from the perspective of her ideas on reality. Mrs. Woolf's approach to the real in literary history resembles Erich Auerbach's, in his book *Mimesis; The Representation of Reality in Western Literature,* trans. Willard Trask (Doubleday Anchor Books, 1957).

tion with her essay "On Re-reading Novels." In "How Should One
Read a Book?" she refers to the idea of perspective, a recurrent critical
term in her essays related to the writer's approach to reality and thus
to the form of his work. If the reader would turn writer, Mrs. Woolf
observes, he would realize the difficulty of imposing form on the fleeting
impressions of life, of creating art out of the chaos of experience. . . .
The most difficult task for the reader is the necessity to compare and
judge; to read, as it were, without the book in front of him in order
to pinpoint the qualities of a work and determine its final worth. He
must "train his taste" not only to read creatively, with insight and
imagination, but to read critically; to evaluate a work in terms of its
internal laws and against the great tradition which was the final
standard for Virginia Woolf.

It is interesting to compare Mrs. Woolf's critic as impressionist-
judge with her father's views on the function of criticism. Though a
follower of Arnold, Leslie Stephen wanted to go beyond the critical
touchstone in order to incorporate a body of critical judgments into a
kind of literary case law. Yet even the positivist-minded Stephen re-
served a place for the critic's emotional response, as he makes clear in
the essay "Thoughts on Criticism by a Critic." "This vivacity and originality of feeling is the first qualification of a critic. Without it no
man's judgment is worth having." And again, from the other direction:
"A good critic can hardly express his feelings without implicitly laying
down a principle." [9] . . . The same conflict between impression and
judgment, thought and feeling, has been noted in the early essays of
T. S. Eliot. The rejection of Arnold and Pater (and his followers) was
behind Eliot's attempt, in *The Sacred Wood,* to deny the dichotomy of
thought and feeling (dissociation of sensibility), which he felt encouraged impressionism (and abstract scientism). Eliot's position is
actually close to Mrs. Woolf's notion of a fusion of critical functions,
though his intention is more rigorous and programmatic in the light
of his poetic aims. . . .[10]

Paradoxically, for Mrs. Woolf, the reader may at last turn to the
great writers and critics, to authority, after he has served his long
apprenticeship in the art of reading. It is only then that he can profit
from the decisions of a great judge, a Dryden, a Samuel Johnson, or a
Coleridge. "But they are only able to help us if we come laden with
questions and suggestions won honestly in the course of our own reading. They can do nothing for us if we herd ourselves under their
authority and lie down like sheep in the shade of a hedge. We can only
understand their ruling when it comes in conflict with our own and

[9] "Thoughts on Criticism by a Critic," *Cornhill Magazine,* xxxiv (November 1876),
564.
[10] T. S. Eliot, "The Perfect Critic," in *The Sacred Wood* (London, 1920; University
Paperbacks, 1960), p. 15.

vanquishes it." [11] Mrs. Woolf's essays, then, reveal a continual effort to resolve the apparent critical conflict between reason and emotion, the individual and authority, abstract rules and the concrete fact of the work of art. . . .

II. *Significant Form*

The concern for the reader as critic leads inevitably to a discussion of form, though Mrs. Woolf seems to avoid the dichotomous monster by approaching the question from the point of view of the reader rather than the writer. In her essay "On Re-reading Novels," [12] Mrs. Woolf gets at the crucial question of form by way of Percy Lubbock's now classic work, *The Craft of Fiction*. Reviewing Lubbock's book when it appeared in 1922, Mrs. Woolf declares that it is a step in the direction of a serious aesthetic for the novel. She agrees with his emphasis on form, on the proper reading of the novel as novel, as pattern, as work of art. But she takes exception to his use of the term "form" itself. It is not only a question of words for Mrs. Woolf, but goes deeper, "into the very process of reading itself." She illustrates her argument with a close reading of Flaubert's "Un Cœur simple." And her sense of the crucial points of the story and the relations set up between these points has to do not with something seen but with something felt. It is the "moments of understanding" that count, even in our second, closer reading of the work. "Therefore, the 'book itself' is not form which you see, but emotion which you feel, and the more intense the writer's feeling the more exact . . . its expression in words." Thus, Mrs. Woolf adds, she has reached her conception of "Un Cœur simple" by working "from the emotion outwards" and "among all this talk of methods, both in writing and in reading it is the emotion that must come first." [13] In "How Should One Read a Book," Mrs. Woolf insisted that reading was a more complex process than seeing. In this essay, "On Re-reading Novels," she clarifies her point by discussing form as an emotional rather than a visual pattern. To better understand Mrs. Woolf's definition of form and her insistence on that definition, it would be instructive to see the connection between Mrs. Woolf's aesthetic and the theories of her Bloomsbury friends, the art critics Clive Bell and Roger Fry.

Clive Bell had formulated his celebrated phrase, "significant form,"

[11] "How Should One Read a Book?" in *The Common Reader*, second series, p. 269.
[12] In *The Moment and Other Essays*.
[13] "On Re-reading Novels," *Ibid.*, p. 130. In discussing Turgenev's fiction, Mrs. Woolf states that he saw his novels not as a "succession of events; but as a succession of emotions radiating from some character at the centre" ("The Novels of Turgenev," in *The Captain's Death Bed*, p. 58).

in 1914, in a book entitled *Art;* though Roger Fry had suggested a
similar idea in 1909, in "An Essay in Aesthetics." [14] Both critics base
their conception of "significant form" on the so-called "aesthetic emotion" which works of art are capable of transmitting. And this emotion
is a response to a significant pattern of relations, the form of the work,
which is in turn the perfect and complete expression of an idea, an
emotion, a "vision of reality," as Mrs. Woolf would say, in the mind of
the artist. In maintaining the balance between form and feeling, Bell
tries to avoid, as does Mrs. Woolf, the so-called "affective fallacy" on
the one hand, and the "intentional fallacy" [15] on the other. . . .

In "An Essay in Aesthetics," Roger Fry defines the same relation
between form and emotion. "When the artist passes from pure sensations to emotions aroused by means of sensations, he uses natural
forms, which, in themselves, are calculated to move our emotions, and
he presents these in such a manner that the forms themselves generate
in us emotional states." [16] Fry repeats his point about the idea, or
state of mind, or emotion behind the "significant form" of the work
of art, in "The Artist's Vision." When we contemplate a work of art,
he says—a Sung bowl, for example—"there comes to us . . . a feeling
of purpose; we feel that all those sensually logical conformities are
the outcome of a particular feeling, or of what, for want of a better
word, we call an idea; and we may even say that the pot is the expression of the idea in the artist's mind." [17] We can see from this
discussion the relation between what Fry calls, in one of his books,
"Vision and Design."

Turning again to Mrs. Woolf's essay "On Re-reading Novels," with
Bell and Fry in the background, we can understand Mrs. Woolf's
insistence on the emotional significance of form. If her account of the
critical (and creative) process is true, there is no possibility, she would
maintain, of establishing the classic dichotomy of form and content.
Only the imperfect works, she insists, allow us to separate the two. In a
great novel, there is a perfect fusion that leaves no "slip or chink";
nothing is left, in fact, but the form of the work entire in the mind.
In answer to Lubbock, she repeats: "There is vision and expression.
The two blend so perfectly that when Mr. Lubbock asks us to test the
form with our eyes we see nothing at all. But we feel with singular
satisfaction, and since all our feelings are in keeping, they form a whole
which remains in our minds as the book itself." [18]

Once Mrs. Woolf has drawn her fine but necessary distinction be-

[14] Included in *Vision and Design* (first published in 1920; reprinted by Meridian
Books, New York, 1956).
[15] For a discussion of these "fallacies," see the first two essays in W. K. Wimsatt's
The Verbal Icon (Noonday edition, 1962).
[16] Fry, p. 37.
[17] Fry, "The Artist's Vision," in *Vision and Design.*
[18] "On Re-reading Novels," p. 130.

tween Lubbock's and her own conception of form, she restores the balance between art and emotion. In Bell and Fry, and in her own essays, we have seen that form is the result of, and results in, emotion. Yet, as Mrs. Woolf has also maintained, form is by definition that controlling, ordering process which we call art. On these terms, she is willing to agree with Lubbock. "Is there not something beyond emotion, something which though it is inspired by emotion, tranquillises it, orders it, composes it?—that which Mr. Lubbock calls form, which for simplicity's sake, we call art?" [19] By insisting on a twofold definition of form, Mrs. Woolf seems to be letting in the back door what she has just pushed out the front. Yet we have seen that her criticism involves a basic counterpoint of form and feeling, art and emotion—saving her from a critical nihilism on the one hand and a rigid, systematic aesthetic on the other.

The emotional or impressionistic pattern ascribed to the novel is of course analogous to Mrs. Woolf's experimental structure in her fiction. Though a Jamesian in her demands for an aesthetic novel, she is unwilling to accept Lubbock's visual sense of form, which derives from James. In this context, J. K. Johnstone's attempt to trace a direct line from Fry's aesthetic to Virginia Woolf's theory and practice of fiction,[20] while valid to some extent, ignores Mrs. Woolf's skepticism toward any visual conception of form, and toward Fry's own plastic approach to the verbal art of fiction.

When Mrs. Woolf refers, in her biography of Roger Fry, to his literary criticism, there is a note of professional skepticism in the midst of praise for an astute, persuasive argument: "As a critic of literature, then, he was not what is called a safe guide. He looked at the carpet from the wrong side; but he made it for that reason display unexpected patterns. And many of his theories hold good for both arts. Design, rhythm, texture—there they were again—in Flaubert as in Cézanne. And he would hold up a book to the light as if it were a picture and show where in his view—it was a painter's of course—it fell short." [21] Yet Fry's insistence on form, pattern, design—inherent in his admiration of Cézanne and the Post-Impressionists—undoubtedly reinforced Mrs. Woolf's belief, inherited from James and Flaubert, in the aesthetic or "well-made" novel. Mrs. Woolf also tells us in her biography of Fry that he had a theory about the influence of Post-Impressionism on literature, which he never had time to work out. Fry appears to have incorporated part of this theory into his essay, "Some Questions in Esthetics," where he attempts to purify painting by purging it of all but plastic values and, at the same time, to create for literature an

[19] *Ibid.*, p. 13.
[20] See the chapter on Bloomsbury aesthetics in J. K. Johnstone, *The Bloomsbury Group*, (New York, 1954).
[21] Virginia Woolf, *Roger Fry: A Biography* (New York, 1940), p. 240.

equivalent purity of form. Since each art, Fry feels, has its own *raison d'être*, its proper criteria for creating and judging it as art, literature should rid itself of those excrescences which Mrs. Woolf decried in her famous essays on the Edwardians.[22] Fry refers to A. C. Bradley's statement on the autonomy of poetry, and goes on to say: "For poetry in this passage we may, I think, substitute the idea of any literature as pure art. The passage at least suggests to us that the purpose of literature is the creation of structures which have for us the feeling of reality, and these structures are self-contained, self-sufficient and not to be valued by their reference to what lies outside." [23] Here then is the belief in the autonomy of art, which Mrs. Woolf consistently endorses in her essays. Fry's friend, the French aesthetician Charles Mauron, had even suggested a way for literature to achieve the formal purity of painting by transposing "the idea of volumes from the dominion of space to the domain of spirit and conceive the literary artist as creating 'psychological volumes'." [24] We can see how the idea of "psychological volumes" fits in with Mrs. Woolf's own subjective novel, which is both formal and psychological.

Mrs. Woolf's insistence on the crucial relation between reason and emotion stems from her role as an artist-critic. Her experiments in the novel, subjective, impressionistic, led paradoxically to a critical struggle with form, and her defense of an emotional structure in the novel— against Lubbock's visual form—parallels her own experience as an intensely subjective yet tenaciously objective literary artist. She was intent upon preserving a balance between form and feeling, and she is careful, as we have noted, to distinguish between the emotional and intellectual or critical basis of form. We have seen that this discussion leads to a denial of the familiar dichotomy of form and content, to an emphasis on organic form, to the perfect fusion of what Mrs. Woolf calls "vision and expression." This account of organic or expressive form is similar, as we have also seen, to the concept of "significant form" developed by Clive Bell and Roger Fry, and may be traced to Coleridge's famous organic theory, with its subjective appeal to the powers of the imagination and its objective reference to the organic relation between the parts and the whole. Mrs. Woolf's reference to an organic form for the novel reveals her again as a follower of Henry James, whose pioneering interest in the novel as art led to his insistence, in "The Art of Fiction," on the organic nature of the novel. "A novel is a living thing, all one and continuous, like any other organ-

---

[22] See especially "Modern Fiction," in *The Common Reader*, first series; and "Mr. Bennett and Mrs. Brown," in *The Captain's Death Bed*.

[23] "Some Questions in Aesthetics," in *Transformations* (first printed in 1926, reprinted in 1956 by Doubleday Anchor Books), p. 11.

[24] *Ibid.* See Charles Mauron's *The Nature of Beauty in Art and Literature* (London, 1927), a book published by the Woolfs and translated by Fry.

ism, and in proportion as it lives will it be found, I think, that in each of the parts there is something of each of the other parts." The American transcendentalists, Emerson, Whitman, Thoreau, stressed the subjective side of Coleridge's theory, using botanical imagery to describe the free or natural development of form out of the artist's vision or inspiration. But for James and Virginia Woolf organic form is an objective pattern of relations, the result not only of emotion or intuition, but of art and the artist's "critical labour," as Eliot terms it in "The Function of Criticism."

III. *The Via Media*

It is not hard to demonstrate that Virginia Woolf, though her essays are informal and impressionistic, really belongs to the modern critical tradition, with its emphasis on the formal, objective values of the work of art. Yet it hardly seems necessary any longer to declare one's adherence to some defiantly modern critical standard. It no longer seems meaningful for modern criticism to insist on its freedom from any romantic-impressionist heritage. If the mythic "old" criticism is dead and the new critical horse has been feeding comfortably in the academic stable, why go on beating either? If time has given us new perspective on the critical propagandists of the recent past, the real value may lie in seeing modern criticism as part of the unending dialectic on classic literary questions.

As Murray Krieger has shown, one crucial dialectic of modern criticism derives from the conflict, first seen in T. E. Hulme and T. S. Eliot, between a belief in the romantic imagination and the classical impersonality of art.[25] Eliot's early emphasis on impersonality, objectivity, and tradition were attempts to resolve the Coleridgeian dilemma of subject and object by pretending to ignore the romantic theory of expression in favor of a classical theory of imitation. Among other things, the classical smokescreen of Hulme and Eliot was a way of escaping the stigma of the Pater-Wilde-Symons impressionist school.

Other critics in the Eliot line had to contend with the Italian aesthetician, Benedetto Croce, whose expressionist theory of art seemed to preclude the kind of analysis demanded by the formalist or "New Critics."[26] Croce's expressionist theory appeared to be a neo-romantic philosophy of art, with the artist's intuition-expression inviolate and essentially untranslatable: "Criticism does not require anything else than to know the true sentiment of the poet is the representative form

---

[25] See especially the first two chapters of Murray Krieger's *The New Apologists for Poetry* (Minneapolis, 1956).

[26] See Murray Krieger's article, "Benedetto Croce and The Recent Poetics Of Organicism," *Comparative Literature*, VII (1955), 253–258.

in which he translated it. Any other demand is extraneous to the question." [27] Croce's expressionism resolves the form-content dichotomy, but with a finality that defends the artist's imagination or intuition against the kind of analysis essential to the modern critic.

I. A. Richards, whose pioneering emphasis on a linguistic analysis of literature had such impact on modern criticism, also produced a kind of embarrassing roadblock for the formalistic critic, with his psychological or affective theory of literature. As a psychologist, Richards seemed, in his early work, to emphasize the therapeutic value of literature: literature as a way of feeling rather than of knowing. But this concern with the emotional value of art—with the reader's response to the work over the work itself, tends to destroy the very value of art as a self-contained approach to reality. In order to emphasize the complexity of modern criticism in its attempts to answer the classic questions, it is only necessary, finally, to refer to John Crowe Ransom's attack on Richards. Though Ransom reproaches Richards for his psychologism and neglect of the objective work, Ransom's own distinction between "structure," or the logical framework of the poem, and "texture," or the rich local details, does not resolve the form-content dilemma but in fact sustains it. [28]

Without venturing further into this labyrinthine problem, we may say, then, that modern criticism has not escaped or resolved the imitation-expression, subject-object dilemma inherited from the nineteenth century. And if we turn back to that prototype of impressionist criticism, Walter Pater, we see the same questions raised and an attempt to find a critical *via media* that anticipates the concern of his modern follower, Virginia Woolf. René Wellek tries to reevaluate Pater as a critic in terms of this dual emphasis on subject and object. In correcting the usual interpretation of Pater's Preface to *The Renaissance,* Wellek remarks: "Pater's theory of criticism stresses not only personal impressions but the duty of the critic to grasp the individuality, the unique quality of the work of art. Pater never advocates the impressionist theory of the 'adventures of the soul among masterpieces,' the 'speaking of myself on occasion of Shakespeare,' as it was formulated by Anatole France." [29] Pater's reaction against the moral criticism of Carlyle, Ruskin, and Morris led to a Coleridgeian concern with form and an endorsement of art for art which may be related to the non-utilitarian ethics of the Bloomsbury philosopher, G. E. Moore, whose insistence that art is an intrinsic or ethical good influenced Bell and Fry

---

[27] Quoted in Brooks and Wimsatt, *Literary Criticism: A Short History* (New York, 1959), p. 515.

[28] See the chapter on Richards in John Crowe Ransom's *The New Criticism* (New York, 1941), and Ransom's article, "Criticism as Pure Speculation," in *Modern Literary Criticism,* ed. Ray B. West (New York, 1961).

[29] René Wellek, "Walter Pater's Literary Theory and Criticism," *Victorian Studies* (September 1957), p. 30.

and Virginia Woolf in their faith in the self-contained values of art. Pater's famous assertion that "all art constantly aspires toward the condition of music" [30] has also been misinterpreted as an extreme example of aestheticism. Yet it is only another variation on the notion of organic or expressive form. Pater refers to music because it is the most abstract of the arts and provides the best example of unity or a fusion of form and content. In expanding upon this point in "The School of Giorgione," Pater anticipates Eliot and Mrs. Woolf and their concern for a combining of thought and feeling, reason and emotion: "but form and matter, in their union or identity, present one single effect to the 'imaginative reason,'" that complex faculty for which every thought and feeling is twin-born with its sensible analogue or symbol. It is the art of music which most completely realizes this artistic ideal, this perfect identification of matter and form." [31]

The modern analytical critics, organic and contextual in orientation, have also been, inevitably, art for art; and Mrs. Woolf's persistent regard for the formal problems of prose fiction and poetry has perhaps been ignored because she has neglected the more rigorous tools of the analysts for the form and style of the essayist. She has suffered a certain neglect as a serious critic for choosing the middle way between the individual, emotional experience and the analytical, evaluative, or judicial responsibility—in a more rigid age where critics are predominantly teacher-specialists rather than practicing artists or reviewers with a very real stake in the critic as common reader. As an essayist, reviewer, and artist-critic; as a Bloomsbury individualist and feminist sensitive to her own Victorian lack of a university education, she reacted instinctively against all prescriptive or positivist-minded criticism as a product of the uncreative academies and academicians whom she suspected and scorned. . . . Mrs. Woolf reflects the impatience and prejudice of the artist-critic, which she shares with T. S. Eliot. Though she was conscious of her own role as a critic and of the formal demands and legitimate aims of literary criticism, there is a growing tendency in her writing to suspect the fallibility of critics and criticism resulting from a too-great dependence upon abstract rules and principles. Her artist soul became skeptical of her critical brain; and though her essays on the novel, for example, reveal a brilliant body of formal criticism, she is conscious of a widening gap between the aesthetic discoveries resulting from her experiments in fiction and the somewhat superficial conclusions she finds in most literary criticism. As artist and Bloomsbury individualist, she blames the academies for the present state of criticism. In "How It Strikes A Contemporary," after praising the great artist-critics of the past, she continues the attack: "Men of

[30] Walter Pater, "The School of Giorgione," in *The Renaissance* (Modern Library Edition), p. 111.
[31] *Ibid.*, p. 114. The phrase "imaginative reason" derives from Matthew Arnold.

taste and learning and ability are forever lecturing the young and celebrating the dead. But the too frequent result of their able and industrious pens is a desiccation of the living tissues of literature into a network of little bones." [32] Mrs. Woolf's dual role as artist and critic merged with a third, wider concern for the common reader and the general state of literature. Since she considered her position as an artist dependent upon a certain intelligent class of common readers, she felt that the academic interest in literature could only lead to a fatal split between the specialized group on the one hand and the reading public on the other, with the artist somewhere in the middle. It is against this possibility of what she considered a sterile literary condition that Mrs. Woolf reacted in her attack on the universities and what she thought was academic criticism. And it is against this background that we can see her growing impatience with the more formal criticism she had herself endorsed in her essays, and a new interest in a more experimental, less formal criticism that would be truer to the work in terms of the creative experience.

In assembling some articles for a second *Common Reader,* she refers in her *Diary* to the possibility of a new critical method that will come closer to what she feels is the aesthetic truth. "There must be some simpler, subtler, closer means of writing about books, as about people, could I hit upon it." [33] And while writing an article on Turgenev, she again refers in the *Diary* to the question of a new critical approach, once more from the writer's standpoint: "The difficulty about criticism is that it is so superficial. The writer has gone so much deeper. T. kept a diary for Bazarov: wrote everything from his point of view. We have only 250 short pages. Our criticism is only a bird's eye view of the pinnacle of an iceberg. The rest under water. One might begin it in this way. The article might be more broken, less composed than usual." [34] Only a year before her death, when she was considering a critical book on English literature, Mrs. Woolf expresses a kind of final disillusionment with the state of literary criticism, which discouraged her from any experiments as well as from the book itself:

No invasion. High Wind. Yesterday in the Public library I took down a book of X's criticism. This turned me against writing my book. London Library atmosphere effused. Turned me against all literary criticism: these so clever, so airless, so fleshless ingenuities and attempts to prove— that T. S. Eliot for example is a worse critic than X. Is all literary criticism that kind of exhausted air?—a book dust, London Library air. Or is it only that X is a second hand, frozen fingered, university specialist don trying to be creative, don all stuffed with books, writer. Would one say

[32] "How It Strikes A Contemporary," in *The Common Reader,* first series.
[33] *A Writer's Diary,* ed. Leonard Woolf (New York, 1953), Monday, 16 Nov. 1931, p. 172.
[34] *Ibid.,* Wednesday, 16 August 1933, pp. 203–204.

the same of the Common Reader? I dipped for five minutes and put the book back depressed.[35]

But we must see this despair against the background of her growing desolation and illness during the war years and just before her final depression and death. Her intense reaction does point up, however, the creative balance she established in her best criticism, between the extremes of abstract scientism and romantic impressionism. And it is from this latter standpoint that we can refuse to further the image of Virginia Woolf as the epitome of the impressionist critic, as the last pale reflection of the decadent spirit, to which literary historians have subscribed.

A fairer estimate of Mrs. Woolf as a critic must take into account the balance or merging of critical functions which I have tried to trace in this study. Against the background of Mrs. Woolf's critical *via media* and her growing disillusionment with contemporary criticism, we should consider again T. S. Eliot's examination of modern criticism and its dominant tendencies. In terms that echo what Mrs. Woolf thought and wrote about the subject, Eliot's essay, "The Frontiers of Criticism," reveals that he has come full circle from his early reaction against impressionism to his present concern for excesses committed in the name of what he calls "understanding." Eliot wants to re-emphasize the relation between "enjoyment and understanding"; again, as in *The Sacred Wood,* he feels that there can be a fusion of the two terms with respect to the critic's function. He traces the transformation of twentieth-century criticism to Coleridge and his interest in "philosophy, aesthetics and psychology," as well as (echoing Mrs. Woolf) to the increasing influence of the teaching of literature in the universities. Though there is not space enough to trace Eliot's discussion of the excesses common to the various critical (and scholarly) methods, his concluding statement attempts once more to strike the kind of creative balance or fusion of functions which describes Mrs. Woolf's most characteristic criticism.

If in literary criticism, we place all the emphasis upon *understanding,* we are in danger of slipping from understanding to mere explanation. We are in danger of pursuing criticism as if it was a science, which it can never be. If, on the other hand, we over-emphasize *enjoyment,* we will tend to fall into the subjective and impressionistic, and our enjoyment will profit us no more than mere amusement and pastime. . . .[36]

For a fitting conclusion, it is also necessary to refer to Henry James's famous portrait of the ideal critic. In many ways, Mrs. Woolf is a direct literary descendant of James, and the kind of critic he describes resembles the image I find reflected in her essays.

[35] *Ibid.,* Tuesday, 17 Sept. 1940, p. 337.
[36] "The Frontiers of Criticism," in *Selected Essays: New Edition* (New York, 1950), pp. 117–118.

To lend himself, to project himself and steep himself, to feel and feel till he understands and to understand so well that he can say, to have perception at the pitch of passion and expression as embracing as the air, to be infinitely curious and incorrigibly patient, and yet plastic and inflammable and determinable, stooping to conquer and serving to direct— these are fine chances for an active mind, chances to add the idea of independent beauty to the conception of success.[37]

In the light of T. S. Eliot's analysis of our critical needs and the Jamesian portrait of the ideal critic, this may be the most rewarding moment in which to turn to the essays of Virginia Woolf.

[37] Henry James, "Criticism," in *Essays in London and Elsewhere* (London, 1893), pp. 276–277.

Feminism in Virginia Woolf

by J. B. Batchelor

The most outspoken critical attack on Virginia Woolf's supposed feminism is in Forster's famous lecture on her; he finds feminism "responsible for the worst of her books—the cantankerous *Three Guineas*—and for the less successful streaks in *Orlando*. There are spots of it all over her work, and it was constantly in her mind." [1] He admires *A Room of One's Own* but feels that there is "something old-fashioned" about her subsequent concern with the status of women. "By the 1930s she had much less to complain of, and seems to keep on grumbling from habit."

To take these two charges—that feminism impairs Virginia Woolf's writing, and that her concern with the status of women is anachronistic —in reverse order, it should be pointed out that Virginia Woolf did not write *Three Guineas* in a vacuum. It is not an out-dated echo of the suffrage movement, but draws on a spirit of resentment which was in some ways peculiar to the 'thirties, intensified as it was by the effects of the depression, by certain aspects of Fascism, and by a popular mis-use of sexual psychology. A contemporary, Ruth Gruber, supports this impression:

> The tremendous battlecry for freedom, for the breaking of chains, which had characterised men like Shelley, is sounded now by women. Just as Nietzsche had proclaimed the men of the future, so Virginia Woolf and her contemporaries, women like Rebecca West and Dorothy Richardson, are making the way for the women of the future. The political emancipa-tion is one step; the intellectual emancipation must follow. [2]

There is no question that by contrast with *A Room of One's Own* (in which lightness of touch is never quite lost) *Three Guineas* is a shrill and angry work. Women may be better off than they were before they gained the right to vote, the right to earn their own livings, and the right to own their own property, but they still suffer intolerable

"Feminism in Virginia Woolf" by J. B. Batchelor. From *English,* XVII (Spring 1968), 1–7. Copyright © 1968 by J. B. Batchelor. Reprinted by permission of the author.

[1] E. M. Forster, *Virginia Woolf* (Cambridge, 1941), p. 23.

[2] Ruth Gruber, *Virginia Woolf: A Study* (Bochum-Langendreer: Heinr. Pöpping-haus, 1934), p. 98.

disabilities and insults from the arrogant male. The declared object of the book is to help men to prevent war;[3] in the course of her examination of male psychology for the factors which make men desire war, her indignation is aroused by the examples of primitive, egotistical vanity and instinctive Fascism that she finds in the educated Englishman, and the tone of the book becomes bitterly rancorous. The disabilities of women seem part of a malignant conspiracy by which educated women are "the weakest of all the classes in the State" (p. 24). Her specific grievances demonstrate that these weaknesses are not illusory: women do not fill the top rank in the Civil Service (p. 81) or the Church, their hold in the universities is precarious (p. 55), they are "stateless" in the sense that they take their nationality from their husbands (p. 197), and their slavery as housewives is unpaid (p. 99).

A study of the status of women by Winifred Holtby (an admirer of Virginia Woolf, admittedly) lends further substance to these protests. Writing in 1934, she complains that "the economic slump has reopened the question of women's right to earn."[4] She points out that the promise of the 1928 Reform Act which gave the full franchise to women is unfulfilled, because the depression has provoked a wave of feeling against women as a potential threat to unemployed men, and they are still far from "equality" with men in the full sense of the word.

Winifred Holtby complains that "the woman who sets out to earn her own living is still expected to content herself with a modest £250 a year" (p. 85)—the same sum that Virginia Woolf quotes in *Three Guineas* as the maximum that a woman can expect to earn in the Civil Service. She makes further points that were to be closely paralleled in *Three Quineas* when she says (on p. 7) that "psychological fashions arouse old controversies about the capacity of the female individual" (which is reminiscent of Virginia Woolf's comment on the "atmosphere" surrounding the words "Miss" and "Mrs." in Whitehall), and that of the high percentage of the population who were found by the Nutrition Board of the British Medical Association in 1934 to be undernourished the greater sufferers were women (p. 87) (cf. Virginia Woolf's angry reference to "ice-cream and peanuts"). Most striking is the relation between Fascism and the social subordination of women found in both *Women* and *Three Guineas,* although Winifred Holtby finds the subordination of women to be an effect of Fascism, and not, as Virginia Woolf finds it, a cause. "The political doctrine of the corporative state in Italy and Germany has inspired new pronouncements upon the function of the women citizens" (p. 7).

To say that Virginia Woolf's rancour in *Three Guineas* has a considerable measure of justification is to defend her only from the charge of anachronism; the broad critical point, that feminism impairs

[3] Virginia Woolf, *Three Guineas* (London: The Hogarth Press, 1938), p. 7.
[4] Winifred Holtby, *Women* (London: The Bodley Head, 1934), p. 7.

(or colours) most of her work, is the point that has yet to be answered. Before and since Forster's lecture there has been critical discussion of feminism in Virginia Woolf,[5] and in particular it has been firmly pointed out that feminism must be distinguished from femininity in her work.[6]

But despite this firm distinction ("one must continuously face up to the fact that she was a woman, and yet be on guard against ascribing to this fact Virginia Woolf's weaknesses")[7] it is nowhere recognized in criticism of Virginia Woolf that she specifically dislikes feminists, and that the implications of feminism are antipathetic to her personality. In the course of *Three Guineas* Virginia Woolf vigorously rejects the concept of "Feminism" because it obscures the ideal of "men and women working together for the same cause" (p. 185). She insists that the crucial adjustment needed in relations between the sexes is not one of "rights," in the public sense, but of psychological acceptance: men and women must make willing emotional acknowledgement of each other as individuals. The word "feminist" is obsolete:

> That word, according to the dictionary, means "one who champions the rights of women." Since the only right, the right to earn a living, has been won, the word no longer has a meaning (p. 184).

That she disliked feminists and was suspicious of organized political activity for women is felt in the caricatures of Evelyn Murgatroyd in *The Voyage Out*, Julia Hedge in *Jacob's Room*, Mr. Clacton and Mrs. Seal in *Night and Day*, and in the decidedly grudging approval allowed to Peggy (the doctor) in *The Years* and Mary Datchet (Virginia Woolf's one feminist in the literal sense) in *Night and Day*. As Ruth Gruber remarked, Virginia Woolf cannot forgive women who adopt a "warrior attitude."

Bernard Blackstone's commentary on Virginia Woolf reminds us, with characteristic sensitivity, that she values individual life irrespective of gender:

> The great duty of the individual is to be himself, to be honest with himself, and not to judge others. Tolerance is the supreme virtue, we must learn to let others alone.[8]

To live one's femininity and to learn to let others alone are tantamount, in *A Room of One's Own*, to a positive activity: that of being

[5] Mary Electa Kelsey, "Virginia Woolf and the She-Condition," *Sewanee Review*, xxxix (1931), 425–44. Herbert J. Muller, "Virginia Woolf and Feminine Fiction," *The Saturday Review of Literature*, xv (6 February 1937), 3–4, 14 and 16. Clara F. McIntyre, "Is Virginia Woolf a Feminist?," *The Personalist*, xli (1960), 176–84.

[6] Ralph Samuelson, "Virginia Woolf, *Orlando*, and the Feminist Spirit," *The Western Humanities Review*, xv (Winter, 1960), 51–8.

[7] *Ibid.*, pp. 51–2.

[8] Bernard Blackstone, *Virginia Woolf: A Commentary* (London: Hogarth Press, 1949), p. 50.

a mute commentator, or commentator-by-example, on the actions of men. Virginia Woolf's instinctive rejection of "the warrior attitude" is present throughout this work: she is indignant with women such as head-mistresses and heads of colleges because they have abdicated the specialized role for which their femaleness equips them by adopting male standards. Women must not emulate men; they have a better role of their own. She says this both explicitly and poetically. Women can give men a "renewal of creative power" by the contact of contrasting ways of life, and for this reason women's education should "bring out and fortify the differences rather than the similarities." [9] In a rare moment of unqualified generosity Virginia Woolf symbolizes the ideal state of men and women, a state in which they live and move in perfect co-operation, in her description of the young couple meeting and taking a cab (p. 95).

There is even less of the "warrior" in *A Room of One's Own* than there is in *Three Guineas*. The essential point of *Three Guineas* (despite its tone) is, itself, relatively pacific; it is that by their presence and "indifference" women can renew a sense of life (and of the importance of life) in men, and thereby protect them from their own instinctual lust for war and death. Yet however pacific the intention, one feels that Virginia Woolf is practising a rather stern justice in this work:

> It is far harder for human beings to take action when other people are indifferent and allow them complete freedom of action, than when their actions are made the centre of excited emotion. The small boy struts and trumpets outside the window: implore him to stop; he goes on; say nothing; he stops (pp. 198–9).

If this is "indifference," then it is the indifference of a school-mistress choking back her anger. In contrast with this mood of rapidly draining patience in the face of recalcitrant stupidity, the spirit of *A Room of One's Own* is meek and retiring. The thing sparkles with satire, but it is the cheek of a pupil rather than the heavy irony of a teacher: Virginia Woolf does not even ask man to co-operate, in this work; she merely asks the liberty to live her own feminine life to the full. Man is asked not to re-order his own life, but to remove the obstacles from hers; specifically, the obstacles that she finds in the way of female writers, such as their lack of education (pp. 20–40), the lack of privacy, the constant distractions, and the interruptions attendant upon life at home (p. 78), the lack of economic independence (p. 39), and the use of chastity as a fetish to prevent women from expressing themselves freely (p. 51). This last is complained of also in the paper *Professions for Women*, where she derides "the extreme conventionality of the other sex." [10] Further obstacles noted in *A Room of One's Own* are the

[9] Virginia Woolf, *A Room of One's Own* (Harmondsworth: Penguin, 1945), p. 87.

[10] Virginia Woolf, *The Death of the Moth and Other Essays* (Harmondsworth: Penguin, 1961), p. 205.

lack of a tradition of significant relationships between women in English fiction (p. 81), and the instinctive male dislike of publicity for women (p. 52).

This concern, that women should be free to make their own unique development, reappears (stripped of its anger, usually) in most of the novels, and to that extent Forster's stricture ("there are spots of it all over her work") has some substance; but far from impairing the novels in which they appear, the tendency of these "spots" is to contribute a salutary firmness to their content. In both *The Voyage Out* and *Night and Day* a young woman escaping from a thwarting domestic world forms the centre of the action. Rachel's education is the "rudiments of about ten branches of knowledge," [11] and Cassandra's (in *Night and Day*) is "short strands of different accomplishments." [12] In the same novel Katharine's talent for mathematics has to be hidden as she is obliged to be "a member of that very great profession . . . the labour of mill and factory is, perhaps, no more severe . . . she lived at home" (p. 39). The effects of the "chastity fetish" are exemplified by Rachel, who when awoken to the facts of life exclaims: "that's why I can't walk alone." She "saw her life for the first time a creeping, hedged-in thing . . . dull and crippled for ever." [13]

In the theme of escape and fulfilment which runs through these two novels, both written before or at the time of the 1918 Reform Act, one feels that the atmosphere of vigour and resentment that surrounded the suffragettes has had some influence. Apart from the portrait of Mary Datchet there is little direct reference to the suffrage movement, but Virginia Woolf conveys a certain indignation when Dalloway, as the average male, says: "may I be in my grave before a woman has the right to vote in England" (*The Voyage Out*, p. 44), or when Hewet comments on the "curious, silent, unrepresented life" of women (p. 258).

I suggest that Virginia Woolf refuses to subscribe more directly to the suffrage movement because the ugliness and humiliation of it, the forcible feeding, the Cat and Mouse act, Emily Davidson's suicide and the rest, repelled her aesthetically.[14] She was at all times fastidious and acutely sensitive to ridicule, and one can sense that however much she might agree in principle, it would be psychologically impossible for her to associate and be identified either in person or in her work with the suffragettes. But one feels that she must have been acutely aware of what was going on, and that these two first novels are, in part, her contribution to the feminist cause with the more grotesque aspects put out of sight.

In the next three novels Virginia Woolf's concern with the obstacles

[11] Virginia Woolf, *The Voyage Out* (London: The Hogarth Press, 1929), p. 31.
[12] Virginia Woolf, *Night and Day* (London: The Hogarth Press, 1960), p. 361.
[13] *The Voyage Out*, pp. 91–2.
[14] Dame Christabel Pankhurst, *Unshackled* (London: Hutchinson, 1958).

in the way of women relaxes, as is appropriate, I would suggest, to the sense of relaxation among all intellectual women following the 1918 act. In Clarissa Dalloway, particularly, we have the portrayal of a woman who has fitted so snugly into the limitations of being a female that the awareness of these limitations shrinks into the background. It makes itself felt only in forms appropriate to Clarissa's sensibility: the characterization of Miss Kilman, for instance. On reflection one can recognize Miss Kilman as a talented woman who has been victimized by a male-oriented society, but the presentation of her in the novel, with her ugliness, her thwarted ambition, and her repressed lesbianism, is designed to affect us as she affects Clarissa; she offends our sense of the aesthetically acceptable. The tone of *Three Guineas* is present only in isolated moments like the characterizations of Holmes and Bradshaw, the psychiatrists who seek to confine Septimus Smith; exempla of the type of male who had been educated in "the arts of ruling, of killing, of acquiring land and capital" (*Three Guineas*, p. 62); and "believes that he has the right whether given by God, Nature, sex, or race . . . to dictate to other human beings how they shall live" (p. 96).

Neither Mrs. Dalloway nor Mrs. Ramsay of *To the Lighthouse* are warriors, yet if Mrs. Dalloway is a woman who is "feminine" within the intention of *A Room of One's Own*—withdrawing her life to the point where she is free to round it out and make it perfect within its own limitations—Mrs. Ramsay is "feminine" within the intention of *Three Guineas*. The way in which the contrasting ways of life of the two sexes are enriched by contact, and the way in which the male and the female modes of creation, the one an agitation of the brain and the other an outpouring of life, must inevitably conflict, is expressed with a surge of conviction in this novel. Mrs. Ramsay's creative power is seen as a "delicious fecundity, this fountain and spray of life" into which "the fatal sterility of the male plunged itself, like a beak of brass, barren and bare." [15] Mrs. Ramsay comforting her husband anticipates, on the domestic level, all the sweetening and civilizing of male life that Virginia Woolf was to urge as the feminine role in *Three Guineas*:

> It was sympathy he wanted, to be assured of his genius, first of all, and then to be taken within the circle of life, warmed and soothed, to have his senses restored to him, his barrenness made fertile, and all the rooms of the house made full of life (*To the Lighthouse*, p. 43).

In *A Room of One's Own*, also, there are passages describing the role of a woman which closely resemble this: the woman renews "creative power" in the man and makes her house a work of art, in which "the very walls are permeated by [her] creative force."

Orlando is a special case. It has been argued so far that "feminism" is inapplicable to Virginia Woolf principally because her art stresses the

15 Virginia Woolf, *To the Lighthouse* (London: Dent, 1960), p. 43.

differences rather than the similarities between the sexes. Yet this fantasy, in which a woman lives three hundred years and spends her first century as a man, seems to be a fable in which Virginia Woolf implicitly denies that there is any essential difference between the sexes. There is the satirical turmoil of her feelings on the boat back from Constantinople:

> "Heavens!" she thought, "what fools they make of us—what fools we are!" And here it would seem from some ambiguity in her terms that she was censuring both sexes equally, as if she belonged to neither; and indeed, for the time being, she seemed to vacillate; she was man; she was woman; she knew the secrets, shared the weaknesses of each. . . . She pitted one sex against the other, and found each alternately full of the most deplorable infirmities, and was not sure to which she belonged.[16]

This would seem to contradict completely the picture of her thoughts as one has formed it so far (that women have to work out a strictly feminine way of life for themselves in order to be fulfilled either as individuals or as members of society). Yet that "for the time being" is an important phrase, and from passages later in the novel (in the eighteenth century) it becomes clear that *Orlando* is to an extent the exception proving the rule suggested by the other novels.

> The difference between the sexes is, happily, one of great profundity. Clothes are but a symbol of something hid deep beneath. It was a change in Orlando herself that dictated her choice of a woman's dress and of a woman's sex. And perhaps in this she was only expressing rather more openly than usual—openness indeed was the soul of her nature—something that happens to most people without being thus plainly expressed (pp. 170–1).

It should be remembered also that *Orlando* was followed immediately by *A Room of One's Own*, and that that work, originally called *Women and Fiction*, was conceived as "a lecture to the Newnhamites about women's writing." [17] Both works, then, are out of the same mould, and the focus of *Orlando* is specifically on woman as writer rather than on woman as entity (as in *Mrs. Dalloway*, for example). The central thread of the work is Orlando's poem, *The Oak Tree*, which takes the full three hundred years of Orlando's life to be written, and the historical settings are taken from literary history, and certainly not from history in the sense in which it is used in *The Years*. Also, the question after Orlando has become a woman is essentially over her liberty to write, and the concern with her liberty to govern her own life is incidental to this.

In *Orlando* the fantasy is designed to lead back to an unacknowledged reality; to "something that happens to most people without being

[16] Virginia Woolf, *Orlando* (London: The Hogarth Press, 1960), p. 145.
[17] Virginia Woolf, *A Writer's Diary* (London: The Hogarth Press, 1959), p. 122.

thus plainly expressed." The technique with which the fantasy is created is that of "extension of reality": time and space are compressed and colours brightened until the effect, especially in the sixteenth-century section, is that of pageantry in miniature on the crowded stage of a toy theatre:

> It was very high, so high indeed that nineteen English counties could be seen beneath; and on clear days thirty or perhaps forty, if the weather was very fine. Sometimes one could see the English Channel, wave reiterating upon wave. Rivers could be seen and pleasure boats gliding on them; and galleons setting out to sea; and armadas with puffs of smoke from which came the dull thud of cannon firing; and forts on the coast; and castles among the meadows; and here a watch tower; and there a fortress; and again some vast mansion like that of Orlando's father, massed like a town in the valley circled by walls (p. 19).

All the fantasy of Orlando, the cumulative hyperboles, the theatrical effect of vivid costumes and scenery, the satirical disparagement of the literary hack (in the person of Nick Greene) and of the morbid "fecundity" of Victorian poetry, and (especially) the discussion and play of wit that centre on the sex change one-third of the way through the book; all these things are arranged round a concern which is integral to all Virginia Woolf's thinking about literature—the androgynous nature of the literary mind. The persistence of this concern is the more interesting for her reluctance to insist on it categorically. "Perhaps a mind that is purely masculine cannot create, any more than a mind that is purely feminine" and "in fact, one goes back to Shakespeare as the type of the androgynous mind," is how she phrases it in *A Room of One's Own* (p. 97), and this is an oddly tentative expression of something that is fundamental in her work. In *Orlando*, to take the immediate case first, the same point is expressed, through the fantasy and the fable, with complete conviction. Orlando as a woman is far more understanding, far more knowledgeable, and therefore far better equipped to write, than if she were wholly female. This is expressed in the knowing conversations she has with Nell the prostitute, whom Orlando (now an eighteenth-century lady) visits disguised as a man (pp. 198–9), and the wide amorous experiences she has as a bisexual Regency rake (p. 200); "for the probity of breeches she exchanged the seductiveness of petticoats and enjoyed the love of both sexes equally." When she meets her Victorian husband (a blend, probably, of all the Romantic poets into "Marmaduke Bonthrop Shelmerdine") they promptly recognize in each other the androgynous writer's mind: "an awful suspicion rushed into both their minds simultaneously. 'You're a woman, Shel!' she cried. 'You're a man, Orlando!' he cried" (p. 227).

Despite the marriage of Orlando and Marmaduke Bonthrop Shelmerdine, we are left with the feeling that the marriage of a woman writer is something of a fraud: "If one still wished, more than anything in the whole world, to write poetry, was it marriage? She had her doubts" (p. 238). This, perhaps accounts for Virginia Woolf's hesitancy over "the type of the androgynous mind." She loves and admires women like the ideal woman of *Three Guineas,* like Mrs. Ramsay, and like old Mrs. Swithin of *Between the Acts;* women who live with men, sweetening them and making life into an art. Yet, taken to its logical conclusion, the position of *A Room of One's Own,* of *Orlando,* and (to a lesser degree) of *Mrs. Dalloway* is at odds with this: in these works woman must withdraw her life from man, rounding it out and making it complete within itself. Virginia Woolf's reluctance to make this act in any way aggressive—to make it an act of rejection—is clear from the stress she places on this "withdrawal"; Mrs. Dalloway mounting the stairs to her narrow bed, Orlando retiring from life into the privacy of his/her look-out post under the oak tree, and the unnamed woman writer of *A Room of One's Own* insisting on five hundred a year and a private room to write in. Yet rejection of the male is necessarily implicit in this withdrawal, and it is more firmly implied in her theme of the androgynous mind. It would be meaningless for mind and emotions to be separated in *Orlando,* and Virginia Woolf courageously accepts this. Orlando as a man has homosexual feelings:

> When the boy, for alas, a boy it must be . . . swept almost on tiptoe past him, Orlando was ready to tear his hair with vexation that the person was of his own sex, and thus all embraces were out of the question (p. 37).

And, correspondingly, Orlando as a woman does not need men in any specific sense; she can have relationships with men and women indiscriminately, or she can live entirely within herself, satisfactorily combining male and female principles within her own mind. The fantastic framework leaves Virginia Woolf free to give Orlando the utmost sexual versatility without confusion, but in *Between the Acts* we find the hard and unequivocal portrayal of a female writer with an androgynous mind, Miss La Trobe, who is lesbian in so far as she has any sexual feelings. Throughout her work Virginia Woolf is interested in homosexual people, and one feels that this interest arises partly from her concern with the androgynous mind, and partly from the feeling (expressed in both *A Room of One's Own* and *Three Guineas*) that there is a harmful lack of significant relationships between women in both English life and English letters. It is as though the relations of a woman and a male homosexual are a half-way stage towards a self-contained relationship between women: Sarah and Nicholas in *The Years* and Isa and William Dodge in *Between the Acts* can talk with an easy intimacy because there can be no hint of sexual threat (and very little of sexual competition) between them. But Virginia Woolf is also prepared to give this relationship on a far less social and cerebral level. Clarissa Dalloway's feeling for Sally Seton is passion in the fullest sense of the word, involving a total (though temporary) rejection of the male, the external, the "public" world:

> She did undoubtedly then feel what men felt. Only for a moment; but it was enough. It was a sudden revelation, a tinge like a blush which one tried to check and then, as it spread, one yielded to its expansion, and rushed to the farthest verge and there quivered and felt the world come closer, swollen with some astonishing significance, some pressure of rapture, which split its thin skin and gushed and poured with an extraordinary alleviation over the cracks and sores.[18]

To return to Forster's original assessment (that the complaints in *Three Guineas* are "cantankerous" and anachronistic, and that feminism impairs much of Virginia Woolf's writing and is constantly in her mind) I have suggested firstly that the protests in *Three Guineas* are legitimate in the context of the 'thirties; secondly that feminism proper is aesthetically unacceptable to Virginia Woolf and hardly appears in her writings; and thirdly that what is "constantly in her mind" is not "feminism" but a passionate concern with the nature of womanhood. This concern takes two slightly contradictory forms; one with women in their relationships with men and with society, and the special roles that they can play (*Three Guineas*, and the portrayals of Mrs. Ramsay, Mrs. Swithin, and others), and the other with the full development of women as individuals and as artists (*Mrs. Dalloway, A Room of One's Own, Orlando*, and in Miss La Trobe and other figures). I would argue further that this double concern, far from damaging Virginia Woolf's art, contributes considerably to its strength and richness. Essentially a private and personal writer, Virginia Woolf does not have an instinctive interest in the "public" aspects of life, as is made clear by the comparative thinness of her writing when she feels obliged to treat them, and by the way in which she will avoid direct description of them. She avoids showing us Eleanor's committee-meeting in progress (in *The Years*), or Richard Dalloway at work (*Mrs. Dalloway*), or the conversations between Ambrose and Pepper (*The Voyage Out*), Ramsay and Tansley (*To the Lighthouse*), Jacob Flanders and Bonamy (*Jacob's Room*); in *Between the Acts*, set against the background of the darkening Europe in the late 'thirties, she avoids giving more than a few emotive references and the emblem of the snake swallowing the toad to represent what Giles Oliver in fact thinks and feels about the approach of war. On the other hand stands the vivid and unforgettable account of Miss La Trobe's agony when illusion fails: "Panic seized her. Blood seemed to pour from her shoes. This is death, death, death, she noted in the margin of her mind." [19]

Also there is the passage quoted above where Clarissa Dalloway dis-

---

[18] Virginia Woolf, *Mrs. Dalloway* (Harmondsworth: Penguin, 1964), p. 36.

[19] Virginia Woolf, *Between the Acts* (London: The Hogarth Press, 1960), p. 210.

covers love between women, in which Virginia Woolf suddenly becomes at one with her subject-matter, and produces this extraordinary flight with its compulsive rhythmic drive (to the climax of "split the thin skin") and its strong, if elusive, sexual imagery. This is Virginia Woolf at her most strong, writing with the whole of her intense range of feeling; throughout the novels her consciousness of what it is to be a woman, both as a member of society and as an individual and artist, emerges as one of her few instinctive and passionate concerns, and is a subject which brings the fullest conviction and engagement in her writing whenever it appears.

Chronology of Important Dates

1878   Leslie Stephen and Julia Jackson Duckworth marry; both for the second time.

1882   Born Adeline Virginia Stephen on January 25; James Russell Lowell her godfather. Leslie Stephen assumes the editorship of the *Dictionary of National Biography* and publishes *The Science of Ethics.*

1883   Julia Stephen publishes *Notes from the Sick Room.*

1895   Death of Julia Stephen; Virginia undergoes the second of the four severe breakdowns of her life; suicide attempt. Educated at home.

1898   Death of Stella Duckworth, her half-sister.

1902   Leslie Stephen knighted.

1903   Publication of G. E. Moore's *Principia Ethica* and Bertrand Russell's *Principles of Mathematics.*

1904   Death of Leslie Stephen. The Stephen children, Vanessa, Thoby, Virginia, Adrian, move to 46 Gordon Square, Bloomsbury.

1905   Death of Thoby Stephen, at 26, of typhoid.

1907   Vanessa marries Clive Bell.

1910   First Post-Impressionist Exhibition in London.

1912   Marries Leonard Woolf, in a civil ceremony, August 10.

1913   *The Voyage Out,* completed in February; publication delayed due to breakdown.

1915   *The Voyage Out* published by her half-brother, Gerald Duckworth. Begins diary on a regular basis.

1917   The Hogarth Press begins operation in the basement of the Woolfs' home in Richmond.

1919   *The Mark on the Wall* and *Kew Gardens,* experimental sketches published by the Hogarth Press. *Night and Day,* published by Duckworth.

1920   *Monday or Tuesday,* experimental sketches. Roger Fry's *Vision and Design.*

1922   *Jacob's Room,* first novel published by the Hogarth Press, henceforth her regular publisher; also accepted by Harcourt, Brace.

1924   E. M. Forster's *A Passage to India.*

1925   *The Common Reader. Mrs. Dalloway.* The Hogarth Press moves to London.

1926   Roger Fry's *Transformations.*

1927   *To the Lighthouse.*

1928   *Orlando;* Clive Bell's *Civilization.*

1929   *A Room of One's Own.*

1931   *The Waves.*

1932   *The Common Reader: Second Series.* Death of Lytton Strachey; also Dora Carrington and G. Lowes Dickinson.

1933   *Flush: A Biography.*

1934   Death of Roger Fry.

1936   Completion of *The Years;* near breakdown.

1937   *The Years.* Death of her nephew, Julian Bell, in the Spanish Civil War.

1938   *Three Guineas.*

1940   *Roger Fry: A Biography.* The first draft of *Between the Acts* completed, February 26.

1941   Death by drowning, March 28, in the River Ouse.

1969   Death of Leonard Woolf.

Posthumously Published Works

1941   *Between the Acts.*

1942   *Death of the Moth and Other Essays.*

1943   *A Haunted House and Other Short Stories.*

1947   *The Moment and Other Essays.*

1950   *The Captain's Death-Bed and Other Essays.*

1953   *A Writer's Diary.*

1956   *Letters: Virginia Woolf and Lytton Strachey.*

1958   *Granite and Rainbow: Essays.*

1965   *Contemporary Writers.*

Notes on the Editor and Contributors

CLAIRE SPRAGUE, the editor of this volume, is also the editor of *Van Wyck Brooks: The Early Years* and *Hamlet: Enter Critic* and the author of *Edgar Saltus*. She teaches at Brooklyn College.

ERICH AUERBACH was Sterling Professor of French and Romance Philology at Yale at the time of his death in 1957. His distinguished career included books and articles on Latin, French and Italian literature.

J. B. BATCHELOR of Darwin College, Cambridge, was formerly Fellow and Lecturer in English at the University of New Brunswick, Canada.

REUBEN BROWER teaches at Harvard University. He is the editor of *On Translation* and the author of *Alexander Pope* and *The Poetry of Robert Frost*.

LEON EDEL is the author of *The Life of Henry James*, a multi-volume work still in progress. Volumes II and III received the National Book Award and the Pulitzer Prize in 1963. Mr. Edel teaches at New York University.

The novelist E. M. FORSTER was a close friend of Virginia Woolf and an original member of "Bloomsbury."

MARK GOLDMAN has published poetry as well as critical essays and is the co-editor of the anthology, *Drama: Traditional and Modern*. He now teaches at the University of Rhode Island.

JOHN W. GRAHAM is a Professor of English at the University of Western Ontario. He is currently editing the manuscript of *The Waves* and plans to return to his study of Mrs. Woolf's longer fiction.

JEAN GUIGUET has published fiction and articles in *Kenyon Review, Etudes Anglaises* and other periodicals and is translating a selection of Hart Crane's poems into French. He is Professor of English and American literature at the University of Aix-en-Provence.

FRANK D. McCONNELL teaches at Cornell University and has published essays on William Burroughs, Byron, Shelley and Flaubert. He is presently writing a book on the criticism of the novel.

JOSEPHINE O'BRIEN SCHAEFER teaches at Western College in Oxford, Ohio. She is preparing her book on Virginia Woolf for American publication. She has also written, with Louise Bogan, the Afterword to the paperback edition of *A Writer's Diary*.

RUTH Z. TEMPLE is at work on a book on the experimental novel. She is the author of *The Critic's Alchemy* and *Nathalie Sarraute* and the editor of *Twentieth Century British Literature*. She teaches at Brooklyn College.

WILLIAM TROY taught for many years at Bennington College before moving to The New School for Social Research where he was teaching at the time of his death in 1961. His articles, still frequently anthologized, are now available in *William Troy: Selected Essays*, edited by Stanley Edgar Hyman.

ANN Y. WILKINSON teaches at the University of California at Santa Barabara. Her published work includes essays on Thackeray and Dickens.

Selected Bibliography[1]

Separate Studies

Bennett, Joan. *Virginia Woolf: Her Art as a Novelist.* Cambridge: Cambridge University Press, 1945.

Blackstone, Bernard. *Virginia Woolf.* London: Hogarth Press, 1949.

Brewster, Dorothy. *Virginia Woolf's London.* London: Allen & Unwin, 1959.

————. *Virginia Woolf.* London: Allen & Unwin, 1963.

Chambers, R. L. *The Novels of Virginia Woolf.* Edinburgh: Oliver & Boyd, 1947.

Daiches, David. *Virginia Woolf.* Norfolk: New Directions, 1942.

Delattre, Floris. *Le Roman Psychologique de Virginia Woolf.* Paris: J. Vrin, 1932.

Hafley, James. *The Glass Roof: Virginia Woolf as Novelist.* English Studies, no. 9. Berkeley: University of California Press, 1954.

Holtby, Winifred. *Virginia Woolf.* London: Wishart, 1932.

Kirkpatrick, B. J. *A Bibliography of Virginia Woolf.* London: R. Hart-Davis, 1957.

Love, Jean O. *Worlds of Consciousness: Mythopoetic Thought in the Novels of Virginia Woolf.* Berkeley: University of California Press, 1970.

Marder, Herbert. *Feminism and Art.* Chicago: University of Chicago Press, 1963.

Moody, A. D. *Virginia Woolf.* Edinburgh: Oliver & Boyd, 1963.

Nathan, Monique. *Virginia Woolf.* New York: Grove Press, 1961 [1956].

Newton, Deborah. *Virginia Woolf.* Melbourne: Melbourne University Press, 1963.

Pippett, Aileen. *The Moth and the Star: a Biography of Virginia Woolf.* Boston: Little, Brown, 1955.

Rantavaara, Irma. *Virginia Woolf and Bloomsbury.* Helsinki: Annales Academiae Fennicae, 1953.

————. *Virginia Woolf's "The Waves."* Helsingfors: Societas Scientiarum Fennica, Commentationes Humanarum Litterarum, XXVI, 2, 1960.

Richter, Harvena. *Virginia Woolf: The Inward Voyage.* Princeton: Princeton University Press, 1970.

Woodring, Carl. *Virginia Woolf.* New York: Columbia University Press, 1966.

---

[1] Does not include works represented in this volume.

Articles

Baldanza, Frank. "Orlando and the Sackvilles." *PMLA,* LXX (March 1955), 274–79.

——. "Clarissa Dalloway's Party Consciousness," *Modern Fiction Studies,* II (February 1956), 24–30.

——. "*To the Lighthouse* Again," *PMLA,* LXX (June 1955), 548–52.

Beach, Joseph Warren. "Virginia Woolf," *English Journal,* XXVI (October 1937), 603–12.

Beck, Warren. "For Virginia Woolf," in *Forms of Modern Fiction.* Ed. William Van O'Conner. Minneapolis; University of Minnesota Press, 1948, pp. 243–54.

Bevis, Dorothy. "*The Waves*: A Fusion of Symbol, Style and Thought in Virginia Woolf," *Twentieth Century Literature,* II (April 1956), 5–20.

Brace, Marjorie. "Worshipping Solid Objects," *Accent Anthology.* New York: Harcourt, Brace, 1946, pp. 489–95.

Cohn, Ruby. "Art in *To the Lighthouse,*" *Modern Fiction Studies,* VIII (Summer 1962), 127–36.

Delattre, Floris. "Virginia Woolf et le Monologue Intérieur," *Feux d'automne.* Paris: Didier, 1950, pp. 225–47.

Doner, Dean. "Virginia Woolf: In the Service of Style," *Modern Fiction Studies,* II (February 1956), 1–12.

Empson, William. "Virginia Woolf," *Scrutinies II.* Ed. Edgell Rickword. London: Wishart, 1931, pp. 203–16.

Fishman, Solomon. "Virginia Woolf on the Novel," *Sewanee,* LI (April 1943), 321–40.

Friedman, Norman. "The Waters of Annihilation: Double Vision in *To the Lighthouse,*" *English Literary History,* XXII (March 1955), 61–79.

Garnett, David. "Virginia Woolf," *American Scholar,* XXXIV (Summer 1965), 371–86.

Gelfant, Blanche. "Love and Conversion in *Mrs. Dalloway,*" *Criticism,* VIII (Summer 1966), 229–45.

Graham, John. "Time in the Novels of Virginia Woolf," *University of Toronto Quarterly,* XVIII (January 1949), 186–201.

Hoffmann, Charles G. "Fact and Fantasy in *Orlando*: Virginia Woolf's Manuscript Revisions," *Texas Studies in Literature and Language,* X (Fall 1968), 435–44.

——. " 'From Lunch to Dinner': Virginia Woolf's Apprenticeship," *Texas Studies in Literature and Language,* X (Winter 1969), 609–27.

——. "Virginia Woolf's Manuscript Revisions of *The Years,*" *PMLA,* LXXXIV (January 1969), 79–89.

——. "From Short Story to Novel: The Manuscript Revisions of Virginia Woolf's *Mrs. Dalloway,*" *Modern Fiction Studies,* XIV (Summer 1968), 171–86.

Johnstone, J. K. "Virginia Woolf," *The Bloomsbury Group*. New York: Noonday, 1954, pp. 320–73.

King, Merton P. "*The Waves* and the Androgynous Mind," *University Review*, XXX (1963), 128–34.

Overcarsh, F. L. "The Lighthouse, Face to Face," *Accent*, X (Winter 1959), 107–23.

Pedersen, Glenn. "Vision in *To the Lighthouse*," *PMLA*, LXXIII (December 1958), 585–600.

Rahv, Philip. "Mrs. Woolf and Mrs. Brown," *Image and Idea*. Norfolk: New Directions, 1949, pp. 139–43.

Ramsey, Warren. "The Claims of Language: Virginia Woolf as Symbolist," *English Fiction in Transition*, IV (1961), 12–17.

"Reminiscences of Virginia Woolf," *Horizon*, III (May 1941). Reminiscences by T. S. Eliot, Rose Macaulay, Vita Sackville–West, William Plomer, Duncan Grant and others.

Roberts, John Hawley. "Vision and Design in Virginia Woolf," *PMLA*, LXI (September 1946), 835–47.

Samuelson, Ralph. "Virginia Woolf: *Orlando* and the Feminist Spirit," *Western Humanities Review*, XV (Winter 1961), 51–58.

Savage, D. S. "Virginia Woolf," *The Withered Branch*. London: Eyre and Spottiswoode, 1950, pp. 70–105.

Toynbee, Philip. "Virginia Woolf: A Study of Three Experimental Novels," *Horizon*, XIV (November 1946), 290–304.